EYES
OF THE
RAF

A HISTORY OF PHOTO-RECONNAISSANCE

By the same author

Woe to the Unwary
Torpedo Airmen
The Strike Wings
Target: Hitler's Oil (with Ronald C. Cooke)
Arctic Airmen (with Ernest Schofield)
Failed to Return
An Illustrated History of the RAF
RAF Records in the PRO
   (with Simon Fowler, Peter Elliott and Christina Goulter)
The Armed Rovers
The RAF in Camera 1903–1939

EYES
OF THE
RAF

A HISTORY OF PHOTO-RECONNAISSANCE

ROY CONYERS NESBIT

ASSISTED BY JACK EGGLESTON

FOREWORD BY
AIR CHIEF MARSHAL SIR NEIL WHEELER
GCB, CBE, DSO, DFC & BAR, AFC, FRAeS, RAF (RET'D)

Bramley Books

First published in the United Kingdom in 1996 by
Alan Sutton Publishing Limited, an imprint of Sutton Publishing Limited

This edition published in 1997 by Bramley Books, an imprint of
Quadrillion Publishing Limited
Godalming Business Centre, Woolsack Way,
Godalming, Surrey GU7 1XW

British Library Cataloguing in Publication Data

A catalogue record for this book is available from the British Library

ISBN 1-85833-389-X

This book was designed and produced by
Alan Sutton Publishing Limited, an imprint of Sutton Publishing Limited,
Phoenix Mill, Thrupp, Stroud, Gloucestershire GL5 2BU

Typeset in 10/13 Sabon.
Typesetting and origination by
Sutton Publishing Limited.
Printed in Great Britain by
WBC Limited, Bridgend, Mid-Glamorgan.

CONTENTS

FOREWORD

BY

AIR CHIEF MARSHAL SIR NEIL WHEELER
GCB, CBE, DSO, DFC & BAR, AFC, FRAeS, RAF (RET'D)

Since the Second World War there have been many books about air operations but the vast majority have confined themselves to the Battle of Britain, the strategic bombing offensive and the Battle of the Atlantic. The general public could be forgiven for presuming that there must have been few other operations of importance. During the early years of the war I was involved in photographic reconnaissance, mostly in Spitfires, as both a Flight Commander and a Squadron Commander. I am, therefore, delighted that a book has been written on the history of photographic reconnaissance, starting even before the First World War. Moreover, it has been written by an author who is experienced in air operations and is also a painstaking researcher. Arguably, photographic reconnaissance made one of the greatest contributions to the Allied victory in the Second World War. I was, therefore, extremely pleased when Roy Nesbit invited me to write the Foreword to his book.

I first came across photographic reconnaissance in the early days of the war when staying with my brother in the Army. In his office I saw an aircraft recognition notice portraying a blue Spitfire. At the time I was a flying instructor on Fairey Battles in Bomber Command, stationed at Benson, and on my return to my unit I decided to find out about blue Spitfires. It was not easy because the unit, then based at Heston just outside London, was regarded as very secret. However, it was the early summer of 1940 and I thought it about time, as a permanent regular officer, that I took a more active part in the war. So, by a highly

irregular visit to the Air Ministry, I managed to wangle a posting to the Photographic Reconnaissance Unit at Heston in the late summer. The unit by then was commanded by Wing Commander Geoffrey Tuttle, although Sidney Cotton still seemed to be on the scene! Roy Nesbit's book refers to 'Sidney Cotton's Air Force' but, rest assured, Heston was a strange place and by then 'Sidney Cotton's Air Force' had become 'Geoffrey Tuttle's Air Force'. Certainly, I had been in the RAF for over five years and Heston bore little resemblance to the RAF stations on which I had served. But there was a terrific spirit!

As this book so graphically portrays, although the operational activity was essentially individual, the morale in PRU was very strong – and not only among the pilots. People speak of the dangers of penetrating deep into enemy-held territory without guns but frankly I do not recall that the dangers loomed large in the minds of the pilots. Moreover, at least we knew that our masters wanted us to get back with the photographs!

I have found reading Roy Nesbit's book most interesting and very nostalgic. It is thorough in its cover of what in the Second World War became a very large area of operations, developing in six years of war from a mere Flight to a Group. The author has clearly carried out exhaustive research into his subject. But it is definitely not a dreary history. Roy Nesbit has made photographic reconnaissance a live and fascinating subject and his book is long overdue. It is a fine tribute to those who did not return with their photographs.

ACKNOWLEDGEMENTS

This book was begun several years ago at the request of the Chairman of the Association of Royal Air Force Photography Officers, who at the time was Squadron Leader Don F. Barltrop RAF. It is based partly on the accumulated material of this Association. I was encouraged by their historians Squadron Leader Paul Lamboit RAFVR and the late Squadron Leader Jack E. Archbald RAFVR, and also urged to embark on the book by the late Air Marshal Sir Geoffrey Tuttle.

In researching and writing the book I have received a great deal of help from the Joint Air Reconnaissance Intelligence Centre (UK) at RAF Brampton, the Joint School of Photography at RAF Cosford, the Joint School of Photographic Interpretation at RAF Wyton, the Air Historical Branch (RAF) of the Ministry of Defence, the Imperial War Museum, the Museum of Army Flying, the Royal Air Force Museum, the Science Museum, the Tangmere Military Aviation Museum, the USAF Archives, the US 8th Air Force Historical Society, the South African Air Force Association, the Italian Ministry of Aviation, 39 (No 1 PRU) Squadron RAF, 42 Squadron RAF, 47 Squadron RAF, RAF Coltishall, RAF Finningley, RAF Leuchars, RAF Lossiemouth, RAF Waddington, RAF Wittering, *Aeroplane Monthly*, *Jet & Prop* in Germany, Carl Zeiss Ltd and members of such bodies as the Medmenham Club and the Boy Entrant Photographers' Association. I have also carried out much research at the Public Record Office at Kew, although of course official documents dating within the last thirty years are not released to the public.

My thanks are due to the following, who have helped with the narrative or contributed photographs from their private collections. Decorations are omitted from this long list.

Mrs Ann Archbald; Brian J. Attwell; Peter Batten; Squadron Leader J.D. Braithwaite RAFVR; Squadron Leader Brian A. Broad RAF (Ret'd); Jack M. Bruce; the late Wing Commander F.E. 'Monty' Burton RAF; the late Wing Commander Geoff J. Buxton RAF; Squadron Leader Ian M. Coleman RAF; Mrs Jane Cowderoy; J. Seb Cox; Wing Commander Gordon J. Craig RAFVR; Warrant Officer Phil G. Crozier RAF (Ret'd); Flight Sergeant E.T. Davies RAF (Ret'd); Sergeant Graham Dinsdale RAF (Ret'd); Bob Docherty; Peter J.V. Elliott; Flight Lieutenant G. Alan Etheridge RAFVR; Wing Commander E.A. 'Tim' Fairhurst RAF (Ret'd); G. Flowerday; Corporal Alan Fox RAFVR; Squadron Leader Don R.M. Furniss RAFVR; Barry Gray; M.H. Goodall; Dr Christina J.M. Goulter; Senior Aircraftman Nigel Green RAF; Dave Hatherell; Dr Eric V. Hawkinson USAF (Ret'd); Roger Hayward; the late Squadron Leader Norman Hearn-Phillips RAF; Flight Lieutenant John P. Hygate RAF; Flight Lieutenant W. Mike Hodsman RAFVR; Ted Hooton; Malcolm Howard; Sergeant Dave J. Humphrey RAF (Ret'd); Flight Lieutenant Norman Jenkins RAF (Ret'd); Sergeant Dave Jenkins RAF (Ret'd); Corporal L. Jewitt RAF (Ret'd); Brian Kervell; Squadron Leader Vic Kinnin RAF; Robert E. Kuhnert USAAF (Ret'd); Paul Lashmar; Art K. Leatherwood USAAF (Ret'd); Squadron Leader Howard W. Lees RAFVR; Bernard Lefebvre; G. Stuart Leslie; Flight Sergeant Ken Loweth RAF (Ret'd); Wing Commander Mike D. Mockford RAF (Ret'd); Sergeant Jim Muncie RAF (Ret'd); the late Squadron Leader Don J. Munro RAF; Ken Murch; John K. Nesbit TA; Flight Sergeant A.W. Orford RAF (Ret'd); Wing Commander David D. Oxlee RAF (Ret'd); Flight Lieutenant George H. Parry RAF (Ret'd); Flight Lieutenant Stan G.E. Payne RAF (Ret'd); Chris Pocock; Dr Alfred Price RAF (Ret'd); Sergeant Alf Pyner RAF

(Ret'd); Squadron Leader E.A. 'Tony' Robinson RAF (Ret'd); Squadron Leader Tom N. Rosser RAFVR; Corporal Norman Shirley RAFVR; Squadron Leader Peter H.R. Singleton RAF (Ret'd); Flight Officer Constance Babington Smith WAAF; Mrs K. Stevens WAAF; Squadron Leader A. Stevenson RAFVR; Flight Lieutenant Andy S. Thomas RAF; Geoff J. Thomas; Squadron Leader Peter J. Thompson RAF (Ret'd); Wing Commander R.G.M. 'Johnny' Walker RAF (Ret'd); Sergeant David T. Watson RAF; Sergeant George M. Webb RAF (Ret'd); Leading Aircraftman Reg F. White RAFVR; Ernie Wickens; the late Group Captain S.G. 'Bill' Wise RAF; G.J. Zwanenburg RNethAF (Ret'd)

My thanks are also due to Air Chief Marshal Sir Neil Wheeler for writing the Foreword and to the aviation artist Charles J. Thompson for allowing the use of his painting on the cover of this book. Two friends who have painstakingly checked and corrected the narrative and captions of this book while it was being written are Squadron Leader Dudley Cowderoy RAFVR and Warrant Officer Jack Eggleston RAF (Ret'd). Any errors which remain after all this expertise are my own responsibility.

CHAPTER ONE

THE OTHER SIDE OF THE HILL

From the beginning of warfare, military commanders have sought to know the disposition and strength of enemy forces, by intelligence or observation. Sometimes visual reconnaissance of a potential battlefield could be obtained by simply climbing up a suitable hill and looking down the other side, provided the enemy had not already occupied that advantageous position. The observer then raced back to report his findings or used some method of signals communication. This was one of the functions of light cavalrymen, while their heavier counterparts were used as shock troops against the enemy. Victory or defeat in battle depended to a great extent on the success or failure of such reconnaissance. Moreover, when the range of artillery increased considerably in the second half of the nineteenth century, an observation post on high ground was often essential if the gunners were to determine whether their shells were falling on the enemy or being wasted.

The first manned ascent in a tethered balloon, by the Frenchman Jean-François-Pilâtre de Rozier on 15 October 1783 over Paris, provided an obvious improvement in military observation. A manned flight of 27 miles by two Frenchmen in a balloon on 1 December of the same year, from the Tuileries in Paris, seemed to offer a new dimension for the art of warfare. A more startling example of the possibilities took place in January 1785, when Jean-Pierre Blanchard crossed the English Channel in a balloon.

The British were somewhat slower to experiment with this form of aerial endeavour, even though it was the English physicist Henry Cavendish who had in May 1776 discovered the density of hydrogen, the flammable gas with which the more successful of the French balloons were filled. An Italian, Vincenzo Lunardi, was probably the first person in Britain to ascend in a balloon, when he made a 20-mile flight from the grounds of the Honourable Artillery Company at Moorfields in London in May 1784. The first military test took place on 3 June when Major John Money, together with George Blake, ascended from Tottenham Court Road in London and came down at Abridge in Essex, a distance of 20 miles. But, by and large, the military establishment in Britain seems to have regarded ballooning as an amusing sport rather than a means of gaining advantage in warfare.

The French took a different view for, in the war against Austria and Prussia which followed their Revolution of 1789, they developed a mobile apparatus for producing hydrogen in the field of battle and so employed military balloons with some success. However, the destruction by Nelson of a ship carrying a balloon company at Aboukir Bay in Egypt in 1798 seems to have discouraged the French from further efforts. With the peace in Europe which followed the defeat of the French at Waterloo in 1815, the military development of aerial observation came to a halt, although in England Sir

The French town of Sèvres, photographed from a balloon by Paul Nadar, the son of the pioneer photographer Gaspard Félix Tornachon, better known as Nadar. (Flight Lieutenant G.H. Parry RAF (Ret'd))

Photograph of the Army camp at Lydd in Kent, taken in 1886 by a camera operating automatically from a small balloon released by Major H. Elsdale of the Royal Engineers. Lydd was an artillery practice camp. (Flight Lieutenant G.H. Parry RAF (Ret'd))

Colonel James L Templer, one of the pioneers of military ballooning from 1878 to 1905, in the wicker car of one of his observation balloons.
(Museum of Army Flying)

George Cayley carried out studies into heavier-than-air flight coupled with the design and testing of gliders.

It was not until 24 September 1852 that the next major development took place, when Pierre Jullien successfully flew a powered airship, 144 feet long and with a 3-hp steam engine, from Paris. A few years later, experiments with aerial photography from balloons began in both France and the USA. A Parisian photographer, Gaspard Félix Tournachon, who was also a caricaturist and journalist with the pseudonym of 'Nadar', attempted in 1858 to take out a patent on his examples of aerial photographs from balloons, although without success. His initial results were disappointing, partly since balloons tended to spin in high winds and partly because the release of hydrogen from the vent valve of the balloon contained impurities which affected the wet collodion plates used in his cameras. These plates needed to be sensitised, exposed and then developed while the balloon was in the air. On subsequent flights, Nadar overcame most of these problems.

In 1859 the enterprising Nadar was offered a commission in aerial photography and by 1863 had built a very large balloon named *Le Géant* for this purpose. Its two-storey wickerwork car contained a photographic darkroom and a small printing room, as well as a dining room. The life of this enormous balloon was short, for it was damaged beyond repair in October of the same year, when its nine occupants attempted to land in a high wind after a journey of 400 miles. But Nadar's enthusiasm was not diminished and he took many successful photographs in the following years.

Similar experiments took place in the USA, where the first satisfactory photographs from a tethered balloon were taken by J.W. Black and S.A. King from an altitude of 1,200 feet over the city of Boston in October 1860.

However, there do not appear to have been attempts to use photography from the balloons employed by the Federal side during the American Civil War of 1861–5.

Balloons were employed extensively by the French during the Siege of Paris in the Franco-Prussian War of 1870. Three tethered balloons were used for reconnaissance, while many others were released to float over the Prussian lines, carrying people and letters. Soon afterwards, the British War Office asked its Royal Engineer Committee to look into the practicability of using balloons with the Army. The War Office was doubtless influenced by the example of the French although two Royal Engineer officers, Captains Grover and Beaumont, had been carrying out many experiments with civilian balloons at their own expense and trying to get ballooning adopted by the British Army. In this period, the problem of sensitising and developing wet photographic plates in the air was overcome by the introduction by the English physician Richard L. Maddox of gelatine dry plates instead of collodion; this improved the sensitivity of the plates and also allowed them to be developed after return to earth.

Initial progress in Britain was slow since no funds were forthcoming from the War Office, but the purse-strings were loosened slightly in 1878 with the setting up at Woolwich of an establishment to develop military ballooning and the employment of an experienced balloonist, Captain James L. Templer, as an instructor. The first Army balloon, named *Pioneer*, made its ascent in the same year, and before long the store at Woolwich Arsenal contained five balloons. In 1882 the balloon establishment moved to Chatham, where the School of Ballooning was formed as part of the School of Military Engineering. Officers and men of the Royal Engineers were trained in aerial reconnaissance, photography and signalling.

The pigeon camera, patented in Germany by Dr Julius Neubronner in 1903. It weighed only 2½ ounces and took negatives of 1½ inches by 1½ inches automatically every 30 seconds. (Flight Lieutenant G.H. Parry RAF (Ret'd))

A man-carrying kite designed by S.F. Cody being raised by a detachment of Royal Engineers at Aldershot, probably in 1906. (Museum of Army Flying)

Stonehenge, taken from a balloon by Lieutenant P.H. Sharpe of the Royal Engineers. This photograph was first published on 6 December 1906. (B. Gray)

Preparing an observation balloon, around 1912 or 1913. (Museum of Army Flying)

The GI building of the Defence and Research Agency at Farnborough (formerly the Royal Aircraft Establishment), photographed in April 1993. This was built in 1907 as the headquarters of the Army's School of Ballooning. It became the headquarters of the RFC in 1913. (B.M. Harris)

The cupboard under the stairs in the GI building of the Defence and Research Agency at Farnborough (formerly the Royal Aircraft Establishment), photographed in April 1993. This was the darkroom used in 1912 by Air Mechanic F.C. Victor Laws of the RFC, who became known later as the 'Father of RAF Photography'. (B.M. Harris)

When in Nova Scotia in 1883, Major H. Elsdale of the Grenadier Guards also experimented with cameras fitted around free balloons and timed by clockwork to take exposures. At long last, balloon flights dedicated to reconnaissance had arrived in the British Army.

One of these units, commanded by Major Elsdale, travelled to Bechuanaland in 1884 as part of an expedition sent to repel Boer incursions, with results which were considered beneficial. Another unit, under Major Templer, was sent to the Sudan the following year, after the fall of Khartoum and the death of General Gordon. The use of balloons in the British Army became assured when successful experiments to correct artillery fire from balloons took place at Lydd in Kent.

The School of Ballooning moved to Aldershot in 1891–2, where there was more space for training. Tethered balloons were flown at altitudes of about 1,000 feet and in winds of up to 20 mph; the operators were also taught how to handle the free-running if the balloons came adrift. Experiments with kites also took place, and in 1894 the first man-carrying kite was raised over Pirbright Camp in Surrey, although this method of aerial observation remained in the experimental stage for some years. Meanwhile the military airship with a rigid frame, developed by Count Ferdinand von Zeppelin, made its first flight in Germany on 2 July 1900 and, after early set-backs, proved successful.

On 17 December 1903 an event occurred which heralded the eventual eclipse of the use of balloons and airships as observation platforms. This was the first powered flight of the biplane *Flyer*, designed by Wilbur and Orville Wright, near Kitty Hawk beach in North Carolina. Although at first this invention received little encouragement from the military in America or Britain, a French syndicate purchased the patent and, with help

from Wilbur Wright, took the lead in aeronautical progress.

In Britain, private enterprise began to wake up to the potentialities of powered flight, and experiments were carried out by engineers such as Charles Rolls, Robert Blackburn, A.V. Roe, Thomas Sopwith, and the brothers Horace and Oswald Short. At this time, these men were not constructing warplanes but were seeking to improve techniques for personal interest coupled with commercial possibilities. Very substantial rewards were offered by newspapers to those men who came first in flying events.

Meanwhile the military establishment continued flying experiments with lighter-than-air craft, its factory moving from Aldershot to Farnborough in 1906. In the same year, a man-carrying kite invented by S.F. Cody was added to the Army equipment. In 1907 the Army's first powered airship, or dirigible as it was sometimes called, made its appearance; it was named *Nulli Secundus* and had a semi-rigid gas envelope. Cody then designed and built an aeroplane powered by a 50-hp engine, which made a flight of about 400 yards on 16 October 1908 and later became Army Aeroplane No 1. The War Office banned further experiments with aeroplanes because of the cost, but events were moving at such a pace that it was soon forced to reverse this decision.

On 25 July 1909, Louis Blériot took off in a monoplane from Les Boraques, near Calais, and landed near Dover thirty-seven minutes later. This startling achievement caused a great stir in the British press, for newspaper editors foresaw thousands of armed Frenchmen, the country's traditional enemies, soaring above the Royal Navy to take coastal defences in the rear. While remaining phlegmatic about this possibility, the War Office set up an Air Battalion in April 1911, consisting of No 1 Company for balloons, airships and kites, and No 2 Company for

The Watson Air Camera was the first camera specially designed for the RFC. It had a 6-inch lens and carried twelve 5-inch by 4-inch plates which were moved into position by pulling a lever. In 1913, the first series of vertical and overlapping photographs was taken with this camera, from HMA *Beta* over the Basingstoke Canal. The airship was flown by Captain J.E. Fletcher and the photographer was Sergeant F.C.V. Laws. (Squadron Leader P. Lamboit RAFVR, courtesy Photogrammetric Record)

The Army airship HMA *Beta* was completed in June 1910, rebuilt from the airship *Baby*. She was a non-rigid machine with a length of 104 feet, powered by a 35-hp Green engine, used mainly for wireless experiments. The airship was rebuilt in late 1912 after an accident, enlarged to 108 feet and fitted with a 50-hp Clerget engine, and renamed *Beta 2*. She was transferred to the RNAS in late 1913. (Museum of Army Flying)

aeroplanes. A White Paper issued by the Secretary of State for War gave details of the Air Estimates: £85,000 for new aeroplanes and dirigibles, with £28,000 for a new shed at South Farnborough in Hampshire to house them. The name of the factory – H M Balloon Factory and Balloon Section, Royal Engineers – was changed to the Army Aircraft Factory, and its engineers began to design and construct aeroplanes.

The Air Battalion formed part of the Royal Engineers, the most innovative and forward-looking branch of the British Army, and of course the principal roles of both Companies were those of reconnaissance and artillery spotting, coupled with aerial photography. No 1 Company received non-rigid airships such as *Beta*, *Gamma* and *Delta*, while 2 Company began to acquire an assortment of aeroplanes, both French and British. The Royal Navy received naval 'Blimps', non-rigid airships of different types, and also began to experiment with aeroplanes.

Public alarm in Britain at the increase in numbers of German Zeppelins and the growing strength of the French Air Force, which in 1911 was able to join in Army manoeuvres with over 200 aeroplanes, forced the War Office to step up the pace of aerial development. It announced a grant of £75 for any officer who learned how to fly an aeroplane, this being the amount charged by private flying schools for tuition. There was no shortage of adventurous young men willing to join this novel, if dangerous, branch of the armed services.

On 13 April 1912, the Royal Flying Corps was formed with the granting of a Royal Warrant by King George V, while the factory at Farnborough became the Royal Aircraft Factory. It was intended that the RFC would have a Military and a Naval Wing, with a Central Flying School common to both. However, the Admiralty refused to take part in such an arrangement and the Naval Wing became known unofficially as the Royal Naval Air Service, a title which eventually became official on 1 July 1914. The Admiralty also set up its own Flying School.

Criticisms of the Royal Aircraft Factory began to appear in journals and newspapers, accusing it of being a government monopoly engaged in unfair competition with private enterprise. In August 1912 a Military Aeroplane Competition, intended to encourage private designs of military aeroplanes, took place at Larkhill on Salisbury Plain. A BE2, built by the Royal Aircraft Factory and flown by Geoffrey de Havilland, gained the highest marks but was considered to be *hors concours* since it was a government design. The competition was officially won by S.F. Cody with his biplane powered by a 120–hp Austro-Daimler engine, but the design was not considered suitable by the Army.

In June and July of 1912 the War Office sent letters to every regiment in the British Army, asking for volunteers to join the Military Wing of the RFC, which was short of ground personnel. One branch which the RFC was anxious to improve was air photography, particularly the adaptation to aeroplanes of the methods of photography used in balloons. In August of that year a young guardsman who was to have a profound effect on the development of air photography was accepted as a First Class Mechanic Air Photographer in the RFC. He was Frederick Charles Victor Laws, twenty-five years of age, who transferred from the 3rd Battalion Coldstream Guards after approximately seven years of Army service. He was a keen photographer who had been able to set up his own darkroom and augment his service pay by selling copies of his photographs, mostly to officers in the Coldstream Guards.

Laws found that photographic facilities at Farnborough were amateurish and ill-equipped, consisting of two men and himself working in a small room under some stairs. However, after a few months he was promoted to sergeant and put in charge of the photographic section of No 1 Squadron and thus became the first non-commissioned officer in charge of photography in the RFC. This squadron had taken over the airships, balloons and kites of No 1 (Airship) Company of the Air Battalion, Royal Engineers. Laws was also disappointed with his first duties, for instead of aerial photography the only use of cameras seemed to be taking pictures of airships emerging from or entering the large hangars at Farnborough. He was keen to become an air photographer, spurred on partly by the extra two shillings a day he would receive whenever he could get into the air, but also genuinely anxious to create a specialised photographic branch for his squadron. He made friends with officers who could allow him to ascend in an airship, a balloon or even a man-carrying kite. Other photographers joined the squadron during the next six months, and he was then in charge of a section of five men.

There were no specialised air cameras in those days and the only adaptable equipment available was the press camera, usually a Pan Ross with a 6-inch lens using 5-inch by 4-inch glass plates. The two methods of air photography were, and still remain, the taking of oblique and vertical photographs. The former are comparable to those exposed from high terrain or a high building, while the latter involve overlapping photographs taken directly downwards. One major advantage of the vertical picture is that it gives an image similar to that of a map, so that the results can be employed for map production. In these early days most air photographs were oblique views, but by mid-1913 it became apparent that verticals were also required for military purposes. A special

camera was needed for airborne use, and this had to be capable of being mounted in the aeroplane as well as sufficiently automatic to provide a series of overlapping photographs in order to ensure continuity of cover for mapping.

The Watson Air Camera, designed in 1913, was the first camera specially produced for air photography in the RFC. It was with this apparatus that the first series of vertical photographs was taken, from the airship *Beta* with Captain J.E. Fletcher as pilot and Sergeant F.C.V. Laws as photographer, together with a sergeant engineer. The photography, carried out along the Basingstoke Canal, marked a major advance in the application of air photography for mapping purposes.

In October 1913 a decision was made to transfer all the airships from the RFC to the Royal Naval Air Service, together with much of the other equipment and many of the personnel. A war in Europe seemed possible by this time, and No 1 Squadron of the RFC was reorganised into an 'Aircraft Park' for the proposed British Expeditionary Force. Laws was more interested in aeroplanes than airships and asked to remain with the RFC. He was transferred to the Experimental Flight at Farnborough under Major Herbert Musgrave. This officer had served in the South African war and, after witnessing the arrival of Blériot at Dover in 1909, had also urged the War Office to interest itself in military aviation. The Farnborough unit carried out experimental work with wireless, ballooning, kiting, bombing, meteorology, photography, armament and artillery co-operation. There were many opportunities for flying and Laws gained much experience in the next few months. With his pilot, Lieutenant F. Joubert, Laws took pictures of such areas as the Royal Aircraft Factory, the Isle of Wight defences and the Solent. Exposures were made from 3,000 feet in a two-seater

F.C. Victor Laws, as a captain in the RFC. He enlisted as a private in the Coldstream Guards in February 1905 and was seconded to the RFC as an air mechanic and photographer in August 1912. He became a sergeant-major and was commissioned in November 1915, rising steadily in rank and prestige, serving after the war and then in the Second World War, before retiring as a group captain in May 1946. He died in October 1975 at the age of eighty-eight, being renowned as the 'Father of RAF Photography'. (Squadron leader P. Lamboit RAFVR)

The Maurice Farman 11, known as the 'Shorthorn', entered service with the RNAS and the RFC shortly before the beginning of the First World War for reconnaissance and bombing duties. In the earlier machines, the observer sat in the rear cockpit with a hand-held machine gun while the pilot sat in the front cockpit, but later these positions were reversed. It was in one of these machines that Sergeant Laws photographed the gathering of the Military Wing of the RFC at Netheravon in Wiltshire, a few days before war was declared. The Shorthorn was withdrawn from front line duties by the end of 1915, but continued in use for training purposes. (*Aeroplane Monthly*)

Blériot XI–2 monoplane and Laws processed the pictures in the back of the aircraft.

In June 1914 the Military Wing of the RFC was gathered into a 'Concentration Camp' at Netheravon in Wiltshire, for a trial mobilisation and practice flying over Salisbury Plain. At the end of July, Laws was transferred to 3 Squadron at Netheravon, and took off from Farnborough with his pilot Lieutenant T.O'B. Hubbard to make the journey. They were flying in an Henri Farman pusher biplane, with the Watson Air Camera mounted in the nose. The engine cut out when they were over Odiham and they came down in a hop field, ending up with the fragile aircraft looking like a broken matchbox, although neither occupant was seriously hurt.

Laws took off again two days later in a Maurice Farman 'Shorthorn', this time piloted by Lieutenant Fitzjohn Porter, and arrived over Netheravon when a great parade and inspection was in progress, for the Secretary of State for War was reviewing the Royal Flying Corps. Photographs were taken of this historic event, and Laws was very pleased with the results, for some of them were so sharp and clear that they showed a sergeant-major chasing an inquisitive dog off the parade ground. The erratic track of the dog and the footprints of the sergeant-major could be seen, where crushed grass presented different angles to the light. These marks were still visible in a later photograph and it was realised that, for example, the overnight movement of troops or vehicles over grass or soft ground might be visible in an aerial photograph up to several days afterwards, even when the tracks were not evident at ground level. The art of photographic interpretation had begun in the RFC.

Laws now felt confident that these results augered well for the future of air photography, and indeed this became a requirement several hours later when, on 4 August 1914, Britain declared war against Germany, the day after that country declared war against France. Nobody could have foreseen the terrible carnage which was to follow.

CHAPTER TWO

CAMERAS AT WAR

The British Expeditionary Force under General Sir John French which arrived in France at the beginning of the First World War was small but, for its size, was a first-class and professional fighting force. Within its ranks were well-trained soldiers, some of whom had had considerable experience of mobile warfare, although not in Europe. The Army had used observation balloons in the past and knew about man-carrying kites, but had little practical experience of the use of aeroplanes or even dirigibles as instruments of war. The idea of photographing the enemy from the air was barely considered. If discussed, some officers even expressed the view that it would be an ungentlemanly intrusion into private affairs, breaching the unwritten code of chivalry in warfare which existed in those days. On the other hand, the French Army had no such inhibitions, and the British notions of a chivalrous enemy were to be shattered when the Germans launched their first gas attack, at Ypres on 22 April 1915.

The whole of the Royal Flying Corps, consisting of 2, 3, 4 and 5 Squadrons and their aircraft park, accompanied the British Expeditionary Force to France. There were sixty-three aeroplanes in all, a collection of BE2s, BE8s, Blériot XIIs, Henri Farmans, Sopwith Tabloids and Avro 504s. They concentrated on Amiens and then, leaving the aircraft park there, moved to Mauberge near the Belgian border. The headquarters went with them, commanded by Brigadier-General

Sir David Henderson. Meanwhile the Royal Naval Air Service, which consisted of seventy-one aeroplanes and seven dirigibles, began to patrol the North Sea and also operated a small wing at Dunkirk in France.

During August and September 1914, the British fought an open and mobile campaign against the Germans. They were positioned on the left flank of the French Army, where there were no trench lines up to the Channel coast, and the fighting took place on Belgian and French soil. The Germans had planned a wide sweep through Belgium and around the northern flank of the French, gaining Paris and trapping the French Army on two sides. Britain's 'contemptible little army', as the Germans called it, stood in their way.

When the RFC squadrons flew to Mauberge they were fired upon by British columns and thus, on arrival, painted Union flags on the undersides of their wings. Since these were not easily distinguishable the insignia were altered later to the roundel which became so familiar. Meanwhile, Sergeant-Major Victor Laws had accompanied 3 Squadron to France and was fully expecting to be sent up in the air to take photographs of the enemy. But nobody seemed to think of this and instead he was sent up the line to work with the first anti-aircraft battery which had arrived in the BEF. This was a horse-drawn carrier on which pom-pom guns were mounted, and Laws's job was to indicate to the gunners which aircraft belonged to the RFC.

The Henri Farman HF20 first appeared in 1913, designed primarily as a reconnaissance aircraft. During the First World War it also served in France, Belgium, Holland, Italy, Romania and Russia. This example was photographed in March 1915 on the island of Tenedos, near Gallipoli. (J.M. Bruce/G.S. Leslie Collection)

The Short 184 seaplane was designed as a torpedo bomber and entered RNAS service in the summer of 1915. On 12 August 1915 one of these machines sank a Turkish merchant vessel in the Dardanelles, achieving the first success of any air-launched torpedo. However, the Short 184 was not wholly successful, being tricky to fly as well as difficult to take off with the load of a torpedo. It served until the end of the war, but primarily for reconnaissance and anti-submarine work. The machine in this photograph, serial 8033, was being hoisted on board the seaplane carrier *Vindex* of 2,950 tons. (J.M. Bruce/G.S. Leslie Collection)

The RFC sent up its first two reconnaissance aircraft on the morning of 19 August 1914, both manned solely by pilots. They were told to keep in company but, intent on looking for signs of the enemy, first lost each other and then themselves. Both landed to ask the way back and eventually returned to Mauberge. After this air observers flew with the pilots, and advancing German columns were spotted on the following day. The British moved into position at Mons in Belgium on 22 August and were ordered to hold this position for a day, in order to guard the left flank of the French Army. Reconnaissance aircraft were sent up and brought back accurate reports of the German dispositions. No wireless sets had been installed in the aircraft, and reports were written in the air and handed in on return. One aircraft crashed, killing both occupants, but the partially written report was brought to the British by Belgian civilians.

On 23 August the Germans attacked the British Expeditionary Force with what appeared to be overwhelming strength but were held back by the accuracy of the British fire. The soldiers had practised rapid firing with their bolt-action rifles to such effect that the Germans believed that every man had been issued with a machine gun. However, the French on their right withdrew unexpectedly, a matter which caused some bitterness with the British. Thereafter, Sir John French gave the RFC the additional task of reporting on the dispositions of the French Army.

The British Expeditionary Force then began a skilful fighting withdrawal and the RFC moved back with them, from Mauberge to Le Cateau, then in turn to St Quentin, La Fère, Compiègne, Senlis, Juilly, Serrit, Pezearches and, finally on 4 September to Mélun, 30 miles south of Paris. During this period the reconnaissance aircraft continued flying over the changing battlefield, where fierce fighting took place with gallant rearguard actions against superior forces. By 4 September the British Expeditionary Force had reached the River Marne and the Germans were unwittingly advancing into a trap, for a new French Army had been mustered and was ready to attack them in the rear. The Battle of the Marne began two days later. The Germans still attempted to attack but communication with their forward area was poor. By then, some of the RFC's aircraft were fitted with wireless sets and the crews were thus able to report immediately on the German dispositions. The Germans were defeated and forced to abandon the battlefield.

In a dispatch of 7 September to the War Office, Sir John French paid a glowing tribute to the work of the RFC during the campaign and also congratulated the squadrons on their air fighting. Although this consisted of little more than firing at German machines with rifles, sporting guns and revolvers, the RFC did succeed in shooting down about five German aircraft. This marked the beginning of aerial combat, for which the RFC is best remembered in the First World War although it comprised only part of its work.

Further battles of movement took place but by November both sides were exhausted. They dug in and a series of trenches extended from near Nieuport in Belgium to the Swiss border. A longer and even bloodier phase of the war was about to begin.

The anti-aircraft battery which Laws accompanied did not shoot down any aircraft at all, friend or foe, but as a result of this exercise he was offered a commission with the Royal Artillery and a letter to that effect was sent to the RFC. In turn, the RFC advised him to stay with them and he agreed readily, for his interest still lay in air photography. In December 1914 he was transferred from 3 Squadron, which by then

The Royal Aircraft Factory BE2c was built to satisfy the requirement of the War Office for an extremely stable reconnaissance aircraft. The first arrived in France in late 1914 but later proved unable to out-manoeuvre German monoplane fighters and too slow to escape them. It was more successful where the opposition was less severe, such as against the Turks in the Middle East. This BE2c was photographed in 1915. (*Aeroplane Monthly*)

was based at Houges, to 9 Squadron at St Omer. This was the same experimental flight in which he had previously served, but enlarged and formed into a squadron. It was equipped with BE2as, Blériot XIs and Maurice Farmans, and still commanded by Major Herbert Musgrave. The squadron came under the direct control of the headquarters of the RFC. Its main occupation was the development of wireless communications but Laws was given the duties of a carpenter, then a motor driver, and finally a motor mechanic. There was still no mention of photography.

A few days before Laws arrived, a new officer joined 9 Squadron. This was 2nd Lieutenant J.T.C. Moore-Brabazon, thirty years of age and a person of considerable experience and influence. He was a skilled mechanic, a balloonist, an acclaimed motor-racing driver, a sportsman, and an aviator who had won many competitions and who held Certificate No 1 issued by the Royal Aero Club, dated 8 March 1910. One of his many friends had been the eccentric genius Charles S. Rolls of Rolls-Royce fame, for whom he had worked as an unpaid mechanic. When Rolls was killed tragically in a Wright aircraft on 12 July 1910, Moore-Brabazon's wife was expecting her first baby and she asked him to cease flying, for he had already suffered a number of accidents in balloons, aeroplanes and on the motor-racing track. He agreed, but on the outbreak of war volunteered to serve as an ambulance driver in France. After several rather unpleasant weeks in that capacity, he decided that he should serve in the RFC and then used his influence in England to obtain a commission and his wings, without any military experience at all.

Moore-Brabazon was not altogether happy with his duties in 9 Squadron, which was non-operational at the time, although he admired most of the other officers, many of whom later achieved great distinction in the RFC as well as in the RAF. However, he did not get along well with Major Musgrave and, on one occasion when he queried an order, was told, 'You will obey your superior officers.' His response was cutting: '*Superior* officer? Senior, if you please, sir.' No disciplinary action was taken against him, and in fact when the various flights of 9 Squadron were dispersed to other squadrons in February 1915, Major Musgrave left the RFC and returned to the Army; he was killed on a patrol behind the German lines on 2 June 1918. His old squadron was re-formed at Brooklands on 1 April 1915 under one of its previous officers, Major Hugh C.T. Dowding, who later commanded the headquarters wing of the RFC in France and twenty-five years on was to earn undying fame as the C-in-C of Fighter Command during the Battle of Britain.

Meanwhile Moore-Brabazon, who was both inventive and enterprising, yearned to do something positive to further the progress of the RFC and help win the war. His opportunity came in early January 1915 after Sir John French had been impressed by a map of the enemy trenches constructed from clear photographs obtained by the French Air Force. The RFC's 3 Squadron had attempted to take photographs of German dispositions during the previous September, during the time Laws was serving with the Royal Artillery, but the results were indistinct. The French map was passed to Sir David Henderson of the RFC, and a staff officer, Major W.G.H. Salmond, was instructed to study the French photographic organisation. Salmond found that the French squadrons were fully staffed with expert photographic personnel, and he recommended to Sir David Henderson that an experimental photographic section be set up in the RFC.

By this time, four of the operational squadrons of the RFC in France had been

The SS (Sea Scout) airship was supplied to the RNAS in March 1915 for coastal patrols around the British coast. It carried a crew of two in a control car constructed from a fuselage such as an Armstrong Whitworth FK3, slung from the non-rigid envelope. This SS airship was photographed on 18 December 1917 while flying over the snow-covered airfield of Waddington in Lincolnshire. (J.M. Bruce/G.S. Leslie Collection)

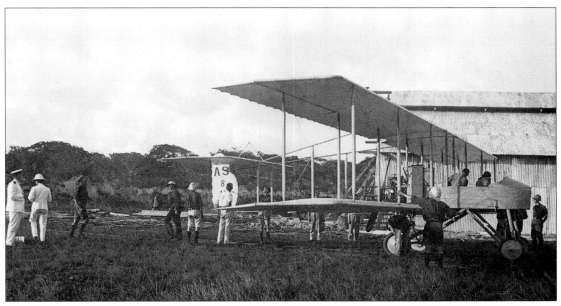

The Henri Farman HF27 was a variant of the HF20, slightly bigger and with a steel airframe. This example of the RNAS, serial 3618, was photographed in early 1915 on the island of Mafia, near the delta of the River Rufiji in German East Africa, where it was engaged on a hunt for the cruiser *Königsberg*. (J.M. Bruce/ G.S. Leslie Collection)

Above, left: Lord Brabazon of Tara, photographed here as Lieutenant John T.C. Moore-Brabazon MC of the RFC, was a pioneer aviator who held No 1 Certificate of the Royal Aero Club. Born on 8 February 1884, he was responsible for the RFC/RAF Photographic Section in the First World War, rising to the rank of Lieutenant-Colonel. He became an MP in 1918 and remained very prominent in aviation circles until his death on 17 May 1964. *Above, right:* Lieutenant Charles D.M. Campbell MBE, who was a founder of RFC photography in the First World War, together with J.T.C. Moore-Brabazon and Sergeant-Major F.C.V. Laws. He rose to the rank of major but died of tuberculosis on 9 March 1918. (Both photos: B. Gray)

The RE5 was the first of the Royal Aircraft Factory's 'Reconnaissance Experimental' biplanes to be put into production. This example, serial 380, was completed in March 1914 as a single-seater with an unequal wingspan. It joined 2 Squadron in France in November 1914, probably converted to a standard two-seater. Most production RE5s were equal-span two-seaters. The air observer sat in the front, armed only with personal weapons. The RE5s was a stable aircraft, but so unmanoeuvrable that it was soon withdrawn from front-line service. (J.M. Bruce/G.S. Leslie Collection)

The A-type camera was built to specifications given to the Thornton-Pickard Camera Company by Lieutenants J.T.C. Moore-Brabazon and C.D.M. Campbell on return from the Western Front in early 1915. It was a tapered and brass-bound wooden box which took 5-inch by 4-inch plates, inserted one after the other by hand. The lens was initially an 8½-inch set at infinity focus. The camera could be mounted on a bracket for vertical photography or the operator could hold it by the straps, leaning over the side into the slipstream. The sight was a simple brass tube with cross-wires. (Flight Lieutenant G.H. Parry RAF (Ret'd))

Lieutenant C.E. Tinne, an air observer in the RFC who was formerly an officer in the Royal Field Artillery, holding an A-type camera in a Nieuport 12 of 46 Squadron. This aircraft also carried a Lewis gun mounted on a Scarff ring. In October 1916, 46 Squadron moved to the Western Front, where it was employed on air reconnaissance and artillery spotting. (Flight Lieutenant G.H. Parry RAF (Ret'd))

formed into two wings, each to operate with two of the four Army Corps of the BEF. The First Wing, commanded by Lieutenant-Colonel Hugh M. Trenchard, comprised 2 and 3 Squadrons while the Second Wing, commanded by Lieutenant-Colonel C.J. Burke, controlled 5 and 6 Squadrons. This arrangement was made in anticipation of a huge expansion of the RFC, for new wings and many new squadrons were planned to co-ordinate with additional Army Corps. The wireless unit, 9 Squadron and 4 Squadron remained temporarily attached to RFC Headquarters, but the new experimental photographic section was set up under the First Wing in the middle of January 1915.

Lieutenant-Colonel Trenchard was an extremely formidable officer who was held in awe and respect by all those who served under him. His Army service had been mainly in India and Africa. During 1912 at the age of thirty-nine he had qualified privately as a pilot at the Sopwith School, paying for his tuition himself. When Sir David Henderson left to take command of the RFC in France, Trenchard commanded the Military Wing at Farnborough, where he had been responsible for much of the planning that led to the later expansion. Confronted with his tall figure and broad shoulders, coupled with his booming voice, junior officers could be reduced to abject misery when subjected to his rebukes. But he was not an unkind person and his attributes of wisdom and farsightedness became startlingly evident as the war progressed and afterwards in the inter-war years. He will always be remembered as the 'Father of the RAF'.

Trenchard sought men with knowledge and experience of photography to staff the new section, and three were available. One of these was 2nd Lieutenant Moore-Brabazon, who had already made up his mind that photography was bound to become an important function for the RFC and had

asked Sir David Henderson's General Staff Officer, Lieutenant-Colonel F.H. Sykes, if he could be considered for work in this specialism. In addition to his other accomplishments, he had previously practised photography on the ground and also experimented with colour systems, X-ray work and high-speed photography in his laboratory. Thus he felt that he was well-qualified in the art of photography. The other candidate was Lieutenant Charles D.M. Campbell, of whom little has been recorded save that he is known to have been proficient as a photographer; he eventually rose to the rank of major but died of tuberculosis before the end of the war.

Neither Moore-Brabazon nor Campbell had had any experience of aerial photography but one man who was proficient in that field was Sergeant-Major Laws. Trenchard sent for the three men, all of whom were based on the airfield at St Omer but had scarcely met before, and asked Laws for his recommendations. Laws suggested that photographic sections should be set up in each wing, and that he should be sent to them in turn, in order to form, equip and run them until they were capable of continuing on their own. The two junior officers supported his opinion, which was accepted by Trenchard. Soon afterwards, Laws began three months with the First Wing. This was followed by three months with the Second Wing and then three months with the Third Wing, which was formed in March 1915.

At the headquarters of the First Wing, which was based within St Omer, Trenchard gave Moore-Brabazon and Campbell the encouragement they needed to develop air photography, and there was much work ahead of them. The majority of cameras in use with the RFC were the folding type with bellows, which were usually held over the side of the cockpit and took rather unsatisfactory oblique pictures, although one

An A-type camera being handed to the air observer of a Vickers Fighting Biplane FB5, a two-seater with a pusher engine which first reached France in July 1915. It was armed with a single Lewis gun and thus the first specialised British fighter, but could also be used for photo-reconnaissance. (Flight Lieutenant G.H. Parry RAF (Ret'd))

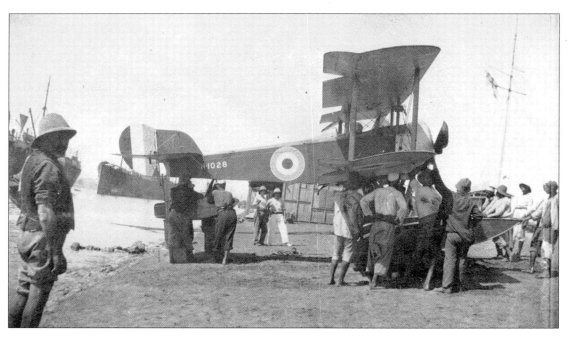

The Sopwith Baby floatplane began to enter service with the RNAS in October 1915. It was a single-seater employed on reconnaissance, anti-submarine work, bombing and fighter patrols. In addition to operating from bases around the British coast, it served on aircraft carriers in the North Sea and the Mediterranean. Serial N1028 seen here operated in the Mediterranean. (J.M. Bruce/G.S. Leslie Collection)

The Caudron GIII was widely used as a photo-reconnaissance aircraft in the early years of the First World War. Most were manufactured in France, and were supplied to the RFC and the RNAS, as well as to Belgium, Russia and Italy. The machine was unusual since it was fitted with a tractor engine but used the nacelle and tailbooms configuration of a pusher aircraft. Like many reconnaissance aircraft, it was vulnerable to enemy fighters. This Caudron GIII, photographed in 1915, carried a vertical A-type camera. (J.M. Bruce/G.S. Leslie Collection)

The Morane-Saulnier BB biplane was developed as an alternative to the parasol monoplanes, as a reconnaissance aircraft. It entered service with the RFC in December 1915. The armament consisted of two Lewis guns, one firing through the propeller and one in the rear cockpit. It was considered a heavy aircraft to handle but continued in service until January 1917. This example was fitted with an asymmetrical bulge on the starboard side for a camera housing. (J.M. Bruce/G.S. Leslie Collection)

The Franco-British Aviation flying boat first appeared in 1915. Some were supplied to the RNAS and were used for photo-reconnaissance and naval patrols. A camera mounting was fitted to the starboard side of this example, serial 3646. (J.M. Bruce/G.S. Leslie Collection)

enterprising observer of 2 Squadron cut a hole in the bottom of his cockpit in a BE2a and took some verticals.

A more robust camera was required, one which could be either hand-held or mounted on the aircraft. Moore-Brabazon and Campbell set about designing one and visited England to invite co-operation with the Thornton-Pickard Manufacturing Company. It was a box-type, built to withstand rough usage, which made use of the Mackenzie-Wishart plates and a Zeiss Tessar lens, and became known as the A-type camera. It could be employed for both oblique and vertical photography and was first used by 3 Squadron over the enemy trenches on 3 March 1915. Although each exposure required ten operations, the results were excellent, and the invention went into production for the RFC.

Even before the introduction of this new camera, however, the tutelage given by Victor Laws to the photographic section of the First Wing bore fruit. In advance of the battle of Neuve Chapelle which began on 10 March, 2 and 3 Squadrons successfully photographed the entire German defences from a depth of 700 to 1,500 yards, in an area where a salient jutted out into the British positions near the junction with the French Army. The enemy trenches shown on the photographs were then traced on a skeleton map in a scale of 1:8,000, and details of the British plan of attack were superimposed.

Copies of the map were used by the artillery, the infantry and the aircrews. The gunners subjected the German forward trenches to a short but intense bombardment and then lifted their fire to fall on the communication trenches and support positions while the infantry attacked. This battle was also notable for the introduction of the 'clock-code' system of artillery spotting by the reconnaissance aircraft. The air observer was handed a celluloid disc with concentric circles radiating from the centre, each circle given a letter, together with the numbers of a clock shown round the outer rim. When the disc was centred on an enemy target shown on the map, he was able to send a wireless message to the battery, giving in letter and figure form the position where the shells were falling, thus enabling the gunners to correct their aim.

Under cover of accurate artillery fire, the British infantry successfully attacked the village of Neuve Chapelle from two sides and consolidated their positions, although further progress was hampered by bad weather, lack of sufficient artillery shells, and stiffening German resistance. For the RFC, the battle was also notable since it marked the first systematic attempt to bomb German positions, using newly introduced bomb racks. These attacks took place at low level behind the German front lines, mainly against railway lines and troop trains, with considerable success.

These beginnings led to the extensive use of photography, interpretation, map construction and artillery spotting in the RFC, and later in the RAF. Before long, Trenchard began carrying aerial photographs in his pockets, displaying them on every possible occasion as evidence of the success of his reconnaissance aircraft and their aerial photography.

CHAPTER THREE

ABOVE THE TRENCHES

The limited success at Neuve Chapelle convinced the British commanders that they had found a formula for defeating the Germans on the Western Front. Firstly, the enemy trenches and supply lines should be covered continually by photo-reconnaissance aircraft, followed by military interpretation of the photographs and the construction of accurate maps. Next, the enemy positions should be subjected to enormous artillery bombardment, as soon as sufficient supplies of ordnance became available from munition factories. This bombardment would be guided by artillery-spotting from aircraft and balloons, enabling the gunners to knock out all German strong points. Then waves of infantry would attack the demoralised defenders and occupy their positions, leading to a breakthrough of the enemy lines. Unfortunately, this planning was to prove tragically flawed, mainly because the Germans were capable of anticipating the British intentions and taking effective counter-measures.

To play its part in these plans, the RFC continued a rapid expansion. By April 1915 there were three wings in France, consisting of seven squadrons and one flight, and an aircraft park. There were about eighty-five aeroplanes in the front line and about twenty in reserve. A much greater expansion had been authorised, now that the vital role of aerial reconnaissance and photography had been recognised. When it was proposed in early 1915 to increase the number of RFC squadrons to fifty the Secretary of State for War, Lord Kitchener, doubled the figure. A similar increase was under way in the RNAS.

However, the Germans did not wage war by the same rules as the British. The Second Battle of Ypres opened in the evening of 22 April 1915 with the infamous release of chlorine gas by the Germans towards a salient occupied by French colonial troops. It was seen from above by a reconnaissance aircraft of 6 Squadron, based at Poperinghe in Belgium, as a bank of yellow-green cloud emerging from the German trenches and drifting in the wind towards the French positions. The victims were not equipped with gas masks and those who were not suffocated fled, leaving a wide gap on the British right flank. German reinforcements moving up to the front were spotted by RFC reconnaissance aircraft and duly bombed, while the 1st Canadian Division counter-attacked and held the line in an epic defence, in spite of enormous casualties.*

This gas attack did not deter the British and the French from continuing a spring offensive, although with limited success. In early May, kite balloons began to arrive on the Western Front, manned by the RNAS but

*The author's uncle, Company Sergeant-Major Thomas O. Nesbit of B Company 10th Battalion, 2nd Brigade, 1st Canadian Expeditionary Force, was killed in this battle. His battalion was one of two which led the counter-attack and of its 750 men only 150 remained after four days of fighting.

A kite balloon, used for spotting by both the RFC and the RNAS, photographed over trenches dug into farmland where the harvest had been gathered. The elongated 'sausage' shape and the drogues on the wire helped to steady the balloon, but observers frequently suffered from airsickness. These balloons were usually flown 3 miles from enemy lines but could be set on fire by gunfire from aircraft or artillery shells. Balloon observers were provided with parachutes. (East Anglian Photographic Collection)

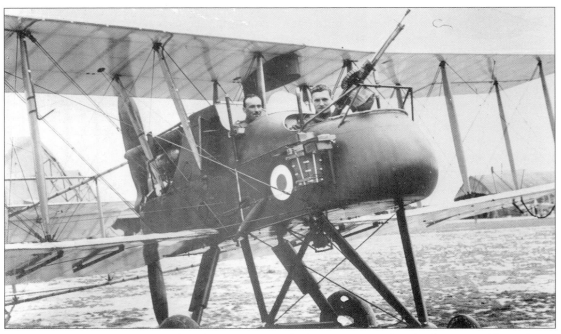

The Royal Aircraft Factory FE2a was a two-seat biplane with a pusher engine which first flew in January 1915. The FE2b, with a more powerful engine, began to arrive in France during the following October. With two Lewis guns, one firing forward and the other upwards towards the rear, the aircraft proved effective against Fokker monoplanes. This FE2b serial 4903 of 18 Squadron, which was equipped with these machines from April 1916 to June 1916, was fitted with a C-type camera. (J.M. Bruce/G.S. Leslie Collection)

Above, left: The WA-type camera was an adaptation of the B-type camera, designed for wide-angle work to cover large areas. It used plates of 8½ by 6½ inches, with lenses of either 6 or 10 inches. Excellent results were achieved by this camera, which could cover a ground area of 3 miles by 2 miles from 20,000 feet. *Above, right:* The C-type camera utilised the body of the A-type but was fitted with a plate-changing top and two magazines. One magazine held about eighteen plates stacked face down over the focal plane. After exposure the plate was slid to a frame in the second magazine, into which it fell. The shutter of the camera, fitted outside the aircraft, was operated by the pilot or observer by a cord attached to the trigger, as shown. Greatly improved results were obtained with this camera. *Right:* A C-type camera fitted to the rear cockpit of a Royal Aircraft Factory BE2c reconnaissance biplane. (All photos: Flight Lieutenant G.H. Parry RAF (Ret'd))

The Royal Aircraft Factory RE7 was designed with a wider wingspan and a more powerful engine than its predecessor, the RE5, to carry a new and large 336-lb bomb as well as to carry out photo-reconnaissance duties. The first RE7 went to France in September 1915 to join 12 Squadron, and many squadrons had a few RE7s by the end of that year. The aircraft was slow and armed with only a single machine gun mounted in the front cockpit. Withdrawal from front-line service began at the end of 1916. This example was fitted with a vertical camera, possibly a WA-type. (J.M. Bruce/G.S. Leslie Collection)

working in co-ordination with the RFC. These balloons were modelled on the German *Drachen*, a sausage-shaped design with the forward segment filled with gas and the rear section with air. The mooring cable was attached to the nose while the observation car was slung from the rear. For stability, the balloon was fitted with a rudder and wind sails, as well as drogue streamers flying from the tail. This design was a great improvement on the spherical balloon, which could not ascend in winds of more than 20 mph and also rotated on its axis, making observation difficult. At the same time, the man-carrying kite could not be flown in winds of less than 20 mph and was also an unsteady platform, so that the kite balloon combined the best attributes of both. They proved of great use for artillery spotting at first, but those employed on both sides later became favourite targets for fighter aircraft.

By the Battle of Loos, which began on 25 September 1915, the three wings of RFC on the Western Front had grown to twelve squadrons with about a hundred and sixty aeroplanes, plus forty aeroplanes in reserve in two aircraft parks, as well as four RNAS Kite Balloon Sections in the front line. The three photographic sections were also equipped with mobile darkrooms, built on the backs of Leyland lorries, which supplemented the darkrooms improvised in cellars and sheds. Five weeks earlier, Sir David Henderson had returned to the War Office and Brigadier-General Trenchard had taken over command of the RFC in France.

The attempts of the British and the French to break the German lines made little progress, and it was in this period that air fighting developed significantly. The summer of 1915 had seen the introduction of a German machine which, for several months, was to prove the scourge of British reconnaissance aircraft. This was the Fokker E-type monoplane, designed by the Dutchman Anthony Fokker before the war but steadily improved until it combined clean lines with a good performance. It was armed with a forward-firing machine gun linked with an interrupter gear, so that the bullets passed the blades of the revolving propeller and enabled the pilot to take direct aim in the line of his flight. A new tactic was evolved for this machine, whereby the German pilot cruised at relatively high altitudes looking for prey and then dived down very steeply, preferably from out of the sun. The pilot fired at his victim and then shot past at high speed, usually before any retaliation could take place. An improvement on this tactic was introduced by Leutnant Max Immelmann, who developed a method of rolling off the top of a loop after the first pass, thus regaining altitude and repeating the attack.

The Royal Aircraft Factory and the Royal Flying Corps had shunned monoplanes after several fatal accidents had occurred in experimental machines, even though they were known to be very manoeuvrable as well as faster than biplanes. Stability and safety for air reconnaissance were the main criteria for new machines rather than air fighting qualities. Even the Blériot monoplane was redesigned as a biplane, being known as a BE, or Blériot Experimental, a type with a tractor engine; the early types had no armament. Another type was the FE or Farman Experimental, with a pusher engine at the rear of the cockpit; this enabled the observer to sit in the front cockpit and fire his machine gun without obstruction by the propeller. The third type was the most stable of all, the RE, or Reconnaissance Experimental, with a tractor engine and the observer sitting in front, supplied in the early machines with only small arms for defence. The last type was the SE, or Scouting Experimental, a single-seater with a tractor engine; the early type was fitted with no more than a couple of rifles angled to fire outside the propeller arc,

A wooden shed built on the side of 'Bocket Winckel' in the Belgian village of Eecke served as a 'cabine photographique' in May 1916. (East Anglian Photographic Collection)

A Leyland mobile photographic 'Prime Mover' of II Wing RFC in France. (East Anglian Photographic Collection)

Ground photographers at the entrance to a photographic workroom at Abeele in Belgium, close to the border with north-east France, in March 1916. RFC photographers were known as 'stickybacks'. (East Anglian Photographic Collection)

A 'Field Developing Box' used by the RFC in France during the First World War. The operator put his arms through the 'sleeves' to develop the plates. Printing was done by light reflected through the mirror. (Squadron Leader P. Lamboit, courtesy Photogrammetric Record)

The Sopwith 1½-Strutter was used widely for photo-reconnaissance as well as for bombing, ground strafing and coastal patrols. It first entered service with the RNAS in April 1916 but was soon in demand by the RFC, being popular as the first British aircraft with a machine gun efficiently synchronised to fire through the propeller. Strutters were replaced with Sopwith Camels on the Western Front during the summer of 1917 but were employed on home defence and on training duties, while others continued on Fleet charge. This example was serial 7777. (J.M. Bruce/G.S. Leslie Collection)

The twin-engined Caudron R4 was designed as a three-seater bomber, with the pilot in the centre cockpit and gunners in the other two. However, it proved too underpowered to carry the intended load and, from April 1916 to April 1917, was used by the French mainly for photo-reconnaissance. This machine had made an unconventional landing on top of a large shed. The French NCO underneath was smoking a cigarette. (J.M. Bruce/G.S. Leslie Collection)

The C (Coastal) airship was another non-rigid and first flew with the RNAS in June 1916. It carried a crew of 5 and had an endurance of about 11 hours at its full speed of 48 mph, or considerably more at lower speeds. This photograph of C9 was taken at Mullion in Cornwall in 1917. (J.M. Bruce/G.S. Leslie Collection)

34

but the later SE5a proved one of the most formidable fighters of the war.

The Royal Aircraft Factory BE2c was the type which most often fell victim to the Fokker monoplane, when the crews were flying over enemy lines for reconnaissance and photography. Its operational ceiling was 10,000 feet compared with the 11,500 feet of the Fokker, while its maximum speed in level flight was about 72 mph compared with 83 mph. By this time, the BE2c was fitted with a Lewis gun in the front cockpit, but the observer had a very limited field of fire above the propeller and wings, or to port and starboard. An additional hazard was the weather, for the crews usually encountered head winds on their return journeys against the prevailing westerlies.

There had always been enemy aircraft, but now the unfortunate BE2c earned the nickname of 'Fokker fodder'. The menace of the Fokker reached its height in October 1915 and continued for several months. The supremacy of this German fighter began to wane when the Nieuport Scout appeared in the spring of the following year and better-armed British reconnaissance machines such as the FE2 and the DH2 were introduced. For the rest of the war, control of the skies over the battlefields swung from one side to the other as new types were introduced, but life expectancy for RFC fliers always remained short, save for the most skilled or the very lucky. While British reconnaissance aircraft usually flew over enemy positions, the method of air photography employed by the Germans consisted mainly of flying low over their own lines and taking distant oblique shots of the Allied positions.

The expansion of the RFC and the replacement of aircrew losses could not have taken place without a huge increase in training facilities. Air photography was one of the subjects which needed to be taught, as well as the equally difficult photographic techniques required on the ground. Here it was Victor Laws who came to the fore once more. After nine months spent forming the photographic sections of the three wings in France and commanding these for six months, he returned to England in September 1915 at his own suggestion to set up a School of Photography at Farnborough.

At this time Laws was still a sergeant-major, having resisted offers of a commission, since this involved a drop in pay as well as the cost of bills in the officers' mess. However, in his new appointment his trainees were to include experienced photographers who had been recruited into the RFC to serve in the new function of photographic officer and in turn become instructors. It was clear that he would have to accept a commission, and on 7 November 1915 was discharged as a non-commissioned officer to become a 2nd Lieutenant in the Lincolnshire Regiment, seconded to the Royal Flying Corps. He was appointed immediately as commandant of the newly created RFC School of Photography at Farnborough.

Meanwhile, Moore-Brabazon and Campbell continued to develop cameras. The B-type was introduced as a modified and enlarged version of the A-type. This used 8½-inch by 6½-inch plates instead of 5-inch by 4-inch and had the means of fitting a tubular extension to the main body, giving longer lenses. This new camera was used mainly for oblique work, but a further adaptation known as the WA-type employed the same plate size and was used for wide-angle work. Another camera, the C-type, used the body and the plates of the A-type but was fitted with a semi-automatic device for changing the plates, using two magazines; this was introduced in the summer of 1915. At the end of 1916 the E-type followed the C-type, being made of metal and fitted with a remote control which facilitated the operation.

The Curtiss H12 flying boat, derived from the American H4, was assembled at Felixstowe for the RNAS, from 1916 onwards, from parts made in the USA. It was fitted with Rolls-Royce engines in place of the original Curtiss engines and carried a crew of four. The airman in this photograph was holding a Houghton-Butcher naval camera. This was a light hand-held camera used mainly for obliques, which employed glass plates and took 7-inch by 5-inch photographs. The cockpit was fitted with twin Lewis machine guns. (J.M. Bruce/G.S. Leslie Collection)

The SSZ (Sea Scout Zero) airship was introduced in 1916. It was provided with a control car modified so that it could float like a boat, in case of landings in the sea. The crew was increased to three and the pusher engine could be started by a mechanic standing inside the rear cockpit. This photograph of SSZ 25, showing a Houghton-Butcher naval camera, was taken at Mullion in Cornwall on 9 January 1918. (J.M. Bruce/G.S. Leslie Collection)

A vertical photograph of a German position on the Western Front taken on 22 October 1916. The interpreters picked out a strong point protected by wire defences at 'A', a passage through the wire at 'B', dugouts in reserve trenches at 'C', trenches marked out but not dug at 'E', and a series of dugouts connected by a trench at 'F'. (The late Squadron Leader J.E. Archbald)

The Martinsyde 'Elephant' was a single-seater biplane designed for long-range escort duty, but it proved too heavy and unresponsive for this role. It first appeared on the Western Front in early 1916, and was soon employed as a bomber, for ground attack and air reconnaissance. In this photograph of serial A6262, a camera mount can be seen fitted beside the pilot's cockpit. (J.M. Bruce/G.S. Leslie Collection)

Above, left: The E-type camera, made from metal, succeeded earlier wooden types which sometimes suffered from distortion during changes of temperature and threw the lens out of focus. It was fitted with a remote control and could be mounted alongside the observer or behind his seat, with the lens through a hole in the fuselage. This E-type camera was photographed on the side of a Martinsyde 'Elephant'. *Below, left:* The L-type camera, which succeeded the E-type, required less attention than any previous models. It could be fitted either inside or outside the cockpit and was operated either by hand or automatically. When working on power, the plate changed every four seconds. This L-type was suspended in a spring mounting which converted vibrations into a mainly vertical movement, minimising blurring of exposures. (Both photos: Flight Lieutenant G.H. Parry RAF (Ret'd)) *Above, right:* An L-type camera fitted to a Sopwith Pup. The flexible cable was connected to a small windmill fitted to the aircraft, providing power drive for the mechanism of the camera. (J.M. Bruce/G.S. Leslie Collection)

The Royal Aircraft Factory FE2d, with a more powerful engine than the FE2b, began to enter service in June 1916. This FE2d serial A6516 of 20 Squadron, which was equipped with these machines from June 1916 to September 1917, was fitted with an L-type camera. (J.M. Bruce/G.S. Leslie Collection)

The Sopwith Pup was a small but robust fighter first delivered to the RNAS in the autumn of 1916, and then in large quantities to the RFC. Fitted initially with a single Vickers gun firing through the propeller, it was well-liked for its excellent flying and fighting qualities. The Sopwith Camel was introduced in the summer of 1917 and the Pup began to be withdrawn at the end of that year. Large numbers of Pups were transferred to training units, such as the example here. (J.M. Bruce/G.S. Leslie Collection)

In January 1916 the RFC in France underwent reorganisation to meet the growing needs of the BEF. It was formed into two brigades, each to support an army in the field. In turn each brigade was divided into two wings, a corps wing and an army wing. The corps wing carried out tactical photographic reconnaissance and artillery spotting for a distance of up to 5 miles beyond the enemy lines, while the army wing carried out strategic photographic reconnaissance and bombing duties beyond this distance. A third brigade was added in mid-February, so that by then there were six wings, each with its own photographic section. In addition, there was the headquarters wing.

By the opening of the notorious Battle of the Somme on 1 July 1916, the RFC in France had grown to four brigades, consisting of twenty-seven squadrons with a front-line strength of 421 aeroplanes, as well as four kite balloon squadrons. There were also 216 aeroplanes in reserve at aircraft parks, while further squadrons were forming in England. By then, the demand for constantly updated photography had become so enormous and urgent that the wing sections could not cope quickly enough. A small photographic section, usually consisting of one NCO and three men, had been established at every front-line squadron. The men had been trained at the School of Photography at Farnborough in such matters as developing and printing of plates, the mixing of chemicals, enlargement of prints, their lettering and numbering, lantern slides, the use and maintenance of aerial cameras, and the method of preparing maps from photographs. The techniques of photographic interpreters had also improved, with the use of shadows to determine height and depth playing an important part. As well as distinguishing trenches and strong points, the interpreters could pick out batteries, mortar and machine gun emplacements, wire, sniper posts, headquarters, tracks of troops and many other points of interest.

In preparation for the British and French assaults, all the German positions had been photographed by tactical and strategic aircraft, and maps had been constructed. A tremendous artillery bombardment opened, with the fire accurately directed from balloons and aeroplanes. This bombardment lasted for a week before 1 July, and then the infantry came out of the trenches and attacked. Unfortunately, the element of surprise which had been so crucial at Neuve Chapelle was lost, for the long bombardment had given the Germans ample warning of what was to follow. Their survivors rose up from their deep dugouts and mowed down the attackers.

These frontal assaults in the area of the Somme continued at intervals until the following November, with little territorial gain. Almost four hundred British aircraft were lost, including many of those employed on photographic reconnaissance duties. The Germans appear to have lost almost the same number of aircraft although, being outnumbered, they ventured over enemy lines far less frequently than the British or the French. Casualties on the ground were appalling: 450,000 British, 340,000 French and 530,000 German.

Back in England, Laws's promotion was rapid, for in September 1916 he was posted as a captain from the School of Photography to the headquarters of the Training Brigade, which had been formed two months earlier. His previous position was taken over by an air observer, Lieutenant Cyril Porri. On arrival in his new post, Laws realised that it would be preferable if he wore pilot's wings, since one of his functions was to give lectures to officers under training for flying duties. Before receiving his commission, he had been the only NCO entitled to wear the air

The NS (North Sea) airships were the last non-rigids constructed in Britain, the first of the series of twelve entering service in February 1917. They had a duration of about 21 hours at the full speed of 57 mph while carrying a crew of ten. This photograph of NS1 was taken at Longside in Aberdeenshire, a crew member seemingly balanced precariously on the gondola. (J.M. Bruce/G.S. Leslie Collection)

The Royal Aircraft Factory RE8 was designed to provide the RFC with a reconnaissance aircraft which was better defended than the BE2 series. It carried a machine gun firing through the propeller and either one or two machine guns mounted on a Scarff ring in the air observer's position. The RE8 entered service in November 1916 and continued until the end of the war. As with other designs from the Royal Aircraft Factory, the insistence on stability resulted in an aircraft which could be out-manoeuvred by enemy fighters. The machine shown here carried a camera mounted vertically. (J.M. Bruce/G.S. Leslie Collection)

Above, left: The LB-type vertical camera was developed when improved anti-aircraft defences forced reconnaissance aircraft to fly higher. The lens cones were up to the length of 20 inches, as shown in this photograph. However, the plates were only 5 inches by 4 inches in size, so that some definition of photographs was lost during enlargement of photographs taken from high level. *Above, right:* An LB-type vertical camera with a shorter focal length, shown here with RFC photographers in 1918. Such cameras were used for reconnaissance at lower level over enemy trenches. (Both photos: Flight Lieutenant G.H. Parry RAF (Ret'd))

observer's brevet, since he had made a number of photographic flights over enemy lines. He applied for a flying course and permission was granted provided he agreed to remain in the photographic branch; he duly passed his course as a pilot and was granted his wings. Within eleven months of obtaining his commission, Laws attained the rank of major.

Laws also took a hand in designing cameras, recognising the need for a type that required as little attention as possible by aircrews who were menaced by enemy fighters. The result was the L-type, which was introduced in early 1917 and represented a further improvement in aerial cameras, for it could be operated either by hand or automatically. The camera could be fitted in any position in the aircraft, since power for changing the plates and resetting the shutter was obtained through a flexible drive connected to a 'windmill' turned by the airflow. The pilot or observer simply pressed a trigger to take an exposure and start the

mechanism. When the camera was set to automatic feed, a locking device ensured that the trigger could not be pressed again until the camera was reset.

The L-type was followed by the LB-type, in which both Laws and Moore-Brabazon collaborated. This employed lenses with much longer focal lengths, up to 20 inches, which enabled aircraft with improved performance to fly above anti-aircraft fire and still obtain reasonable results. The camera was also easier to maintain, since the various sections of the mechanism could be removed with less difficulty for overhaul.

The heavy losses of photo-reconnaissance aircraft in 1916 resulted in some rethinking of tactics by the RFC. Fighters were employed to escort the camera-carrying aircraft but, when losses continued in the whirl of dogfights, cameras were mounted in some of the fighters on the assumption that these were better able to look after themselves. However, this did not prove satisfactory, for it was always necessary to fly straight and level while photographing and at such a time any aircraft was vulnerable. The idea of stripping a single-seater fighter of its armament, fitting it with a camera and then flying at altitudes which armed fighters could not reach, does not seem to have occurred to the planners. It was not until the Second World War that this very successful method was employed.

The Russian Revolution began in March 1917 and it became apparent to the Allies that the Germans would be able to transfer troops to the Western Front. Although the USA declared war on Germany the following month, she was unable to train and equip a large expeditionary force immediately. The RFC had increased its strength to about fifty squadrons by this time, and the Allies continued their attacks throughout the year, through the Battle of Arras, the Third Battle of Ypres and the Battle of Cambrai. Enormous losses were sustained while little was gained. By December, when the Russo-German Armistice was signed, the exhausted troops of the Allies faced a very ominous situation. In the same month, Major Victor Laws was posted to France as Senior Photographic Officer in General Headquarters, replacing Moore-Brabazon who returned to England as a lieutenant-colonel in order to take charge of photographic requirements at the War Office. By this time a vast photographic map of the whole of the Western Front had been built up, constantly amended as new photographs were brought in almost daily. With the aid of this map, the Allied commanders watched enemy preparations while battle-hardened German troops poured across from the Eastern Front.

When the Germans began their spring offensive on 21 March 1918, their movements behind the lines had been shrouded by fog for several days, enabling them to bring forward in secrecy troops and aircraft to key sectors. Their assault was heralded by an intense but short artillery bombardment: the infantry attack broke through the Allied lines and threatened to roll up and entrap whole armies. Suddenly, trench warfare was replaced by mobile battles, with the German positions reported only intermittently in the continuing bad weather. For a while, it seemed that even the fall of Paris was possible.

On 1 April 1918 the Royal Air Force was formed by merging the RFC and the RNAS, partly to unite their heavy bombers in an 'Independent Bombing Force' which it was expected would exact retribution on Germany for the bombing of London by Gothas. This RAF bombing force was located in France and commanded by Major-General Hugh Trenchard, who had been replaced during the previous January by Major-General John Salmond as General Officer Commanding the RFC. However, it was the less dramatic work of the photo-reconnaissance aircraft over the Western Front which was to prove of far greater importance to the Allies. Ten days after the formation of the RAF the Allied position on the Western Front had become so perilous that the British commander, Field Marshal Sir Douglas Haig, delivered a somewhat desperate 'backs to the wall' order of the day to his troops. On the following day the weather cleared and RAF photo-reconnaissance aircraft brought back precise details of the German positions, which were bombed and machine-gunned with considerable effect, and then subjected to artillery bombardment which was accurately directed from the air. More photographs were taken on that day than on any other since the outbreak of war. From this time, air surveillance was continuous. The German attacks were checked and, although further thrusts were made over the next three

The BM-type camera was an enlarged version of the LB-type, with a plate size of 9½ inches by 7 inches. It gave results of fine detail but its disadvantage was the weight, 85 lb with one magazine and 12 plates by comparison with 52 lb for the LB-type and 18 plates. This BM-type camera was installed in a Bristol F2B Fighter. (Flight Lieutenant G.H. Parry RAF (Ret'd))

months, enemy casualties became so severe that a halt was made in a salient between Soissons and Reims.

When the British and the French, reinforced by American divisions, began the first of their counter-attacks on 18 July, they possessed an air superiority of about five to one. The Germans had lost about half a million men during 1918 in their final bid to win the war, and could only fall back while fighting stubbornly. Their positions were recorded assiduously by photo-reconnaissance aircraft. In the course of 1918, over 10 million prints were delivered to the armies on the Western Front. Assaults fell on the Germans from different sectors in turn, by Allied armies who by then enjoyed

such an overwhelming strength with tanks, artillery and aircraft that they could frequently achieve surprise. The German artillery commanders knew that they had lost the war and that it would be only a matter of time before the fighting reached the Fatherland. The Armistice of 11 November 1918 ended the bloodiest fighting recorded in the history of mankind.

Of course, the Western Front was not the only theatre of the First World War in which the British carried out aerial photography, although by comparison the others were known as 'sideshows'. Of these, the débâcle of the landings at Gallipoli which began on 25 April 1915 is perhaps the most notorious. This operation was intended to deal a blow

The Royal Aircraft Factory BE12a was designed as a single-seat fighter and began to appear in December 1916. However, the few that were sent to France were not successful in their intended purpose and were transferred to the roles of photo-reconnaissance and light bombing. They served in Palestine, Macedonia and in some Home Defence squadrons. The aircraft shown here, serial A579, was fitted with a camera which may have been a LB-type for high-level photography. (J.M. Bruce/G.S. Leslie Collection)

The Hythe gun camera was invented in the First World War by Major David Geddes of the RFC, the commanding officer of the Hythe Gunnery School. It incorporated a shutter and a lens in a barrel casing which replaced the normal barrel of a Lewis gun. A film box contained a ruled glass screen on which the position of the target was recorded each time the gun was cocked and the trigger depressed. From the photographs, it could be ascertained whether the trainee was allowing the correct amount of adjustment for distance and deflection when aiming at a target aircraft, either from a stationary position on the ground or from a moving aircraft during training flights. (J.M. Bruce/G.S. Leslie Collection)

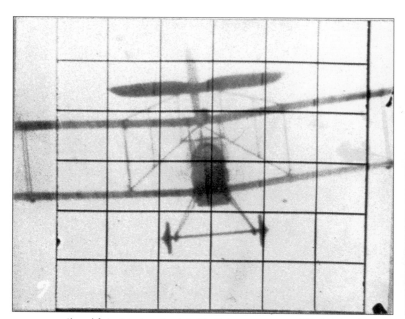

Above, left: An air-to-air practice shot with a Hythe gun camera on a DH2 of 20 Squadron. It was taken in July 1917 during training at Bailleul in France. (East Anglian Photographic Collection) *Above, right:* A vertical photograph of RAF Boscombe Down in Wiltshire, taken on 24 February 1918. This station was opened in 1917 as a training unit but closed at the end of 1919. It was re-opened in 1930 as a bomber station but on the outbreak of the Second World War became the home for the Aeroplane and Armament Experimental Establishment, which moved from Martlesham Heath in Suffolk. (J.M. Bruce/G.S. Leslie Collection)

The Airco DH4 was designed for day bombing and photo-reconnaissance at high speed, being capable of climbing above enemy fighters and thus operating without fighter escort. The first machines arrived in France in March 1917, when some were allocated to 2 Squadron. This was renumbered 202 Squadron on 1 April 1918. This DH4 of 202 Squadron was photographed at Bergues, near Dunkirk. It carried a camera housing beneath the fuselage. (J.M. Bruce/ G.S. Leslie Collection)

The Curtiss JN series was produced in the USA and Canada in response to a requirement of the US Army in 1914 for a biplane trainer with a tractor engine. The JN–3 was the first major version, becoming known as the 'Jenny'. This example, serial A3277, was fitted with a camera and employed at the School of Photography at Farnborough. (J.M. Bruce/G.S. Leslie Collection)

The Armstrong Whitworth FK8 arrived in France during January 1917, designed for photo-reconnaissance and bombing. Well-defended with a machine gun firing through the propeller and another on a Scarff ring, it was liked by aircrews, who considered it superior to the contemporary Royal Aircraft Factory RE8. The cameras in this photograph were an L-type mounted vertically beside the pilot and a P-type being handed to the air observer. (J.M. Bruce/G.S. Leslie Collection)

against Turkey after she entered the war in October 1914 as well as to relieve pressure on the Russians on the Eastern Front. Air reconnaissance and photography were carried out by the RNAS, which at the outset could muster only six seaplanes of dubious reliability, together with two aeroplanes which flew from the nearby island of Tenedos. The aircrews were inexperienced and communications with the ground were poor, so that the British and ANZAC troops who made the first landings were given little idea of the Turkish dispositions in the hills above and suffered heavy casualties. Thereafter reconnaissance improved until by June the enemy trenches had been photographed and maps prepared. Further landings, at Sulva Bay on 6 August, were almost unopposed, but the favourable situation was not exploited and the Allies evacuated their positions during the following December and January.

Reconnaissance aircraft of the RNAS and RFC supported the British, South African, and Belgian forces in German East Africa, now Tanzania. On 25 April 1915 an RNAS seaplane located and photographed the cruiser *Königsberg* in the Rufiji river, where she had been hiding since the previous October. The German cruiser was badly damaged by monitors on 4 July and then sunk a week later. Air photographs were also taken of the German forces, while routes through the featureless bush were mapped by the aircraft for use by the Allied troops. Nevertheless, the Germans waged a skilful guerilla campaign and some elements were able to continue fighting until the Armistice.

British and French divisions arrived in southern Macedonia, or Salonika, to help the Allied cause against the Bulgarians, who entered the war on the side of the Central Powers on 12 October 1915. The early air reconnaissances were made by the RNAS, but RFC aircraft arrived in July 1916. In addition

to reconnaissance, photography and artillery spotting, the BE2cs and BE12s of the RFC carried out bombing attacks and air combats. The Bulgarian positions in the mountains were so well concealed, however, that the Allies were unable to detect the true deployment of artillery from dummies until winter, when tracks in snow showed up in photographs. The fighting continued until Bulgaria surrendered on 29 September 1918.

Italy entered the war on the Allied side in May 1915 and fighting took place in the mountains and plains against Austrian troops. The Italians held their ground for over two years but began to collapse when German forces joined the Austrians in October 1917. British and French troops were sent to reinforce the Italians, together with the RFC in brigade strength. Air superiority over the Austro-German Air Force was gradually achieved and the RFC's reconnaissance of enemy positions helped the Allies to regain lost ground and check further advances by the enemy.

In Palestine, the Turkish forces advanced across the Sinai Desert in early 1915 with the objective of taking the Suez Canal. Their movements were detected by a small number of British and French aircraft, and the attack was repulsed. An RFC wing arrived in November 1915, but the BE2cs were outclassed a few months later by German fighter aircraft which arrived to support the Turks. Nevertheless, the RFC continued its work of reconnaissance and photography, and the British began to advance in the spring of 1916, assisted by Arab guerillas who were in rebellion against Turkish rule. The RFC in the area was built up to brigade strength by 1 July 1916 and slowly began to gain ascendancy over the German fighters. In the following year the RFC commenced photographing the whole of the area facing the British, which hitherto had not been surveyed in detail. In spite of primitive

A vertical photograph of Valenciennes taken on 2 February 1918, with pit slag heaps showing as conical shapes. (The late Squadron Leader J.E. Archbald)

An oblique view of the airfield of Coudekerke, near Dunkirk, photographed in 1918. This was the home of the Handley Page 0/100 and Short landplane bombers of the RFC's 5th Wing. (J.M. Bruce/G.S. Leslie Collection)

Airmen of 15 Squadron, commanded by Major H.V. Stammers, receiving reconnaissance reports on 25 March 1918, during the first battle of Bapaume. The squadron was equipped with Royal Aircraft Factory RE8s and based for that day only at Le Houssoye in France. (Flight Lieutenant G.H. Parry RAF (Ret'd))

Towards the end of the First World War it was decided to give all plate cameras the prefix 'P', all film cameras the prefix 'F', and gun cameras the prefix 'G'. The LB-type camera, as in this photograph, became the P7. (Flight Lieutenant G.H. Parry RAF (Ret'd))

The P18 camera was similar to the P14, but it was made from metal and wood and could be fitted with 6-inch, 8-inch and 10-inch lenses. The P18 (without magazine) in this photograph was demonstrated in April 1993 by Brian C. Kervell, Curator and Archivist of the Museum at the Defence and Research Agency, Farnborough. (B.M. Harris)

The P14 camera was developed as a replacement for the A-type hand-held camera, for the purpose of taking oblique photographs. It was made entirely of metal and fitted with a 10-inch lens. The P14 (without magazine) in this photograph was demonstrated in April 1993 by Brian C. Kervell, Curator and Archivist of the Museum at the Defence and Research Agency, Farnborough. (B.M. Harris)

Photographic processing in the desert during the First World War. (Flight Lieutenant G.H. Parry RAF (Ret'd))

A mobile photographic laboratory employed by the RFC in Palestine. (The late Wing Commander H. Hamshaw Thomas MBE)

A photographic mosaic, prepared by the RFC in Palestine, being rephotographed. (The late Wing Commander H. Hamshaw Thomas MBE)

conditions in the desert, the photographic officer of V Wing, Lieutenant Hugh Hamshaw-Thomas, earned a high reputation for his work in building up mosaics from which accurate maps were constructed. The British advance continued and by early 1918 the Turkish forces had been ousted from Palestine.

In Mesopotamia, a small force from India landed at Basra in November 1914, in order to protect the oil wells in the area of the Persian Gulf, and advanced up the Tigris and Euphrates rivers towards Baghdad during the following spring. Air reconnaissance was rewarding in the flat terrain, but only a handful of RFC and RNAS aircraft were available and these flimsy machines suffered from the extreme heat while a high sickness rate among the airmen caused additional problems. The arrival of German fighter aircraft gave the enemy temporary air superiority. One Indian division was surrounded at Kut on the Tigris and forced to surrender in April 1916. It was not until early in the following year that the British troops, aided by reconnaissance aircraft which photographed and mapped extensive areas of enemy territory, resumed the offensive. The Allies occupied Baghdad on 10 March 1917, and newly arrived aircraft such as Spads, Bristol Scouts and SE5As steadily overcame the German Air Force. The Turks withdrew northwards in good order and the fighting continued until, in September 1918, two of their armies were trapped in defiles and the men, bombed and machine-gunned by the RAF, were slaughtered in their thousands. Turkey surrendered the following month.

CHAPTER FOUR

BETWEEN THE WARS

The RAF ended the First World War with over 25,000 aircraft, more than 100 airships, and about 316,500 uniformed personnel, including airwomen. It is estimated that there were some 4,000 aerial cameras in the front line areas in addition to about 5,000 being used for training in England. However, the RAF was rapidly run down from about 200 squadrons to only 33, with those based in the UK being divided into a Northern Area, a Southern Area and a Coastal Area. The Independent Bombing Force, which was still being built up at the end of the war, was disbanded. It seemed that the RAF could no longer remain as a separate force, for the War Office coveted the old RFC squadrons as an air arm while the Admiralty hoped that it would resume control of the old RNAS squadrons. Hugh Trenchard was given a gratuity and a baronetcy, and contemplated retiring to civilian life.

In January 1919 Winston Churchill became Secretary of State for War and Air, and had the foresight to see the potential of the RAF. He invited Trenchard to resume the position of Chief of Air Staff which he had held briefly in April 1918. Trenchard set about the task of revitalising the RAF and raising its esteem in the eyes of the public. He was aided by events abroad, for it became apparent that control of territories such as Iraq, which had been mandated to Britain, could be exercised most effectively by the combination of RAF squadrons and armoured cars. Moreover, this method proved far less expensive than maintaining a considerable force of ground troops in parts of the British Empire, and was thus favoured by the government. Trenchard, who was eventually successful in expanding the RAF, occupied the position of Chief of Air Staff for nearly eleven years, before retiring with the undying reputation as the 'Father of the Royal Air Force'.

Within the post-First World War RAF, air photography did not receive a high priority, in spite of a memorandum written by Trenchard in 1919 which recognised that photography was one of the 'prime necessities' for which training was 'of extreme importance'. Training continued at the School of Photography at Farnborough but Trenchard decided that all photographic officers should be recruited from the General Duties, or flying, branch. Those officers who qualified from the long course were entitled to appear in the Air Force List with the letters PH after their names. Very few pilots or navigators were interested in this subject, however, preferring to qualify in subjects such as engineering, armament or wireless, as their specialisms. Similarly, the non-commissioned ranks who qualified at the School of Photography found that there were few opportunities for promotion. Military interpretation of aerial photographs remained in the hands of the Army, and officers were attached to RAF units for this purpose.

Nevertheless, the RAF gained a high reputation for its ability to provide

The F5 was the last of the Felixstowe flying boats, entering service soon after the end of the First World War. It became the standard flying boat of the RAF for the next seven years. This Felixstowe F5 serial N4198 was on the strength of 480 (General Reconnaissance) Flight at Calshot in Hampshire. (J.M. Bruce/ G.S. Leslie Collection)

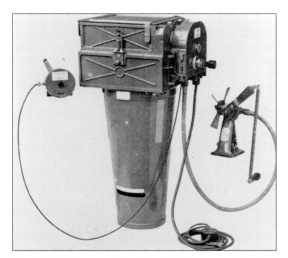

Above, left: The F8 camera, designed primarily for air survey, was introduced in 1919. It could be used for automatic overlapping of vertical photographs or for individual exposures. Power was supplied by either a windmill or an electric motor. Fixed-focus lenses of 7, 10, 14 and 20 inches could be fitted to the camera body. The film magazine contained 100 exposures of 7-inch by 7-inch, plus space for flight instrument recording, taken on a mean exposure of 1/90th of a second. Exposure was set by adjusting the lens aperture. The camera used a fixed-slit focal plane shutter and was fitted with a capping blind which screened the film during the shutter rewinding and film-changing operation. It was built on the unit principle, each unit being inter-changeable with the corresponding unit of any F8 camera. *Above, right:* An F8 camera on a gun mounting. (Both photos: Flight Lieutenant G.H. Parry RAF (Ret'd))

The Supermarine Southampton entered RAF service in August 1925 with 480 (Coastal Reconnaissance) Flight, replacing the long-serving Felixstowe F5s. This flight became 201 Squadron in January 1929. Four other maritime squadrons were also equipped with Southamptons, which remained in service for over ten years. They became famous for their long-distance flights, particularly a cruise to the Far East in 1927. This photograph is of Southampton II serial S1123. (J.M. Bruce/G.S. Leslie Collection)

The F24 camera, first introduced in 1925, could be either hand-held or installed in vertical and oblique positions with the operation fully automated. The picture size was 5-inch by 5-inch and the magazine contained rolls of film which gave up to 125 exposures. Three lenses were initially available, 6-inch, 8-inch and 10½-inch. The focal plane shutter speeds could be adjusted between 1/40th and 1/120th of a second, by adjusting the shutter spring tension. It was a reliable instrument which became the RAF's main general-purpose camera during the Second World War, and remained in service for thirty years. (Flight Lieutenant G.H. Parry RAF (Ret'd))

Ken Murch of the Tangmere Military Aviation Museum demonstrating the use of a hand-held F24 camera, without magazine. The rubber eye-piece is missing from the camera sight and the front of the lens has been modified. (B.M. Harris, courtesy Tangmere Military Aviation Museum)

A photographer handing a camera magazine to the air observer of an Airco DH4. (*Aeroplane Monthly*)

Lawrence of Arabia, photographed as an aircraftman. He joined the RAF on 30 August 1922 under the assumed name of John Hume Ross and, after basic training at Uxbridge, was posted in November 1922 to the RAF School of Photography at Farnborough where he began training as a photographer, a trade which interested him. His identity was discovered by the press and he was forced to leave the RAF in January 1923. He joined the Tank Corps as Thomas Edward Shaw in March 1923 but in the following year was hounded again by the press. Under this name (confirmed by deed poll in 1927) he transferred back to the RAF in August 1925. He then served at clerical duties and on seaplanes and motor boats, at home and abroad. His last station was RAF Bridlington in Yorkshire, where this photograph was probably taken. He left the RAF at the end of his engagement on 25 February 1935 and was killed in a motorcycle accident on 19 May 1935, at the age of forty-seven. (The late Wing Commander G.L. Buxton MBE)

photographs for the construction of mosaics, maps and charts. In one project from 1920 to 1922, the Egyptian Government funded a survey of the Nile. This was carried out from 14,000 feet by the DH9As of 47 Squadron and the Bristol fighters of 208 Squadron, over a stretch of 618 miles. The main objectives were to provide the Department of Irrigation of the Public Works Ministry with hydrological records of the behaviour of the Nile with respect to its ever-changing sandbanks, erosion of the river banks and the effect of the annual flood on the protection works.

In another scheme, the DH9As of 60 Squadron based at Risalpur in India undertook during 1923 a photographic reconnaissance of vast areas of the Baluchistan and Afghan borders. Three years later the DH9As of this squadron, by then based at Kohat, photographed an area of the Indus river from 12,000 feet, using P7 cameras with glass plates. A mosaic was prepared from the results, to assist the Indian Government in building dams to conserve water for agricultural purposes.

Another mapping survey was carried out in 1924 by the DH9As of 84 Squadron based at Shaibah in Iraq, when the Anglo-Persian Oil Company requested a mosaic of their Abadan refineries. Such photographic survey flights made in difficult conditions by overseas squadrons of the RAF preceded the work undertaken in later years by civil air survey companies.

Meanwhile, Squadron Leader Victor Laws was posted after the war to a newly created branch of the Directorate of Scientific Research at the Air Ministry, with the brief of producing a specification to meet the photographic necessities of the post-war RAF. His first step was to design a camera with a larger picture format and to replace glass plates with roll film.

Before the war, the companies of Dallmeyer in Britain, Goerz–Anschutz in Germany and Kodak in the USA, had dominated the field of lens and camera making. In the course of the war various British companies improved the difficult techniques of making the lenses and also produced most of the cameras used in British aircraft. Together with Harry B. Stringer of the Royal Aircraft Establishment, Laws designed in 1919 the excellent F8 camera, which used roll film with a 7-inch by 7-inch picture format and could be fitted with lenses of various focal lengths.

To the disappointment of Laws, the Air Ministry considered that the camera was too large and heavy for the aircraft in service at the time, as well as too expensive at £200 each, and by 1924 only thirty had been made. Some of these were sent to India for testing under tropical conditions, where, as will be seen later, they proved of immense value when the Japanese invaded Burma in 1942. Others were used in a photographic survey of the boundaries of British Somaliland in 1929. For this work an Air Survey Flight was formed under Flight Lieutenant G.S. Shaw, consisting of two Fairey IIIFs with seventeen personnel including four aircrew. The length of the survey area was 350 miles and excellent results were obtained, despite extreme climatic conditions. With day temperatures of 50°C, processing was carried out in tents at night when photographic solutions dropped to 25°C.

The Air Ministry required a smaller and lighter camera than the F8, and in 1925 the Royal Aircraft Establishment produced the F24, which gave a picture of 5 inches by 5 inches. This proved a highly reliable camera which, although it was not capable of the higher definition which Laws knew would be required in times of war, became the mainstay of the RAF's photographic equipment for many years. It fulfilled only limited requirements for military mapping, but the Archaeological Office of the Ordnance

Fairey IIIF Mark IVs of 47 Squadron, serials J9796, J9809 and J9802, fitted with floats, on the River Nile. The squadron was equipped with these general-purpose machines from December 1927 to January 1933 while based at Khartoum in the Sudan. It was employed on photo-reconnaissance while exploring the Cape to Cairo route. (The late Squadron Leader J.E. Archbald)

King George V and Queen Mary visiting the RAF's School of Photography at Farnborough on 16 May 1928, accompanied by the commanding officer, Wing Commander Victor Laws. (The late Group Captain F.C.V. Laws CB, CBE, FRPS)

Group Captain F.C. Victor Laws CB CBE FRPS. He was also mentioned in despatches twice and awarded the US Legion of Merit and the French Croix de Guerre. (The late Group Captain F.C.V. Laws CB, CBE, FRPS)

The Armstrong Whitworth Atlas, the first aircraft designed for Army co-operation, entered service in October 1927. Its duties included artillery spotting, photo-reconnaissance, reporting by W/T, picking up messages by means of a hook on the undercarriage, and attacking with bombs or machine guns. The observer in this Atlas serial J9956 was busy taking photographs from his exposed position. (*Aeroplane Monthly*)

The Hawker Audax entered RAF service in 1931, as the Army co-operation version of the Hawker Hart. It had a message-collecting hook on the undercarriage and could be distinguished from the Hart by its long exhaust pipes. In this photograph of an Audax trainer and photography pupils at Farnborough, taken in 1934, Flight Sergeant Don Munro had his hand on the leading edge of the lower wing while the engine was running. (The late Squadron Leader D.J. Munro)

An F24 camera being handed to a leading aircraftman photographer in a Hawker Audax trainer, with another F24 (manually operated, with sight) on the ground. (*Aeroplane Monthly*)

The Vickers Vildebeest, originally designed in 1928, remained the only torpedo bomber available to front-line squadrons of the RAF in the years immediately before the Second World War. It was also employed on maritime reconnaissance. This Vildebeest III serial K4589 was a three-seater on the strength of 22 Squadron before Bristol Beaufort torpedo bombers arrived at the end of 1939. (The late Squadron Leader N. Hearn-Phillips AFC, DFM)

Vickers Vincent serial K6364 of 47 Squadron, one of those which replaced Fairey IIIFs from July 1936 onwards and continued in service with the squadron until July 1940. This modified version of the Vickers Vildebeest could carry a long-range tank in the place normally occupied by the torpedo. With an endurance of up to nine hours, Vincents helped survey the route along the Nile used by flying boats of Imperial Airways. (*Aeroplane Monthly*)

Survey used the camera for recording sites from the air. Almost all aircrew trained with this camera before, during, and even after the Second World War, and looked upon it with considerable affection.

Victor Laws became dissatisfied with his lack of advancement at the Air Ministry but in October 1924 was posted back to Farnborough, once more to take charge of the School of Photography, where he remained for six more years. He was promoted to wing commander in January 1927 and became a revered figure to his staff and the trainees, being known as 'Daddy' Laws – although not to his face, for he was a severe but fair disciplinarian. His next posting was in October 1930 when he moved away from the photographic branch to become the commanding officer of the Aircraft Depot at Hinaidi in Iraq.

When Laws returned to England in February 1933 to take up the post of station commander of Farnborough, he decided that RAF photography was, in his own words, 'at a dead end'. Very little was being done to develop cameras and air photography, while the skill of photographic interpretation remained with the Army. The only minor encouragement had occurred the previous year when the Under-Secretary of State for Air, Sir Philip Sassoon, announced an annual competition and trophy for 'any regular unit in the home commands normally carrying out air photography', other than the School of Photography.

At this time Britain had not yet recovered from the Great Depression, and all public spending was severely restricted. The RAF still numbered only about forty squadrons, in spite of a proposed expansion to fifty-two which had been decreed in 1923. It was still equipped with biplanes and, although some of these machines were beautiful in appearance and a pleasure to fly, most were little more than advanced versions of those which had

flown in the First World War. In September 1933, Laws retired from the service to take up a lucrative civilian post in charge of a photographic survey in Western Australia.

As it happened, Laws left the RAF at a time when public awareness of the need for strong armed services was beginning to stir. The assumption of power in Italy during 1922 of Benito Mussolini and the fascist dictatorship had caused little disquiet in Britain, but the appointment of Adolf Hitler as Chancellor of Germany in January 1933 was potentially a different matter. It soon became known that German aircrews were receiving military flying training as 'civilians' and that German civil aeroplanes were easily capable of conversion to warplanes, in spite of the conditions of the Treaty of Versailles which prohibited the formation of a German Air Force. The National Socialist philosophy of the German rulers, with its extreme nationalism and overtones of race hatred, gave people in Britain pause for thought. Perhaps the terrible conflict of 1914–18 had not been a 'war to end all wars' after all. RAF bomber stations were concentrated in the south of England, against any enemy across the Channel, but in the mid-1930s it became apparent that a far greater threat was developing from across the North Sea.

In 1934 the British Government decided to increase the strength of the RAF as rapidly as possible to seventy-five squadrons, and then to one hundred and twenty-eight squadrons within five years. Specifications for new aircraft were prepared, and these were to lead eventually to the development and construction of monoplanes such as the Hawker Hurricane, the Supermarine Spitfire, the Bristol Blenheim, and the Short Stirling. In February 1935 Hitler defied the League of Nations by creating the Luftwaffe, and the race to re-arm began. Mussolini invaded Abyssinia in October of that year and started bombing villages as well as using poison gas.

Fairey Gordon serial K1776 of 35 Squadron, which was equipped with these machines from July 1932 to August 1937 and based in the Sudan for part of this period. The Gordon was employed as a day bomber and as a general-purpose aircraft, including reconnaissance. The aircraft in this photograph was converted from a Fairey IIIF, being fitted with a Panther radial engine in place of the Napier Lion. (*Aeroplane Monthly*)

A photographer handing an LB-type camera with a 4-inch or 6-inch lens to the air observer of a Fairey Gordon of 40 Squadron, which was equipped with these aircraft from April 1931 to November 1935. The photograph is dated 13 May 1932, when the squadron was based at Upper Heyford in Oxfordshire. It seems that some squadrons of the RAF were still using this camera of First World War vintage (renumbered the P7 after the war) although the F24 had come into service a few years earlier. (*Aeroplane Monthly*)

Hawker Harts of 39 Squadron flying over the Himalayas from their base at Risalpur in India. These were light day-bombers which first entered RAF service in 1930, and their duties also included photo-reconnaissance. Harts proved very successful and continued with 39 Squadron until July 1939. (The late Wing Commander F.H. Isaac DFC)

Hawker Hind serial K5558 of 107 Squadron, photographed at Andover in Hampshire in 1936. The Hind was a general-purpose aircraft, developed from the Hart, and was employed on Army co-operation work as well as on light bombing duties. (Flight Lieutenant S.G.E. Payne C Eng., MRAeS, RAF (Ret'd))

The RAF moved squadrons to Malta, Somaliland and Egypt. Requests were received from the Chiefs of Staff for vertical and oblique photographs of a number of Italian islands in the Mediterranean and areas of land along the coast of North Africa and the Red Sea. Some results were achieved by 1936 and then, in the following year, there were reports that the Italians were building an underground air base on the island of Pantellaria. On 15 May 1937 the Air Officer commanding RAF Malta was asked to obtain distant air photographs to determine the state of construction. The Italians had imposed a 6-mile prohibited zone around the island and care had to be taken to avoid any infringement. Two Supermarine Scapa flying boats of 202 Squadron from the seaplane base of Kalafrana were allotted the work but the first results, taken on 25 May with F24 cameras, were too indistinct to be of any use. Another attempt on 15 July by two Scapas of the same squadron proved somewhat more successful.

In the same year anxiety arose about threats to passage through the Suez Canal, and British Forces Aden requested photographic coverage of the island of Dumeirah in the Red Sea to verify reports of Italian military construction. The task was given to 8 Squadron, equipped with Vickers Vincents and based at Khormaksar in Aden. Pictures were taken in July from outside a 6-mile radius from 10,000 feet, using F24 cameras with 14-inch lenses, but the definition was so poor that they were almost useless. Fresh supplies of panchromatic film and filters were ordered, but did not arrive for two months. Better coverage took place on 1 October and the negatives were sent to the School of Photography for interpretation, perforce by an Army officer. In the subsequent report sent to the Air Ministry, Wing Commander Cyril Porri, who was once more the Commandant of the School of

Photography, pointed out that there were no RAF officers trained in photo-interpretation. This revelation followed a report earlier in 1937 when, at a conference of Command and Group photographic officers held on 16 April, it had been stated that the RAF had little knowledge of photographic requirements in times of war.

One person who was alerted to the inadequacies of RAF photography was Squadron Leader Fred W. Winterbotham of the Air Ministry. Winterbotham had flown as a pilot with the RFC and on 13 July 1917 had been shot down in a Nieuport 17 of 29 Squadron behind German lines. After the war he had entered RAF Intelligence and became involved with MI6, a branch of the Secret Intelligence Service. He had met many of the German military leaders and had even become a honorary member of the Luftwaffe Club which was formed in Berlin in 1935.

Winterbotham was convinced that air photographs could provide a prime source of intelligence concerning the German defence system in the west, and discussed the matter with his French counterparts. The French were also interested in extending their espionage system in western Germany, and their Deuxième Bureau de l'Armée de l'Air approached Alfred J. Miranda Jr of the American Armament Corporation for advice. In turn, Miranda was a friend of Lieutenant Commander F. Sidney Cotton, an Australian pilot who had flown on reconnaissance flights with the RNAS during the First World War. He was the inventor of the warm 'Sidcot' flying suit which later became standard issue to RAF aircrews.

After the war, Cotton had pursued an adventurous career in civil aviation and had also been a director of Dufaycolor, the camera film company. Miranda flew over from the USA to London in September 1938 and took Cotton to Paris to meet Paul Koster, the European representative of the American

The Westland Wapiti first appeared in 1927 as a replacement for the DH9A, which had given faithful service for many years. It was a general-purpose aircraft, employed on reconnaissance and light bombing. This all-metal Wapiti V serial J9754 was on the strength of 5 Squadron, which was equipped with Wapitis from May 1931 to June 1940 while on the North West Frontier of India. The photograph was taken at Miramshah in March 1938, during Army co-operation sorties, with Pilot Officer C.D. Lavers as pilot and Aircraftman S.G.E. Payne as gunner. (Flight Lieutenant S.G.E. Payne C Eng., MRAeS, RAF (Ret'd))

The airfield, on the upper left, at RAF Quetta, photographed in June 1935 from a Wapiti IIA of 5 Squadron. (Flight Sergeant A.W. Orford RAF (Ret'd))

Ground practice with the Mark III Hythe gun camera mounted on a Scarff ring, being carried out by a leading aircraftman in the mid-1930s on a day when the weather was obviously very chilly. (The late Squadron Leader N. Hearn-Phillips AFC, DFM)

The Supermarine Scapa was an improved version of the Southampton, first entering squadron service in May 1935 and continuing until December 1938. This Scapa, serial K4200, served with 202 Squadron. (*Aeroplane Monthly*)

The Saro London entered service with 201 Squadron in April 1936, replacing the Southampton flying boat. It continued in squadron service until June 1940. (*Aeroplane Monthly*)

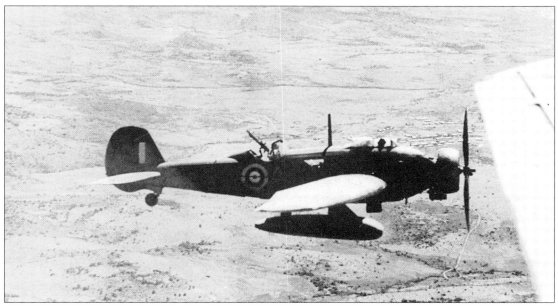

The Vickers Wellesley entered squadron service in April 1937 as a long-range bomber and became famous the following year when three aircraft broke the world's long-distance record, flying non-stop from Egypt to Australia. After the outbreak of the Second World War it was employed by 47 Squadron on reconnaissance work in Egypt. (The late Squadron Leader J.E. Archbald)

When the Westland Lysander entered service in May 1938, the RAF believed that it was the most suitable aircraft for carrying out tactical reconnaissance and photography for the Army. This Lysander II serial L4742 was on the strength of 4 Squadron, which went to France on the outbreak of war as part of the Air Component. By 1942 most Lysanders had been withdrawn from front-line duties, although they continued for the remainder of the war in air-sea rescue squadrons, as target-towers, and in special duty units. (*Aeroplane Monthly*)

Fitting an F24 camera in an oblique position beside the observer of a Westland Lysander. (*Aeroplane Monthly*)

Armament Corporation. The men discussed the possibilities of clandestine reconnaissance flights over Germany and agreed that these should be carried out in a civil aircraft.

The day after Cotton returned to London, he received a telephone call from Winterbotham, and the two men met on several occasions. They decided that the Lockheed 12A was the most suitable aircraft for the proposed flights. Although the normal range of this civil aircraft was about 700 miles, it could be fitted with extra fuel tanks which added another 900 miles. It was in a modified Lockheed 12 that during the previous year Amelia Earhart had attempted to circle the world along an equatorial route, although the enterprise ultimately led to her death. Miranda arranged for one of these machines to be sent from America, and it arrived at Southampton in January 1939. A pilot with engineering qualifications was required to work with Cotton and Winterbotham chose a Canadian who was nearing the end of his short-service commission with the RAF, Flying Officer Robert H. Niven. A private company was formed as a cover, the Aeronautical Research and Sales Corporation.

Cotton and Niven flew from Heston to Toussus-le-Noble, a small airfield about 15 miles south-west of Paris, where they were welcomed by a liaison officer from the Deuxième Bureau. On 25 March 1939 the two men flew at an altitude of about 15,000 feet over Krefeld, Hamm, Munster and the Dutch border, using a French camera with a focal length of 30 cm. The Black Forest was covered on 1 April and Wurtemburg six days later. On 9 April they covered the outskirts of Karlsruhe, Bruchsal, Heidelberg, Mannheim, Ludwigshafen and Ebersbach, taking evasive action from an approaching German fighter at one stage. Later in the month they flew to Tunis and, on 25 April, covered the Italian port of Tripoli, the airfield of Castel Benito,

several other airfields and a number of gun positions. In the course of this series of flights, Cotton was annoyed to find that the French were not prepared to show him the photographs he had taken and decided that it was impossible to work with them.

The Lockheed was handed over to the French and two more of these machines were ordered, one for the French and one for the British. Winterbotham told Cotton and Niven that their first task would be to carry out photographic reconnaissance in the Middle East. The Lockheed 12As arrived at Southampton in early May and Cotton took charge of one of them, which was given the civil registration letters G-AFTL. He installed extra fuel tanks behind the cockpit, similar to the arrangement in Amelia Earhart's machine, and had three F24 cameras with lenses of 5-inch focal length fitted in the fuselage, one vertically and two obliquely, so that he could photograph a strip 11½ miles wide from an altitude of 21,000 feet. The holes in the fuselage were cut slightly larger than the camera lens, so that warm air from the interior was sucked out over them and prevented condensation. They were covered with small sliding panels when not in use, and these and the cameras were controlled electrically from the cockpit. Next, he invented and installed a Perspex pear-shaped window so that he could look downwards from the cockpit; this 'tear-drop' window proved so successful that over 100,000 were manufactured for RAF aircraft during the Second World War. Finally he had the Lockheed painted in a light duck-egg green, which he considered provided the best camouflage at higher altitudes, and registered this colour as 'Camotint'.

On 14 June 1939 Cotton and Niven flew to Malta, where they met Flying Officer Maurice V. 'Shorty' Longbottom, a pilot who had been involved with the reconnaissance flights during 1937 and was convinced of the

The Short Sunderland I entered service with the RAF in June 1938 as a general reconnaissance and anti-submarine flying boat. It proved an excellent platform for photography and the interior was sufficiently spacious to include an F24 developing tank, enabling a photographer to carry out inflight processing. The films were dried by festooning them along the lower deck. This photograph of a Sunderland of 210 Squadron was taken at Pembroke Dock in 1939. (Flight Lieutenant G.H. Parry RAF (Ret'd))

A Supermarine Stranraer I serial K7292 of 228 Squadron at Pembroke Dock in 1939, with a Sunderland in the background. Stranraers served with 228 Squadron from April 1937 until April 1939, when they were replaced with Sunderlands. (Flight Lieutenant G.H. Parry RAF (Ret'd))

RAF trainee photographers receiving instruction in the installation of the F24 camera in a section of a fuselage, during May 1938. (*Aeroplane Monthly*)

RAF trainee photographers attending a lecture on the construction and assembly of the F8 camera, with a demonstration F24 camera on the right. The photograph was taken in September 1938. (*Aeroplane Monthly*)

importance of air photography in times of war. Cotton, who was now in the guise of a wealthy Englishman with a penchant for photographing ancient ruins, needed someone to help with the cameras and the films, and Longbottom was allowed to join his clandestine team for a single day. On 15 June they flew to Sicily and covered Comiso, Augusta, Catania and Syracuse before returning to Malta, where the photographs proved to be excellent, but Longbottom was not allowed to accompany them on further flights. Nevertheless, the three men were able to discuss their ideas concerning the most suitable RAF aircraft for photographic reconnaissance, and their conclusions were to produce very significant results a few months later.

At dawn on 16 June, Cotton and Niven left Malta to photograph the Italian-held islands of Cos and Leros in the Dodecanese and then headed for Cairo, where they landed. On 19 June they covered the port of Massawa in Italian Eritrea, but after flying inland, found that Asmara was swathed in cloud. They turned to land at the British island of Kamaran in the Red Sea, and then continued to RAF Aden. On the following day, Cotton took off to examine a possible submarine base on the peninsula of Hafun in Italian Somaliland, and returned with some photographs showing the construction in progress. On 21 June they flew back to Kamaran and then, on the following day, photographed some parts of Massawa which they had not covered on their previous run, before landing at RAF Atbara in the Sudan, where the results of their work were collected by a Blenheim and flown to RAF Heliopolis. They then flew to Cairo and headed back to Malta on the following day, en route photographing Italian airfields and military installations at El Adem, Tobruk, Derna, Bernice and Benghazi. From Malta, they landed back at Heston on 25 June.

The next task was to take some further photographs over Germany. Fortunately, Cotton had been given the sales rights for Dufaycolor film in Europe, and a German combine was interested in this product. Cotton and Niven flew the Lockheed to Berlin on 26 July 1939, but did not carry cameras on that occasion. However, the aircraft had been modified to take two Leica cameras in the wings, concealed by sliding panels, and these were carried on a 'business' trip to Frankfurt on 28 July, where there was also an international air meeting. The Lockheed was much admired at Frankfurt, and they took the Commandant of Tempelhof airfield, who was at the gathering, for a pleasure flight during the following day. They passed over Mannheim, where Cotton secretly took a series of photographs. On the return trip to Heston, Cotton and Niven took photographs of the Siegfried Line.

A further flight to Berlin took place on 17 August, and on the return trip the two men managed to take pictures of targets north of Berlin. The cameras were removed from the wings for another trip on 22 August but on the return flight they used hand-held Leicas to take photographs of German warships at Wilhelmshaven. These were received so enthusiastically by the Admiralty that Cotton was asked if he could take some photographs of the German Frisian islands, Heligoland and the island of Sylt. He took off with Niven on 27 August, accompanied by a young lady photographer to help with the Leicas, under the guise of a business group heading for Copenhagen. They photographed airfields in the Frisian group and took some excellent shots of Sylt, but Heligoland was covered with fog.

On the morning of the day that Hitler sent his troops into Poland and received an ultimatum from Britain, 1 September, Cotton was asked by the Admiralty for information about the German fleet in its home ports. A

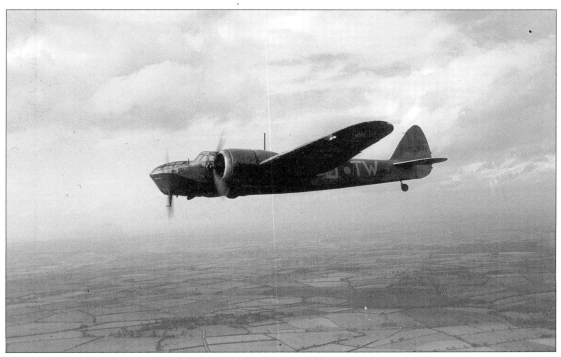

Before the outbreak of the Second World War, the RAF allocated the task of long-range strategic photography to the Bristol Blenheim IV, known as the 'long-nose Blenheim'. Attempts were made to operate over Germany in daylight but the aircraft was far too lightly armed and could not fly high enough; many were shot down by German fighters. This photograph is of a Blenheim IV of 90 Squadron, a training squadron based at Upwood in Huntingdonshire from 19 September 1939 to 4 April 1940. (The late Squadron Leader J.E. Archbald)

A vertical F24 camera being handed to the observer of a Blenheim IV. (Flight Lieutenant G.H. Parry RAF (Ret'd))

Above, left: F. Sidney Cotton in 1941. (The late Wing Commander F.S. Cotton OBE) *Above, right:* Squadron Leader Maurice V. 'Shorty' Longbottom DFC. In June 1939, when he was a flying officer, he accompanied Sidney Cotton and Flying Officer Robert Niven on a clandestine flight over Sicily in a Lockheed 12A. The following August, he submitted to the Air Ministry a memorandum recommending the use of unarmed Spitfires for strategic reconnaissance deep in enemy territory. After the outbreak of war he joined the new Photographic Development Flight which was formed at Heston. He was later attached to Vickers-Armstrong as a test pilot and in April 1943 was partly responsible for testing 'Upkeep' mines in Lancasters and 'Highball' mines in Mosquitos, the bouncing bombs invented by Dr Barnes Wallis. He was killed at Weybridge on 6 January 1945 when testing Vickers Warwick V serial PN778, one of the general reconnaissance versions used by Coastal Command for anti-submarine work. (Flight Officer Constance Babington Smith MBE, WAAF)

Sidney Cotton's Lockheed 12A at Spaceport Executive Airport, Titusville in Florida, photographed on 11 March 1991 by Graham Dinsdale, who had retired from the RAF a few months previously. It had been restored to flying condition. Although displaying registration NC116IV, the correct registration was N12EJ. Owned by Steve R. Oliver, the former spy-plane is in natural metal overall with an orange cleat line and orange on the nose and engine cowlings. When flown by Sidney Cotton before the Second World War, it was painted in Camotint, a light duck-egg green. (Sergeant G. Dinsdale RAF (Ret'd))

few hours later, Niven took off in a single-engined Beechcraft monoplane, which had been painted in Camotint and added to the Heston flight, on a further flight to these ports and came back with some photographs of Wilhelmshaven. These last three photographic flights impressed on the Admiralty the advantage of frequent coverage in order to determine the movements of enemy units.

While these events were taking place, Longbottom had been recording his discussions with Cotton and Niven in Malta. These were submitted to the Air Ministry in August 1939 in a memorandum entitled 'Photographic Reconnaissance of Enemy Territory in War'. Longbottom concentrated on strategic reconnaissance, which at the time was considered by the RAF to be the province of the new Bristol Blenheim IV. He argued that the use of a single light bomber to photograph deep in enemy territory was extremely dangerous, for it invited the attention of enemy fighters and anti-aircraft fire, and the results might not be brought back to base. He recommended the employment of a fast single-engined machine, stripped of radio and armament so that it could carry extra fuel tanks. The aircraft would be camouflaged and fly high enough to be almost invisible from the ground in clear weather. Its operating altitude would be beyond the reach of anti-aircraft fire while reliance would be placed on speed to avoid enemy fighters. In cloudy weather, it would descend low enough only to take photographs and then take cover once more. Longbottom assumed that the best aircraft for such stategic photographic reconnaissance was the new Spitfire I.

This was a remarkable document to be written by a junior RAF officer, and no immediate action was taken. The proposals seemed revolutionary at the time, although after a few months they were to become standard practice in the RAF. Longbottom was blessed with the gift of foresight, as was Generaloberst Werner Freiherr von Fritsch of the Werhmacht who forecast in 1938 that 'the military organization which has the most efficient reconnaissance unit will win the next war'. Neither Longbottom nor von Fritsch were to survive the conflict which began with Britain's declaration of war on 3 September 1939, but the words they left behind were to prove absolutely correct.

CHAPTER FIVE

Sidney Cotton's Air Force

The ability of the RAF to reconnoitre and photograph enemy activity on the outbreak of the Second World War was not of the highest order. Of course, most bomber and maritime aircraft could carry the F24 camera on daylight operations and the aircrews were trained in its use. Systematic photography for the purpose of gathering intelligence was, however, vested mainly in two types of aircraft. Within the Air Component of the British Expeditionary Force which was sent to France, tactical reconnaissance and photography was one of the functions of five squadrons of Westland Lysanders, while strategic reconnaissance and photography behind the German lines as far as the Rhine was entrusted to four squadrons of Bristol Blenheim IVs. Whatever the merits of these two aircraft, it is certain that both were very vulnerable to the attentions of Messerschmitt Bf109 fighters, particularly when flying alone. The Lysander depended mainly on manoeuvrability at low level to escape German fighters. The Blenheim was even less fortunate, for its service ceiling was only 22,000 feet, bringing it within the range of heavy anti-aircraft fire on long-distance flights as well as attack by enemy fighters, which were about 100 mph faster than their quarry. Moreover, the use of the F24 camera with its limited definition compelled aircrews of the Blenheim to fly at no more than 12,000 feet, so that in clear weather their missions became almost suicidal; when they were partially protected by cloud cover

photography was often impossible.

However, a few high-ranking RAF officers were aware of the defects in the service's photo-reconnaissance and were receptive to ideas for improvement. In July 1936 the home-based RAF, consisting of the Air Defence of Great Britain and various Area Commands, had been reorganised into Bomber, Fighter and Coastal Commands, to meet the steady expansion of the service. The nucleus of a photographic interpretation section, known as AI 1(h), had been formed at the Air Ministry in March 1938 under Squadron Leader Walter H.G. Heath. Soon afterwards, Bomber Command had set up a similar section, commanded by Squadron Leader Peter J.A. Riddell and staffed by graduates of the Army Interpretation course at Farnborough. A small photographic interpretation team, consisting of three Army officers trained at Farnborough, accompanied the RAF to France.

During the first few weeks of the 'phoney war' which characterised the beginning of the conflict, the photographs brought back by RAF aircraft did not provide adequate intelligence of the enemy's activities and possible intentions. In this early period, Bomber Command was prohibited from attacking the German homeland, for fear of retaliation on British cities by the Luftwaffe, so that its sorties were mostly confined to dropping propaganda leaflets at night. Only the warships of the Kriegsmarine were considered legitimate targets for attack by

The premises of Aerofilms Ltd and the Aircraft Operating Company at Wembley, photographed in 1936 or 1937. The photo-interpretation skills of the staff were used by the RAF's Photographic Development Unit at the beginning of the Second World War, and both companies were taken over by the Air Ministry in April 1940. (Squadron Leader P. Lamboit RAFVR, courtesy Hunting Aerofilms of Borehamwood)

Civilian photo-interpreters using mirror stereoscopes, which gave the impression of depth and solidity to aerial photographs. (Squadron Leader P. Lamboit RAFVR, courtesy Hunting Aerofilms of Borehamwood)

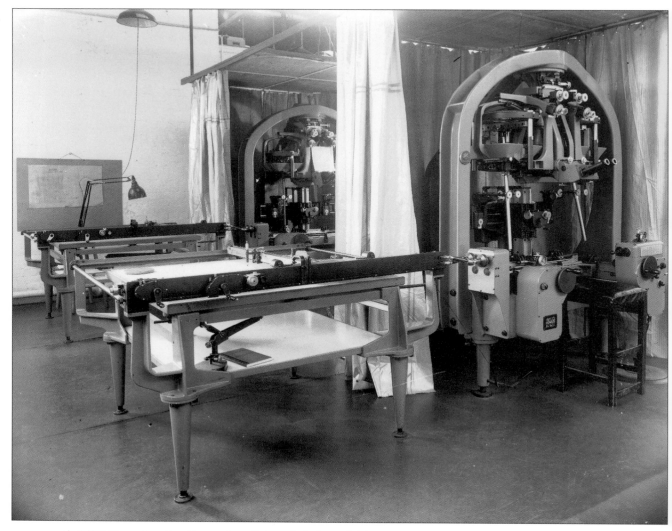

The Wild A5 'Stereo-autograph' machine, manufactured in Switzerland and originally belonging to the Aircraft Operating Company. It was taken over by the Air Ministry and used for map production by the Central Interpretation Unit. (Squadron Leader P. Lamboit RAFVR, courtesy Hunting Aerofilms of Borehamwood)

The Wild A5 'Stereo-autograph' machine being used by a civilian operator. (Squadron leader P. Lamboit RAFVR, courtesy Hunting Aerofilms of Borehamwood)

both the RAF and the Royal Navy. Of course, Sidney Cotton's exploits were known to the intelligence services and the Admiralty had no hesitation in approaching him for help with a somewhat delicate matter. The personal assistant to the Director of Naval Intelligence, Ian Fleming (who was later to achieve fame as the author of the James Bond novels), suggested that Cotton use his private aircraft to investigate the possibility that the Germans had set up refuelling bases for U-boats along the west coast of neutral Eire.

Cotton and Niven made a reconnaissance sortie in the Lockheed 12A at 10,000 feet on 12 September 1939, but no refuelling bases showed up on the photographs. They were asked to make another at 2,000 feet but meanwhile Wing Commander Fred Winterbotham had made an arrangement for Cotton to visit the Director General of Operations at the Air Ministry, Air Vice-Marshal Richard Peck, on 15 September. On the morning after this meeting Cotton was introduced by Peck to the Vice-Chief of the Air Staff, Air Marshal Sir Richard Peirse. The two senior officers discussed with Cotton the difficulty the RAF was experiencing in obtaining photographs of Dutch ports, where movements of German naval units had been reported, primarily because the F24 cameras kept 'freezing up' at medium level.

Cotton explained that the trouble was probably caused by condensation, not freezing, and decided to demonstrate his own proficiency. Without obtaining authority, he took off with Niven in his Lockheed during the same afternoon and came back with excellent photographs of Flushing and Ymuiden, which he showed on 17 September to a meeting of RAF officers, all of whom were astonished and some rather indignant. The outcome was Cotton's appointment on 22 September 1939 to the RAF, as a squadron leader with the acting rank of wing commander and the duty of commanding a special photographic

reconnaissance flight under Fighter Command's 11 Group, operating from Heston, which at that time was a civil airport. Authority for the formation of this unit, part of the Secret Intelligence Service, had been granted on 15 September. Winterbotham had hoped to assume this command, but Cotton was chosen. The initial establishment provided for a commanding officer, a photographic officer, an adjutant, four officers for flying duties and nineteen other ranks.

The new unit, known as the Heston Flight, was opened on 23 September. Squadron Leader Alfred 'Tubby' Earle, a pilot/photographer who had been an instructor at the School of Photography at Farnborough where he had done a great deal to launch and foster a Boy Entrant's training scheme, was appointed to take charge of the photographic development. Flying Officers Bob Niven and 'Shorty' Longbottom were the first of the four operational pilots, and they were later joined by Flying Officers Hugh C. Macphail and S. Denis Slocum, as well as other pilots when the unit expanded.

The first photographers in the unit were Sergeant S.R. 'Wally' Walton and Leading Aircraftmen Whinra Rawlinson, Ron Mutton and Jack Eggleston, all of whom had passed through the School of Photography at Farnborough and were also available for aircrew duties. There were also five fitters, three flight mechanics, two flight riggers, an electrician, an instrument maker and three general aircraft hands.

The only aircraft on the strength of the new unit were Cotton's Lockheed and Beechcraft, both of which carried out further flights along the west coast of Ireland as well as off Belgium and Holland. Although Cotton had protested that they would be of little use, two Blenheim IVs were sent to Farnborough on 21 September for modification. These were rubbed down to a smooth finish, with all airflow spoiling cracks blocked up.

Group Captain Fred Winterbotham CBE. Born on 16 April 1897, he served as an RFC pilot in the First World War and became a PoW after being shot down behind German lines while flying a Nieuport fighter of 29 Squadron. He entered RAF Intelligence at the Air Ministry in the 1920s and managed to ingratiate himself with prominent Nazis in Berlin during the 1930s. He was associated with Sidney Cotton's clandestine flights over Italian and German installations before the Second World War and later helped to organise the RAF's new Photographic Development Unit. In April 1940 he organised the decryption of German 'Ultra' signals at the Government Code and Cypher School at Bletchley Park and then he liaised with the Allied high command with the flow of information from these decrypts. He died in January 1990. (Flight Officer Constance Babington Smith MBE, WAAF)

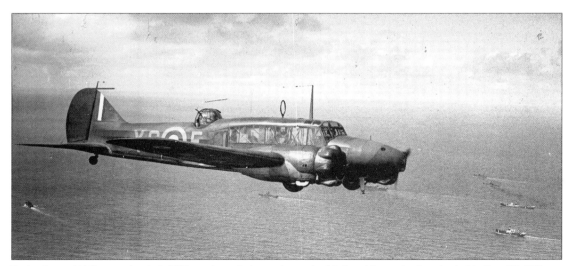

The Avro Anson, which first entered service in 1936, was the standard reconnaissance aircraft in Coastal Command at the outbreak of the Second World War. With a range of only about 790 miles and an armament consisting of a single machine gun firing forward and another in the turret, it was not adequate for its duties. After the German Blitzkrieg it was relegated to the roles of trainer and transport. Nevertheless, it was liked for its reliability, being known as 'Faithful Annie', and remained in RAF service until 1968. The Anson on convoy duties in this photograph was from 502 Squadron, which was equipped with these machines from January 1939 to November 1940 when based at Aldergrove in Northern Ireland. (The late Squadron Leader J.E. Archbald)

The Lockheed Hudson, modified from the Lockheed 14 Super Electra civil aircraft, began to replace Coastal Command's Avro Ansons in May 1939 for maritime reconnaissance and anti-shipping work. With a range of 2,160 miles and an armament of seven machine guns, it was a great improvement on its predecessor, the Anson. The Hudson in this photograph was on the strength of 48 Squadron when operating from the north of Scotland and the Shetlands. (The late Squadron Leader J.E. Archbald).

Oblique and vertical F24 cameras fitted in the fuselage of a Lockheed Hudson. (Flight Lieutenant G.H. Parry RAF (Ret'd))

Spinners were fitted to the propellers, the tail-wheels were made retractable, and tear-drop windows were installed. It was found these measures increased the airspeed by about 20 mph, and Cotton believed that the commander-in-chief of Fighter Command, Air Chief Marshal Sir Hugh Dowding, was so impressed by this result that he agreed to allocate two Spitfires Is to the new unit. In fact these two aircraft, serials N3071 and N3069, did not come from Fighter Command but were delivered to Heston on 30 October from Maintenance Command, by arrangement with Air Vice-Marshal Peck.

In his memoirs written in 1991 one of the airmen photographers, Jack Eggleston, wrote:

'The modification of aircraft for wartime photography involved experimenting with different cameras having focal lengths from five to forty-eight inches and varous camera fits. This was done in liaison with Mr Harry Stringer together with the aircraft and photographic experts of the Royal Aircraft Establishment at Farnborough, about twenty miles south-west. F24 cameras were fitted in vertical positions, as split pairs, forward-facing, and as side obliques. Cameras could be mounted in the wings, housed in small pods, or positioned in the fuselage. They were protected from condensation and the effect of cold by electrically-heated muffs or by air ducted from the engine. Particular attention was paid to obtaining vibration-free mountings for the fixed cameras. All experiments aimed for a camera fit which would be best for the particular conditions of air photo recce anticipated.

Modification also consisted of stripping the aircraft of all armament facilities and unwanted weight. An extra twenty to forty knots was obtained by minimising air-spoiling protuberances and by creating a smooth-polished skin surface. Even rivet heads were smoothed over. This task was carried out with a will by all airmen of the unit regardless of rank or trade. The Spitfires in particular were treated in this way and were experimentally sky-camouflaged for high or low level photography with variations of pale pink, light blue, duck-egg green and later a darker blue which was generally adopted. The pilot's cockpit canopy was modified with tear-drop extensions each side for visual navigation, and with marks to aid oblique target sighting. Extra fuel tanks were fitted and on later Spitfires the wing units were converted to hold many more gallons of fuel. It was said that the PR Spitfire was like a flying petrol bowser with cameras attached. This aircraft modification for wartime air photo recce was called "Cottonising".'

The Heston Flight was renamed No 2 Camouflage Unit on 1 November, in an additional attempt to preserve secrecy. The first two Spitfires retained only the normal tanks of 84 gallons, however, being known as Spitfire PR IAs. It was decided to test N3071 in operational conditions and the aircraft was flown on 5 November by Longbottom to Seclin, near Lille in France, while other personnel arrived in the Lockheed. The unit in France was named the Special Survey Flight and was kept isolated from RAF squadrons. Longbottom flew the first sortie in the Spitfire on 18 November, refuelling at Challerton near the Luxembourg border and then flying over the German frontier as far as Aachen. He brought back some excellent pictures from 33,000 feet, although Aachen itself was covered by cloud. After a period of settling into the French environment, part of the unit moved on 20 November to Coulommiers, about 30 miles east of Paris. The photographic section, under Sergeant S.R. Walton, was also based near there, at the village of Tigeaux. Jack Eggleston described the morale of the personnel back at Heston:

This example of the excellent aerial photographs taken by the Luftwaffe shows part of Hamburg in early 1939. The eight large vessels in the centre are moored in the Kaiser-Wilhelm Hafen, with eight more large vessels in the Kuhwerder Hafen above. The Vulkan Hafen is bottom left while the large buildings on the right are the Howald Deutsche Werke. The river Norder-Elbe is outside the photograph. (The late Squadron Leader J.E. Archbald)

The port of Bremen photographed in early 1939 by the Luftwaffe. The heavy cruiser *Lützow* of 12,750 tons displacement, under construction, was moored centre left, while the cruiser *Seydlitz* of the same displacement was under construction in the dry dock bottom left. The cruiser *Lützow* (not to be confused with the pocket battleship *Schweren Kreuger Lützow* which was renamed from *Deutschland* by Hitler and sunk by the RAF on 16 April 1945) was rebuilt as an aircraft carrier but not used in the Second World War. The cruiser *Seylitz* was not completed. (The late Squadron Leader J.E. Archbald)

'In the early days the unit was very informal, not at all like the regular air force we were used to. Some pilots, particularly the ex-bush pilot types, often wore desert boots, spotted neck scarves, and wore their caps at jaunty angles with their tunic top buttons undone. We young airmen delighted in this informality. No Station Warrant Officer to harass us, no working parades, no kit inspections and minimum saluting. We were "Sid Cotton's Air Force", working on and with the aircraft, all mucking in together and the end product was good quality intelligence-producing photography.'*

Although the pilots were flying fighter aircraft, they were expected to possess qualities which were different from those required by the men who flew on short missions hunting for enemy aircraft to attack. Their sorties were for long distances in conditions of extreme cold, while breathing oxygen most of the time. They needed to fly very steady compass courses and to be capable of pilot-navigation without any aids other than map-reading. Above all, they were expected to avoid combat and to bring their precious magazines of photographs safely back for interpretation.

Some RAF officers did not approve of Cotton's working methods, especially when the unit began to expand. The photographic officer at Heston, Squadron Leader 'Tubby' Earle,† asked to be transferred, leaving Cotton with the problem of finding a replacement. He selected a civilian

photographic technician, Paul Lamboit, who was then working with Dufaycolor in the USA. Lamboit was asked to return to Britain and duly commissioned as an acting pilot officer on 23 November but found, on Cotton's insistence with his superiors, that he was elevated to the rank of squadron leader in early January 1940.‡

Another who disapproved of Cotton was Victor Laws, who had finished his work in Australia and returned home to become managing director of the Williamson camera company. He was called up soon after the outbreak of war and posted as a wing commander on 24 November to the headquarters of the Air Component of the British Expeditionary Force in France, where he took charge of photography. In his own words, Laws regarded Cotton as 'quite out of control', although he rather grudgingly admitted that the 'one good thing Cotton did' was to introduce Spitfires into photographic reconnaissance.

In the knowledge that the static 'phoney war' could not last indefinitely, the Royal Aircraft Establishment at Farnborough formed its Mobile Photographic Printing Unit. This consisted of a 'J'-type trailer for processing and printing contact prints, a generator mounted on another trailer, and a vehicle containing a Graber multi-printing unit for mass production. Another vehicle carried a copy camera for enlarging or reducing, mounted on rails for ease of scaling. A stores vehicle completed this mobile unit, which moved to France in December with Sergeant Len Eades in charge, and set up in a village near Arras. Very bad weather hampered activity in the last weeks of 1939 and Eades received orders to move

---

* After retirement from the RAF, Jack Eggleston became an instructor and also worked in a voluntary capacity as the curator of the museum at the Joint School of Photography at RAF Cosford. In 1993–5 he helped the author to write his book.
† Alfred Earle continued his distinguished career in the RAF and also opened the School of Photography at RAF Cosford in 1965. He retired with the rank of Air Chief Marshal in 1966 and died in 1990.

‡It was Paul Lamboit, as the historian for the post-war Association of RAF Photography Officers, who first persuaded the author to embark on this book.

A photo-reconnaissance Spitfire of 212 Squadron on an airfield in France, possibly Seclin or Coulommiers. It seems to have been a warm day in late spring, with some of the airmen in shirt-sleeves. (Squadron Leader P. Lamboit RAFVR)

Spitfire PR IB serial N3117 of 212 Squadron, with a leading aircraftman leaning on it. Experiments were made with camouflaging these early reconnaissance Spitfires in light blue, light green and even light pink. This photograph was taken at Seclin in France before the German Blitzkrieg of May 1940. (Warrant Officer J.H. Eggleston RAF (Ret'd))

Two of the earliest pilots of the Photographic Development Unit, photographed at Heston in 1940. Left to right: Pilot Officer Spencer L. Ring, Pilot Officer S.G. 'Bill' Wise. Later, both commanded photo-reconnaissance squadrons. (The late Group Captain S.G. Wise CBE, DFC).

The Lockheed Hudson which was given the civil registration G—AGAR and used for the spy flights over Baku and Batum in March and April 1940. Conversion of a Hudson for photo-reconnaissance was made by removing the gun turret and other armament so that the aircraft's configuration closely resembled the original Lockheed 14 Super Electra civil aircraft. It was then fitted with cameras and an extra fuel tank in the fuselage. This aircraft was flown back to the Middle East in June 1940, where it was sometimes known as 'Cloudy Joe'. It was written off on 4 April 1941 after being badly damaged by an Italian CR42 while on the ground in Crete. (Wing Commander R.G.M. Walker DFC, RAF (Ret'd))

into Arras, where the equipment was installed in a building while the vehicles were jacked up. This move proved to be unwise in the light of later events.

The bad weather restricted the operations of the solitary Spitfire PR IA in France, but by 26 January 1940 Cotton was able to claim that it had photographed 5,000 square miles of enemy territory without loss, whereas up to the end of 1939 the RAF Blenheim IVs had photographed only 2,500 square miles and lost 16 aircraft in the process, while the French had photographed 6,000 square miles with the loss of 60 aircraft. In order to obtain the photographs, however, the Spitfire had frequently flown without authority over the neutral countries of Belgium and Holland. These statistics, which Cotton had obtained partly from the French, made a deep impression on the Air Staff as well as Air Marshal Sir Arthur S. Barratt, who commanded the British Air Forces in France.

Meanwhile, on 16 January 1940, the first Spitfire fitted with an auxiliary fuel tank of 29 gallons, behind the pilot, arrived at Heston. This was known as the Spitfire PR IB, the radius of action being increased from about 240 to 325 miles. It was painted in medium blue, which became the standard camouflage for photo-reconnaissance aircraft. On 10 February, Longbottom flew it from Debden in Essex and photographed Wilhelmshaven, for the Admiralty was particularly anxious to verify whether the powerful new battleship *Tirpitz* was still in dry dock.

Cotton had begun to fall out with the Air Staff, who pointed out that RAF interpreters could not cope with photographs taken from 33,000 feet with the F24 camera, since the small 5-inch by 5-inch format lacked definition. However, Cotton was equal to any problem. He had already made contact with Major Harold 'Lemnos' Hemming, AFC, the managing director of a survey organisation located at Wembley in Middlesex. This was the Aircraft Operating Company, which had considerable experience of surveys for oil companies in the Middle East and employed a number of photo-interpreters. Together with its associated company Aerofilms, it was equipped with a sophisticated photogrammetric mapping machine made in Switzerland, the Wild A5. This remarkable machine gave eight times magnification, so that far more information could be obtained from the F24 photographs than by using a hand stereoscope.

Without obtaining permission, Cotton had already begun to use the staff in these two civilian companies for the interpretation of RAF photographs, the work being carried out in strict secrecy. One of the photo-interpreters, Michael Spender, was able to verify that the *Tirpitz* was still in dock. Cotton passed this information to the Admiralty, where it came to the attention of the First Sea Lord, Winston Churchill. The Air Staff had little option but to accept the approval of the Admiralty, but resentment of Cotton's unorthodox methods was growing. Negotiations began for bringing the Aircraft Operating Company and Aerofilms, together with their staff, under the authority of the RAF, but were not completed until 31 May.

The titles of the reconnaissance units were changed yet again. On 17 January 1940, No 2 Camouflage Unit was renamed the Photographic Development Unit, and on 10 February 1940 the detachment in France known as the Special Survey Flight became 212 Squadron. To the cheerful and industrious airmen in both units, however, these alterations were made solely to confuse the enemy, and they still served in 'Sid Cotton's Air Force'. A step was taken to bring both units in conformity with regular RAF practice by the appointment on 9 February of Squadron Leader Geoffrey W. Tuttle as second-in-command. Tuttle was a former fighter pilot who had earned his DFC in north-west India and was also a qualified aeronautical engineer. He proved the ideal choice for the position, handling the administration with great skill but at the same time ensuring that the spirit of enterprise was not stifled.

In the first months of 1940 the Spitfires in France were employed on essential work for the British Expeditionary Force under Lord Gort. It was fully appreciated that the Germans would try to attack through Belgium, around the northern flank of France's Maginot Line, but the maps available dated back to 1914. A photographic survey was required and this was begun by the Spitfires of 212 Squadron, operating from Seclin, without authority from the neutral country of Belgium. The 'cover story' was that the pilots were engaged on training flights but made errors in navigation or experienced compass trouble. The whole of Belgium was photographed in this way and up-to-date maps were duly constructed.

Meanwhile, the unit at Heston concentrated mainly on work for the Admiralty. In February, it was allocated three Lockheed Hudsons, the RAF's name for the Lockheed Super Electra 14 civil airliner. Cotton devised a scheme whereby these aircraft, without gun turrets or armament but with auxiliary tanks in the fuselage, went out and reported on weather conditions over enemy territory. If the skies were sufficiently clear, a Spitfire then took off and continued at high level over German targets. In cloudy weather, the Hudson came down briefly to take photographs and then climbed back into cover. But a tragedy occurred on 3 March when one of the aircraft, with its livery of duck-egg green, was shot down over Kent by a puzzled Hurricane pilot. The machine was flown by Flying Officer Denis Slocum, who was killed with the photographer Leading Aircraftman Mutton and the wireless operator Leading Aircraftman Butcher, although the co-pilot managed to bale out.

On the day before this tragedy, 2 March, the new Spitfire PR IB was employed on a task which the short-range Mark IA had been unable to perform. Bob Niven took off from Heston and flew over neutral Holland making for the Ruhr, a target which had been too distant and too dangerous for the reconnaissance Blenheims of Bomber Command. He photographed Duisburg from 30,000 feet, turned east as far as Dortmund and then made a reciprocal run back to the Rhine. German fighters pursued him over Luxembourg but he managed to outstrip them and landed safely at Heston. A mosaic of the photographs was prepared from this successful sortie, which Cotton showed triumphantly to the Commander-in-Chief of Bomber Command, Air Marshal Sir Edgar Ludlow-Hewitt. The C-in-C was so astonished and impressed that he put forward a proposal that his command should take over the whole photographic unit, but this was not accepted by the Air Staff.

The first loss of a Spitfire occurred on 22 March when Flying Officer Claude M. Wheatley took off from Stradishall in Suffolk for north-west Germany but did not return. He was reported to have been shot down by an enemy fighter and lost his life. It is possible that his 'tell-tale' condensation trail, which was one of the inevitable hazards of the high-flying Spitfires, was spotted by the Germans in time to arrange an interception.

One of the Hudsons at Heston, serial N7364, was fitted with extra fuel tanks in the fuselage and used for an exploit which in retrospect seems almost bizarre. At the time, Russia was still bound by the Non-Agression Pact which had been signed with Germany on 24 August 1939 and was supplying large quantities of oil from the Caucasus region to Germany, which had almost no natural sources of its own and was forced to rely mainly on synthetic oil derived from coal for its military forces. Russia was regarded as a potential enemy by the British

Above, left: Squadron Leader Hugh C. Macphail DFC, one of the early pilots in the Photographic Development Unit. In March and April 1940 he commanded an expedition to spy on the Russian oilfields at Baku and Batum. In March 1941 he took over command of No 2 Photographic Reconnaissance Unit at Heliopolis in Egypt. (The late Squadron Leader H.C. Macphail DFC). *Above, right:* Flying Officer Frederic E. Burton DFC. He was the captain of the Hudson, or Lockheed 14 Super Electra serial N7364, which was given the civil registration G—AGAR and made spy flights from Iraq over the Russian oilfields at Baku and Batum in March and April 1940. (The late Wing Commander F.E. Burton OBE, DFC). *Right:* Flight Lieutenant R. Idris Jones, who made detailed interpretations of the photographs taken during the spy flights over Baku and Batum in March and April 1940. The Germans sentenced him to death *in absentia* following their discovery of the Anglo-French plans after the fall of France, but could not carry out their sentence. Afterwards, RAF interpretation reports were no longer signed. (The late Squadron Leader R.I. Jones)

and French, and their Combined Chiefs of Staff devised a scheme which they thought might knock out both Germany and Russia in a single blow. This was no less than the destruction of the Caucasus oil supplies by bombing, employing five squadrons of Martin Marylands of the French Air Force to be moved to northern Syria, and four squadrons of Blenheim IVs and one of Vickers Wellesleys of the RAF to be moved to northern Iraq. Both the French and the British expressed optimisim about the likely results, probably unwisely, and the British ordered the Photographic Development Unit to carry out a preliminary photo-reconnaissance of the main Russian production centres at Baku, Batum and Grozny.

Slocum had been the only pilot in the unit qualified to fly the Hudson, but 224 Squadron at Leuchars in Fifeshire had been equipped with these machines since May 1939. A call was sent to this squadron for a pilot to fly on a secret mission and Flying Officer Frederic E. 'Monty' Burton, DFC, was chosen. Burton had flown Hudsons operationally since the outbreak of war and had participated in the destruction of two Dornier flying boats, including a Dornier 18 which was shot down on 5 September 1939, the first victory of the RAF in the war. He travelled to Heston and crewed up with Squadron Leader Hugh Macphail, who was put in charge of the mission whereas Burton was the captain of the aircraft. Together with a photographer, Leading Aircraftman Alan J. 'Tubby' Dixon, and a fitter, Leading Aircraftman Bissett, they took off in the early morning of 23 March 1940 for the destination of RAF Habbaniya, near Baghdad in Iraq.*

* Before his death in 1984, Wing Commander Freddie Burton, OBE, DFC, discussed this matter in great detail with the author, using his pilot's log book and other memorabilia. Details of the plan of attack can be found in the Public Record Office, under AIR 14/770 and AIR 23/980.

They arrived at Habbaniya three days later, having made overnight stops at Marseille, Malta, and Helwan in Egypt. Here they changed into civilian clothes and put aside their service documents, for they had been issued with civilian passports. The RAF markings were painted out of the machine, using a pot of Camotint brought with them for the purpose, and the civil registration G-AGAR was painted on the fuselage and wings. Burton took the aircraft up for a fuel consumption test on the following day, and it was decided that Baku and Batum were within range but that they could not make a return trip to Grozny.

They photographed the whole of Baku on the coast of the Caspian Sea, in brilliantly clear weather on 30 March, making a series of line overlaps to provide a mosaic, although the town proved to be far bigger than it appeared on the thirty-year-old map which had been given to them. The photographs were developed on their return to Habbaniya and they flew them down to the RAF headquarters in Heliopolis. Returning once more to Habbaniya they took off on 5 April and crossed the neutral country of Turkey making for Batum on the coast of the Black Sea. On this occasion flak opened up on them as they began their photographic runs at 20,000 feet, although it burst harmlessly beneath them. After the first run Macphail spotted an Me109, probably one of a batch provided to Russia by Germany, climbing towards them. They beat a hasty retreat to the safety of the Turkish border and returned to Habbaniya with the target only partially covered. The RAF men returned to Heston, arriving on 13 April. Three copies of the developed photographs were brought back and interpreted by Flying Officer R. Idris Jones for distribution to the Intelligence Section of the Air Ministry, the British Secret Service and the French Secret Service. The photographs were accompanied by a target map and details of the plan of attack.

While these strange events were taking place, a new long-distance version of the Spitfire arrived at Heston. This was fitted with a 30-gallon blister tank under the port wing as well as the 29-gallon tank behind the pilot, giving a radius of action of about 410 miles. The wing tank was counter-balanced by a blister under the starboard wing, housing two F24 cameras with 8-inch lenses. On 7 April, Longbottom took off in one of these machines, which was known as a Spitfire PR IC, and photographed Kiel for the first time, to the intense interest of the Admiralty, for the pictures disclosed preparations for the anticipated invasion of Norway which began two days later. One result was the shelving of the proposed attacks on the Russian oil fields, for the British and the French became engrossed in matters of more immediate importance.

The Germans began their anticipated attack through Belgium on 10 May and the British and French Armies advanced to meet them. In the campaign which followed, the front-line strength of the Blenheim and Battle squadrons was wiped out and the Lysander squadrons also suffered badly, in spite of the astonishing bravery of the aircrews. The Allied Forces reeled back from the Blitzkrieg and on 16 May Cotton received orders from London to evacuate to Heston. He chose to ignore this order but it was repeated on the following day and some of the personnel were flown back by various means.

Cotton's photo-reconnaissance aircraft continued to operate over the German lines for the next three weeks, even after Dunkirk fell on 4 June, and some aircraft which were sent down to Corsica and the south of France to photograph targets in Italy did not return home until 15 June, four days after that country entered the war. Unfortunately, Spitfire PR IB serial P9331 was left behind in France and captured intact by the Germans, giving them a clear appreciation of the techniques developed by the RAF's reconnaissance unit. On 16 June, in a railway train at La Charité-sur-Loire, the Germans captured the French copies of the photographs taken over Baku and Batum by Burton and Macphail, together with the Allied plan of attack. They duly sent copies to Stalin and made a great show of righteous indignation on behalf of their 'ally', causing some embarrassment to the British Government. The photo-interpreter who signed these reports, Flying Officer R.I. Jones, was sentenced to death *in absentia* by the Germans. Future interpretation reports were therefore not signed, but of course the Germans were never able to carry out their threat.

Meanwhile, the RAE's Mobile Photographic Printing Unit was put back on the road and the vehicles set off towards Boulogne and then Cherbourg. However, the men were forced to abandon their vehicles and eventually returned home in a French aircraft, with their films, or from ports in western France.

The men of 212 Squadron set off on 9 June in the direction of Poitiers, while Cotton circled above in his Lockheed 12A. Cotton flew down to Marseille on 11 June to arrange the evacuation of his party by Hudson and also made other flights back to Heston. Some of the men patched up a damaged Battle which they found at Poitiers and then drove on to a small grass airfield at Fontenay-le-Comte, near the port of La Rochelle, arriving on 16 June. Cotton flew to this airfield to see that all was well with the men, whose morale remained astonishingly high, and then flew on to the airfield at Le Luc, near Marseille. Here he found that a Hudson sent to evacuate his men had been destroyed on the ground by an Italian air attack, but he arranged for them to be brought back by the

Photographic vehicles in June 1940 at the airfield of Fontenay-le-Comte, near the port of La Rochelle, ready to be blown up by the RAF men. They consisted of photographic trailers, trucks, a petrol bowser, a power unit and a van. After destroying the vehicles, the RAF men who were unable to take off in aircraft headed for Bordeaux. They boarded a collier and reached the UK in July. (The late Corporal C.E. Lloyd)

On 20 June 1940, five men from 212 Squadron escaped from France in Fairey Battle I serial L5360 of 88 Squadron. The aircraft had been attacked and forced down at Poitiers airfield, where it was abandoned. Some of the men from 212 Squadron patched up the bullet holes and replaced a damaged wing tip with a tree branch and some fabric. The aircraft was flown down to Fontenay-le-Comte, north-east of La Rochelle, by Flight Lieutenant L.D. 'Tug' Wilson, where the ground personnel cut cards for the privilege of flying back to England. The winners were (left to right): Leading Aircraftman Cook, Sergeant Walton and Sergeant Ward. The other was Leading Aircraftman Jim Muncie, who took the photograph. Wilson took off with his four passengers and reached Heston after a flight of four hours. (Sergeant J. Muncie RAF (Ret'd))

Fleet Air Arm. Back at Fontenay-le-Comte later that day, he and his men slept in the open and he then arranged for the evacuation of some of the party in a Bristol Bombay transport aircraft, while a few returned in the Battle and others in a collier from Bordeaux. By these and other means, all the men managed to return to England.

Cotton flew back to England on 17 June, together with Niven and four other passengers, landing at Jersey for the night and then on to Heston the following day. He sent his two remaining Hudsons back to Bordeaux to pick up other passengers and opened a letter which had been written to him on 16 June by the Permanent Under-Secretary of State for Air, Sir Arthur Street. The content was terse but polite, expressing appreciation of his work but informing him that the Photographic Development Unit was to be removed from his command and taken over by Wing Commander G.W. Tuttle, to serve under the orders of the Commander-in-Chief, Coastal Command.

CHAPTER SIX

BRITISH INTELLIGENCE

The replacement of Sidney Cotton as the commanding officer of the Photographic Development Unit was inevitable. He was a good master, to whom most of his RAF officers and airmen were devoted, but he was also a bad servant. A photo-interpreter who met Cotton when she was a young trainee in the WAAF, Constance Babington Smith, described him in her very readable book* as 'tall, quick, wolf-like, with horn-rimmed glasses and thick grey-white hair'. It is unlikely that a man of Cotton's entrepreneurial talents and impatient nature could have fitted into a service environment for the duration of the war, obeying orders he thought unsuitable or misguided. He was unable to accept the delays which were inevitable in an organisation which had been drastically run down between the wars. In his own words, attempts to make the RAF satisfy his requirements for equipment was 'worse than trying to extract diamonds from the Crown Jewels'.

Whatever his defects as an RAF commanding officer, however, Cotton deserved better treatment than was meted out to him. He was placed on the RAF Reserve List and made an Officer of the Order of the British Empire. This award, although prestigious, was not thought by his friends to have been sufficient recognition of the value of his achievements. After months of frustration he was invited on 3 March 1941 by Sir Arthur Street to resign his commission, and had no alternative but to do so. Thereafter, all his attempts to offer help with various ideas for improving Britain's prosecution of the war were steadfastly blocked by the authorities, which was considered to have been a shameful waste of his talents.

On the other hand, the appointment of Wing Commander Geoffrey Tuttle† to succeed Cotton was wholly admirable. He had been responsible for running the unit at Heston for several months and was highly respected by his officers and airmen. He was an experienced pilot, a qualified aeronautical engineer, and an excellent administrator. He was also fortunate in some respects, for the way ahead had been charted by Cotton while the value of his unit had come to be recognised at the Air Staff and even by the War Cabinet headed by the new Prime Minister, Winston Churchill. On 13 May 1940 the Commander-in-Chief of the Home Forces had advised the Chiefs of Staff that 'the most effective method of keeping a watch by air on German movements will be high altitude reconnaissance as often as practicable'. With the threat of an imminent invasion after the fall of France, the RAF heeded this advice.

---

* Constance Babington Smith, *Evidence in Camera*, London, Chatto and Windus, 1958.

† During several meetings before his death in 1989, Air Marshal Sir Geoffrey Tuttle KBE CB DFC FRAeS, was kind enough to encourage the author to write this book.

Above, left: Group Captain Peter J.A. Riddell, who commanded Bomber Command's air photographic section at the beginning of the Second World War. He devised the highly successful photo-interpretation procedures which were later followed by the RAF. In May 1944 he became the Senior Air Staff Officer for No 106 (Photo-Reconnaissance) Group when it was formed to co-ordinate and control all RAF and USAAF strategic reconnaissance work. *Above, right:* Air Marshal Sir Geoffrey W. Tuttle CBE CB DFC FRAeS, photographed as a Wing Commander. Born on 2 October 1902, he was awarded the DFC in 1937 while serving on the North West Frontier of India. After the outbreak of the Second World War, he served with the Advanced Air Striking Force in France. He took over command of the Photographic Reconnaissance Unit at Heston in June 1940 and was mainly responsible for its expansion before he was promoted and moved to other duties in November 1941. His distinguished career in the RAF continued until he retired in 1960. He died on 11 January 1989.

Wing Commander Douglas N. Kendall, a former staff member of the Aircraft Operating Company Ltd, who was commissioned in the RAF in January 1940. He was sent to join the small detachment of 212 Squadron in France, engaged on photo-reconnaissance over German territory. After the fall of France, he devised the procedures for the RAF's photo-interpretation and trained its personnel, with great success, and commanded the Photographic Interpretation Section at Medmenham in Buckinghamshire. From mid-1943 onwards, he co-ordinated the reconnaissance work on German 'V' weapons. (All photos: Flight Officer Constance Babington Smith MBE, WAAF)

The Spitfire PR ID entered service in October 1940. It was a modification of the Spitfire V, carrying 114 gallons of extra fuel in wing tanks as well as 29 gallons behind the pilot. It carried two F24 or F8 cameras. The type was later designated the Spitfire PR IV and became the mainstay of No 1 Photographic Reconnaissance Unit during 1941 and 1942. This photograph was taken in a blast pen at St Eval in Cornwall in 1941, where B Flight No 1 Photographic Reconnaissance Unit was based. (Sergeant J. Muncie RAF (Ret'd))

Spitfire serial N3117, converted to a PR IE from a PR IB, with two cameras in the wings pointed outwards for low-level work. It is believed that this was the only Spitfire converted to this configuration. It was first flown in this form on 3 July 1940 by Wing Commander Geoffrey Tuttle of No 1 Photographic Reconnaissance Unit. On 7 July 1940, Flying Officer Alistair Taylor flew the machine to Boulogne, where he took some excellent photographs below cloud at 300 feet. (The late Squadron Leader J.E. Archbald)

A Spitfire PR IV of B Flight, Photographic Reconnaissance Unit at St Eval in Cornwall, with the photographer Leading Aircraftman Jim Muncie sitting on the nose. This aircraft, serial P9385, began life as a Mark I but was later converted to a Mark IV. The 'teardrop' window on the cockpit hood, which gave the pilot a much better view, was invented by Sidney Cotton; over 100,000 were made. (Sergeant J. Muncie RAF (Ret'd))

Above: Split F24 cameras with 8-inch lenses, installed forward-facing in a 90-gallon 'slipper-type' drop-tank fitted to a reconnaissance Spitfire. (Flight Lieutenant G.H. Parry RAF (Ret'd))

Tuttle took over the unit on 21 June 1940. Seventeen days later, on 8 July, there was yet another change of name when it became the Photographic Reconnaissance Unit. On the same day, it was placed under the control of Coastal Command's No 16 Group. This was also a wise choice, for a number of reasons. By this time, the Germans controlled the whole of the European coastline from the north of Norway to the Franco-Spanish border. The likelihood of invasion necessitated continual reconnaissance of enemy ports while the seriousness of the threat to Britain's shipping lanes from German U-boats and capital ships was equally acute. If the Spitfires were to achieve maximum radius of action, it was necessary for them to operate from coastal airfields. Moreover, if the unit had been transferred to Bomber Command, there is little doubt that its limited resources would have been concentrated on bombing assessment flights, the matters being of less immediate importance than reconnaissance devoted to Britain's survival in her most critical period.

British Intelligence inherited from Cotton the nucleus of another organisation which was to play a prominent part in the war. This was the photo-interpretation unit which had been set up on 31 May 1940 when the Aircraft Operating Company at Wembley was taken over by the RAF. Originally known as the Photographic Development Unit (Interpretation), its name was changed on 6 July to the less clumsy Photographic Interpretation Unit. The functions of photographic processing and interpretation, hitherto carried out by the Royal Aircraft Establishment at Farnborough, were transferred to this unit. It had been joined on 26 June 1940 by Squadron Leader Peter Riddell, the most experienced interpreter in the RAF, who had already been recruited by Cotton from Bomber Command.

Riddell set about organising this strange new unit with an unquenchable energy, knowing that he had to satisfy the demands of the Admiralty and the Army as well as the three operational Commands of the RAF. It had already been recognised that women possessed the qualities of patience and perception which were required by photo-interpreters, and a number of young women in the WAAF had been recruited as trainees.

At the outset, Riddell was the only RAF officer in the unit, and one of his first actions was to ask for the Army interpreters who had escaped from France. He was also able to use the services of the civilian experts who had previously worked for the Aircraft Operating Company, some of whom were commissioned into the RAF. With the help of one of these men, Michael Spender, he was successful in attracting into the RAF unit a number of eminent academics who specialised in such subjects as cartography, mathematics, archaeology, geology and geography. In addition, Flight Lieutenant Hamshaw Thomas, who had been responsible for the success of photo-interpretation in the Middle East in the First World War and had since worked as a botanist at Cambridge, eventually joined the unit. One of Thomas's first tasks was to revise the Air Ministry's manual of photographic interpretation.

Riddell devised a method of interpretation which he divided into three phases. In the first phase, a preliminary report was prepared almost immediately after the aircraft had landed and the contents of the camera magazines were developed, sometimes from the negatives before they were printed. The second phase resulted in a report which was made within the following twenty-four hours, giving a more detailed appreciation of the enemy activity by comparison with earlier photographic cover. The third phase was made by the experts who specialised in various fields, providing discerning reports of

Gun cameras were superseded by ciné cameras when Hurricanes and Spitfires entered service. Although designed to assist in training, they also provided a record of air combat. The first to be electrically operated was the G42B, which carried a magazine containing 25 feet of 16-mm film and took 1,000 exposures. It was usually installed in a fixed forward position and operated automatically when the pilot pressed the firing button, but it could also be used as a free-handling camera by an air observer. (B.H. Harris, courtesy Tangmere Military Aviation Museum)

The G45 ciné camera was designed to replace the G42B ciné camera after numerous RAF fighters had been lost in the Battles of France and Britain. The intermittent drive of the latter was difficult to machine and production could not keep up with requirements. The G45 was designed to be loaded from the top or the side and could also be fitted in turrets in addition to the fixed-forward and free-handling positions. (B.H. Harris, courtesy Tangmere Military Aviation Museum)

This 35-mm ciné camera was donated by the film industry and fitted to the Spitfire VA serial W3185 flown by Wing Commander Douglas Bader. It was lost when this celebrated pilot was shot down or collided over Béthune on 9 August 1941 and taken prisoner. (Flight Lieutenant N. Jenkins RAF (Ret'd))

This posed photograph was intended to encourage recruitment into Group 2 trade of the WAAF, which included the maintenance of photographic equipment. The young lady was aiming a G28 gun camera, which was based on the Vickers K machine gun and produced negatives of 2½-inch by 2½-inch from a roll film. (The late Squadron Leader J.E. Archbald)

strategic value. For the second and third phases, these experts were eventually put in charge of interpretation sections entitled Airfields, Aircraft and Aircraft Industry, Army, Naval, Industries, Wireless, Communication, Camouflage, Damage Assessment, Plotting, Enemy Decoys and Photogrammetric. Supporting sections dealing with models and target material, press and public relations, and a print library were also added to this growing organisation.

The interpreters used small stereoscopes to view stereo pairs of vertical photographs, so that buildings and other objects stood up quite startlingly in three dimensions. Each became familiar within his or her specialised subject from a succession of photographs, and learnt to look for any unusual alteration among a mass of other details. Shadows were particularly important, and one of the interpreters, Squadron Leader Claude Wavell, later invented a spheroid device which he named an 'Altazimeter' for measuring the heights of objects in relation to the shadows they threw on the ground. On this the interpreter set the declination of the sun (i.e. the angle above the horizon) for the date, time and latitude of the object, together with the azimuth of the sun (i.e. its direction). These details were readily available from Air Almanacs and Astronomical Navigation Tables. The device then gave the height of an object by comparison with the length of its shadow, which was known from the scale of the photograph.

The Photographic Interpretation Unit soon became an indispensable source of intelligence for the Chiefs of Staff. The other main provider of intelligence was the Government Code and Cypher School, the nucleus of which had been set up by the Cabinet in 1919 and moved to Bletchley Park in Buckinghamshire on the outbreak of the Second World War. Its purpose was the protection of British cyphers and the decryptanalysis of enemy cyphers, usually obtained from the British 'Y' service which monitored enemy wireless transmissions.

In the 1920s the Germans had introduced a commercial version of an 'Enigma' machine, an electro-mechanical device which encyphered messages with a system of wired drums and wheels. This machine was adopted by the German Navy in 1926, the Army in 1929 and the Air Force in 1935, after some modifications had been made which were considered to render the system safe even if a machine was captured. The Germans were too sanguine in this belief, for considerable advances in breaking the various codes were made by Polish mathematicians before the war and this information was passed to the French and the British. However, the Germans made certain additional changes to the wheels and the codes, and it was not until their invasion of Norway that the British succeeded in breaking the codes used by the Army and the Air Force, although the Enigma used by the Navy, which employed additional wheels, remained impenetrable at this time.

Decryptanalysis and photo-interpretation, in both of which Wing Commander Winterbotham was closely involved, provided the Allies with their main sources of intelligence throughout the war. Of course, additional information was obtained through diplomatic channels, as well as from agents and very courageous resistance fighters in occupied countries, but these sources could not cover the great spectrum of information gleaned by the two main intelligence bodies.

Meanwhile, the photo-reconnaissance Spitfires and Hudsons continued to fly. On 1 July 1940, Tuttle moved A Flight to Wick on the north-east tip of Scotland for operations over the Norwegian coast, while B Flight was sent to St Eval in Cornwall to cover the west coast of France. C and D Flights remained at Heston to cover the enemy ports in the English Channel as well as the Belgian,

Dutch, Danish and German coasts. E Flight, formed for training on 27 July, was also based at Heston. Six months later, sections engaged on first phase interpretation were also set up at Wick and St Eval.

At the beginning of July 1940 a Spitfire IA was modified to carry an F24 in a blister under each wing, angled outwards at about 15 degrees below the horizontal so that photography could be carried out at extremely low level. On 3 July Tuttle flew the first operation in this machine, Spitfire PR IE serial N3117, but cloud covered the target. Flying Officer Alistair L. Taylor took off three days later and photographed Boulogne from 300 feet, then making a run in the other direction with the other camera.

At the end of July, another variant of the Spitfire arrived. This was the 'super long-range' Spitfire PR IF, which carried a 30-gallon tank in each wing as well as the 29-gallon tank behind the pilot. Fitted with two F24 cameras in the fuselage, it had a radius of action of about 650 miles, but this was still not sufficient to meet the demands of the Air Ministry or the Admiralty. By this time the unit consisted of only twelve Spitfires, of which eight were PR IBs, three were PR ICs and one was the PR IE. Nevertheless, these could carry out a surprisingly large number of sorties.

While the Battle of Britain raged in the summer and early autumn of 1940, the men of the Photographic Reconnaissance Unit flew 327 sorties, 183 of them in September. Reports that invasion fleets were being assembled in western France, Belgium, Holland, Germany and even southern Norway were checked by the Spitfire pilots, and their photographs revealed that invasion barges were assembling at Channel ports such as Dunkirk. Bomber Command carried out a number of daylight raids with light bombers against enemy ports and airfields, suffering severe losses on occasions. These attacks were made in addition to night operations over Germany itself. The threat of invasion petered out when intelligence reports confirmed that Hitler had suspended the military operation on 12 October 1940, after the Luftwaffe had failed to overcome the RAF.

Of course, there were casualties among the Spitfire pilots and Hudson crews, but the morale and spirit of the unit remained high, for the men were very proud of their role in the war. Some of these men lost their lives but others fell into enemy hands. Flying Officer Peter L. Dakeyne failed to return in a Spitfire on a low-level operation over the Belgian coast on 14 September 1940 and wrote to Tuttle from Dulag Luft, the German interrogation centre for the RAF at Oberursel near Frankfurt:

'I rather foolishly ran into AA fire whilst preoccupied and also distracted by a third factor. A direct hit stopped the prop, so rolled and fell out to land among troops! The machine made a spectacular crash full out! The prospect of a year or two here is infuriating but I hope that I will see you again – the last month or two had been to me – ideal! The best of luck!'

A letter also arrived from the same German PoW centre, from Flight Lieutenant James R.T. Smalley DFC, who had been shot down in a Spitfire over Kiel on 8 October 1940:

'Sorry I couldn't finish the job, Sir! Don't quite know what happened – big bang and fireworks. I just managed to get out, a bit battered but safe and sound and as happy as can be expected. Very good treatment, good quarters, food and company here – but of course I'm worried about and anxious for all my friends back home and long for news and long to be back with you all again. My love to all the boys, Sir – thank you for a very happy stay in your unit.'

The Consolidated PBY-5 of the US Navy was known as the Catalina I when it entered RAF service early in 1941. In spite of its slow speed, it proved a very effective reconnaissance aircraft in home waters and abroad. When fitted with long-range tanks, it had an endurance of up to twenty-seven hours. This example, Catalina IVA serial JX574 of 210 Squadron, was fitted with a Leigh Light for illuminating U-boats detected at night by radar. The photograph was taken in 1944, at a time when the squadron was based at Sullom Voe in the Shetlands. (*Aeroplane Monthly*)

The effect of a German parachute mine on the Imperial Airways hangar at RAF Heston on the night of 19/20 September 1940. Five reconnaissance Spitfires were badly damaged, as well as Sidney Cotton's Lockheed 12A which had to be shipped back to the USA for rebuilding. Most of the photographic equipment was recovered. (The late Corporal C.E. Lloyd)

Danesfield, the country house at Medmenham taken over by the RAF after the Photographic Interpretation Unit at Wembley received a direct hit from a German bomb on 2 October 1940. Nissen huts and other temporary buildings were erected as expansion continued. After the war the house was occupied by several organisations. It was opened as a five star hotel by a Dutch chain in 1989 but severely damaged by fire. (Squadron Leader P. Lamboit RAFVR, courtesy Hunting Aerofilms of Borehamwood)

Hudson N7301 was shot down on 26 October 1940 on an operation over the Scheldt estuary and the pilot, Flight Lieutenant Arnold A. Rumsey, wrote to Tuttle from Oflag IXA on 7 November:

'You will be glad to know Phillips, Williams, Dixon and Broome, also myself, landed by parachute. I have not seen Broome since he landed but all the others are well. We jumped between 600 and 200 feet so were lucky to escape from the burning kite. Sorry to disappoint you in not turning up for the party.'

Unfortunately, Pilot Officer Charles G. Broome did not survive. Leading Aircraftman Alan Dixon was the photographer who had flown with Burton and Macphail over Baku and Batum during the previous March and April, and he and the others remained in PoW camps for the rest of the war.

By this time, the Germans were fully aware of the photo-reconnaissance flights, from the presence of high-flying Spitfires over Europe and the wreckage of some aircraft. They also used the device of hidden microphones in their interrogation centre, as did the British in their centre at Cockfosters, and ensured that there were two prisoners in the same cell so that they could eavesdrop on their conversations. They were also experts at breaking the British codes used in wireless transmissions. Heston airfield and the Photographic Interpretation Unit at Wembley became obvious targets, and these were doubtless picked out by photo-reconnaissance Ju86 P2s. The German *Knickebein* system of radio beacons provided accurate navigation for bombers, not yet having been jammed by the British, while the winding Thames enabled bomb aimers to make good visual checks at night. Attacks against Heston culminated in a raid on the night of 19/20 September 1940, when the main hangar was hit by a parachute mine and five Spitfires as

well as Cotton's Lockheed were badly damaged. In the early hours of 2 October 1940, the interpretation section at Wembley was almost demolished by a bomb. St Eval on the north coast of Cornwall was also bombed on frequent occasions, although these attacks were probably directed mainly against the bomber aircraft of Coastal Command which were operating from this airfield.*

It became evident that the units at Heston and Wembley would have to move to safer localities. The airfield at Benson in Oxfordshire was chosen by Coastal Command, but the aircraft and crews did not begin moving to this new base until 27 December 1940. The photo-interpreters continued to work at Wembley, in a row of shabby and unheated houses opposite their bombed premises. On 7 January 1941 it was renamed the Central Interpretation Unit and the first section moved to Danesfield House at Medmenham in Buckinghamshire, the main party following on 23 May 1941.

Meanwhile, two new variants of the Spitfire were employed at Heston. One was the Spitfire PR IG, which was inspired by the PR IE which took large-scale photographs from low level. This retained the eight machine guns of the fighter version, since it was recognised that the pilots might be involved in combat or be able to take a quick squirt at ground targets. The machine was fitted with the 29-gallon tank behind the pilot and three F24 cameras, two verticals and one in the fuselage arranged obliquely to either port or starboard. From early October 1940 these PR IGs were employed on dangerous short-range sorties, most being painted in a very light pink instead of blue or the light green Camotint.

---

*In the evening of 25 January 1941, a few days after the author arrived at St Eval as a newly commissioned pilot officer, a bomb fell on an air raid shelter and killed twenty-one RAF men. Another man died the next day.

Personnel of the WAAF working on a continuous film processing machine at Medmenham, with the drying drum on the right. (The Medmenham Club)

Personnel of the WAAF working on a multiprinting machine at Medmenham. (The Medmenham Club)

The other was the Spitfire PR ID, two of which were completed in late October 1940. This variant arrived out of alphabetical sequence since the structural alterations originally requested by Sidney Cotton took more than three months to complete. It was the type known as the 'extra-super-long-range' Spitfire or the 'flying petrol bowser', since it carried 114 gallons of petrol in special tanks fitted into the leading edges of the wings. Together with the extra tank containing 29 gallons behind the pilot, they gave a radius of action of about 875 miles. The machine carried two F24 cameras with 8-inch or 20-inch lenses or two F8 cameras with 20-inch lenses, the latter having been designed by Victor Laws and built in the early 1920s. On 29 October 1941 Flying Officer Samuel J. Millen took off in Spitfire PR ID series P9551 and covered the distant targets of Stettin and Rostock in the Baltic, a sortie of five hours twenty minutes which earned him the DFC. Sadly, Millen lost his life the following month.

There was a strange episode at Heston on 21 November 1940 when a Polish pilot, Flying Officer Richard Drygalla, taxied Spitfire I serial P9426 out over the grass airfield with a fitter, Aircraftman H. Rhodes, sitting on the tail and then took to the air before the airman got off. The pilot managed to avoid a spin on two occasions, unaware that someone was clinging desperately to the tail, and finally dropped the machine back on the ground from 100 feet. Rhodes shot into the air and rolled over and over, breaking two ribs and suffering concussion. The Spitfire was badly damaged and Drygalla was also knocked out but, when he came to, complained that the aircraft was 'tail heavy and not stable'.

In the latter part of 1940, the activities of the PR Spitfires were directed primarily at naval targets. This concentration of effort gave rise to some annoyance on the part of Bomber Command, who justifiably required damage assessments after their raids. On 16 November, No 3 Photographic Reconnaissance Unit was formed at Oakington in Cambridgeshire, consisting of a number of Spitfires transferred from Heston under Squadron Leader Pat B.B. Ogilvie. Two Wellingtons were added for night photography. The unit came under the authority of Bomber Command's No 3 Group, and it began work over targets in Germany and occupied Europe. The results began to cause considerable perturbation, for it seemed that many of the bombing attacks were ineffectual.*

The unit at Heston was renamed No 1 Photographic Reconnaissance Unit, No 2 being reserved for the Middle East, as will be recounted in the next chapter. The flights at Wick, St Eval and Heston (later at Benson) were rotated every three months or so, to give the air and ground crews a change of environment. The pilots were required to bring back evidence of U-boat construction, and a steady stream of photographs was provided for the photo-interpreters. They also confirmed the Admiralty's worst fears when they discovered that the battleships *Scharnhorst* and *Gneisenau* had left Kiel on 27 December 1940, thus adding to the perils of Britain's life-line, the Atlantic convoy system. In the words of Winston Churchill, these were 'dark days' for Britain.

When these warships were photographed in Brest on 28 March 1941, having sunk about 120,000 tons of British shipping, they received almost daily attention from No 1 PRU as well as nightly bombing attacks. On 5 April *Gneisenau* was photographed outside the safety of dry dock at Brest, having been moved into the harbour to avoid danger from an unexploded bomb, and a flight of Beauforts from 22 Squadron was despatched from St Eval early the following morning.

*See Chapter Eleven, Night Bombing and Photography.

Constance Babington Smith joined the RAF in July 1940 and was commissioned six months later. In April 1941 she began work as the only photographic interpreter in the aircraft section of the RAF's Central Interpretation Unit (later the Allied Central Interpretation Unit), and continued in charge of this section until VE-Day. She was mentioned in despatches in January 1942 and was awarded the MBE in 1945. She was then attached to the USAAF for interpretation work in the Pacific theatre and in December 1945 became the first British woman to receive the US Legion of Merit. (Flight Officer Constance Babington Smith MBE, WAAF)

Charles Sim, who served as a photographer/air gunner in the pre-war RAF, joined the *Aeroplane* magazine and later served as a photo-interpreter during the Second World War. He is seen here as a flight lieutenant, checking air photographs with a factory plan at Medmenham. (The Medmenham Club)

A leading aircraftman of the Support Section at Medmenham, annotating a map showing the movements of the battleship *Tirpitz* from Germany to Norwegian fjords. (The Medmenham Club)

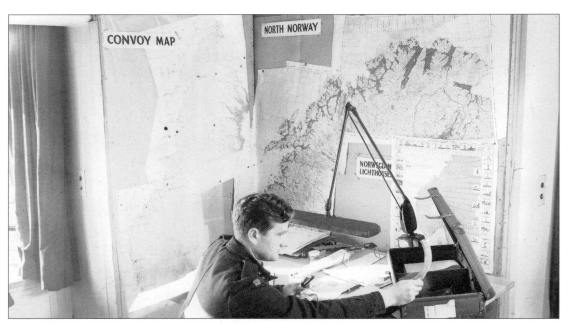

A Norwegian officer working in the Shipping Section at Medmenham, examining photographs of German coastal vessels and U-boats. Coupled with the decrypting of German signals at the Government Code and Cypher School at Bletchley Park, precise information of enemy movements was made available to the Royal Navy and strike aircraft of Coastal Command. The lighthouse charts on the wall were compiled from photo-reconnaissance and were used by aircrews for navigational purposes along the indented coast of Norway. (The Medmenham Club)

First-phase interpretation being carried out on reconnaissance photographs at Medmenham by a WAAF section officer with a pocket stereoscope.
(The Medmenham Club)

Only one aircraft, flown by Flying Officer Kenneth Campbell, found the target in atrocious weather. He dropped a torpedo which blew a 40-foot hole in the side of the battleship before his aircraft was destroyed by flak. The battleship was out of commission for six months and Campbell was awarded a posthumous Victoria Cross.

The Spitfire PR ID ranged far afield, and Flight Lieutenant Peter Corbishley flew P9551 to Malta in a single hop on 19 January 1941, in order to photograph the Italian battle fleet. Unfortunately, he was shot down over Genoa on 2 February, but survived to become a prisoner of war. In April 1941, when fitted with the more powerful Merlin 45 engine instead of the Merlin III but still without the comfort of cockpit heating, the Spitfire PR ID was redesignated the PR IV. A total of 229 of these Spitfires were built, becoming the standard single-engined machines employed by photo-reconnaissance units until the end of 1942. They were painted in cerulean blue, a deep shade which became known as 'PR blue'.

In March 1941 a new unit was formed at Hendon, on the insistence of the Army. This was No 1416 Flight, equipped initially with six Spitfire PR IGs, their main task being to reconnoitre British beaches in the event of invasion. This was soon extended to include photography of the enemy coastline, and the unit became 140 (Army Co-operation) Squadron on 17 September 1941, based at Benson.

On 21 May 1941 the most powerful battleship in the world, *Bismarck*, arrived at Grimstadfjord, south of Bergen. Her companion, the heavy cruiser *Prinz Eugen*, sailed further north to Kalvanes Bay. These two warships had already been spotted by a Swedish cruiser while en route from Gdynia and the information had been passed to British intelligence. On the same day as their arrival, two Spitfires of No 1 PRU were despatched from Wick for a sweep over the Norwegian fjords. One of these, Spitfire PR IC serial X4496 flown by Flying Officer Michael M. Suckling, located both vessels and brought back photographs from high level. It became evident that the Atlantic convoys faced their greatest threat of the war, and the Royal Navy ordered heavy warships to patrol the Denmark Strait between Iceland and Greenland. The German battleship was damaged during an engagement in which she blew up the battle cruiser HMS *Hood*, and headed for St Nazaire. The Royal Navy lost contact with her during the subsequent chase but she was located in the morning of 26 May by Catalina I serial AH545 of 209 Squadron from Loch Erne in Northern Ireland, flown by Pilot Officer Dennis A. Briggs. The British warships closed in and, after being crippled further by torpedoes dropped by Fairey Swordfish from HMS *Ark Royal*, the enormous German battleship was destroyed by gunfire and more torpedoes. She went down with her colours flying.

No 3 PRU and its interpretation section were disbanded on 21 August 1941 and their resources brought back into No 1 PRU, in spite of bitter protests from Bomber Command. It was discovered that the two units were duplicating their operations to some extent, although it was recognised that some additional effort would have to be put into bomb damage assessment in future. More distant targets came within range of the unit a week later when de Havilland Mosquito PR Is began to arrive at Benson. Ten of these new machines, serials W4053 to W4062, were the first to enter RAF service in any capacity, although a lengthy fitting-up process took place. This machine had a radius of action of about 1,100 miles, carried one oblique and two vertical cameras in the bomb bay, could reach 35,000 feet, and was capable of outstripping any German fighter sent up to intercept it.

The heavy cruiser *Admiral Hipper* in dry dock at Brest, photographed by a Spitfire of No 1 Photographic Reconnaissance Unit from St Eval in Cornwall on 26 January 1941. The warship entered the port with machinery defects and slight damage inflicted by British cruisers, after commerce raiding in the Atlantic. The hull, funnel and bridge were dazzle-painted, while the hangar (which housed three aircraft) was open. (The late Squadron Leader J.E. Archbald)

An oblique photograph of a model of Lorient, facing south, used by the author in 1941 as a target map for low-level bombing attacks agains the port. (R.C. Nesbit)

A strange event with beneficial consequences for British intelligence took place on 27 August 1941 when a Hudson of Coastal Command's 269 Squadron from Kaldadarnes in northern Iceland straddled a U-boat in the Atlantic with depth charges. This was a Type VIIC, *U-570*, and the inexperienced crew decided to surrender. This was accomplished with the aid of a Catalina from 209 Squadron and an armed trawler of the Royal Navy, the U-boat being towed to Iceland. The intelligence obtained from this U-boat added to the information obtained from *U-110*, which had been abandoned by her crew after being depth-charged by the Royal Navy on 9 May 1941; British seamen had been able to board her before she sank, and vital code books used in the German naval Enigma machine were obtained.

By September 1941, No 1 PRU was equipped with thirty-seven Spitfires, two Mosquitos and two Marylands, the latter being used occasionally for high-level photography. The first successful sortie in a Mosquito took place on 20 September 1941, when Flight Lieutenant Alistair L. Taylor in serial W4055 covered Bordeaux, Pauillac, Le Verdon and La Pallice. Three Mosquitos were sent up to Wick during the following month, but serial W4055 was lost on a sortie to Trondheim and Bergen on 4 December. It was flown by Alistair Taylor and both he and his navigator Sergeant Sidney E. Horsfall were killed. Taylor had been regarded as the 'ace pilot' of the unit, for he was the first officer in the RAF to have been awarded the DFC and two bars.

On 5 December 1941, an audacious sortie was carried out by Flight Lieutenant A.E. 'Tony' Hill in Spitfire PR IV serial R7044 from Benson. During a visit to the Central Interpretation Unit at Medmenham, he had learned that a Scientific Officer on the staff of the Air Ministry, Dr R.V. Jones, was intensely interested in an object which had been photographed from high level near the village of Bruneval at Cap d'Antifer near Le Havre. It had been known since 22 February 1941, from photographs taken from a Spitfire flown by Flying Officer K. Manifould in a low-level sortie over Auderville, near Cherbourg in the Hague peninsula, that the Germans employed radar equipment known as the *Freya*. It seemed to British scientists that this radar gave the direction of an aircraft but not its altitude. Another radar known as the *Würzburg* had been identified from its transmissions and was believed to give range, direction and altitude to German nightfighters.

Tony Hill made his first low-level sortie over Bruneval on 4 December, but his camera did not function. Undeterred, he went back the next day and returned with perfect photographs. It was evident, however, that more information was required about the nature of the German equipment than could be disclosed from photographs. The newly formed 1st Airborne Division was alerted and the Model Section at Medmenham began work on a model of the locality, including the coastal cliffs at Cap d'Antifer.

Wing Commander Tuttle finished his long stint as commanding officer on 24 November 1941 and was replaced by Wing Commander J.A.C. Stratton, who in turn was replaced on 25 April 1942 by a Canadian with much experience of flying with the unit, Wing Commander Spencer L. Ring.

In January 1942 the first new camera of the Second World War was fitted to aircraft. This was known as the F52, and by coincidence the prototype took fifty-two days from design to completion. It utilised the mechanism of the F24 but was fitted with lenses of up to 40 inches for high-altitude photography, while the format was increased to 8½ inches by 7 inches. Most of the credit for this very successful camera went to Harry Stringer of the Royal Aircraft Establishment but Group Captain Victor Laws, who had

Right: Flying Officer Michael F. Suckling, the Spitfire pilot who photographed the battleship *Bismarck* and the heavy cruiser *Prinz Eugen* in the Norwegian fjords on 21 May 1941. He was known as 'Babe', owing to his name and youthful appearance. He lost his life on a photographic sortie over La Pallice on 21 July 1941. (Flight Officer Constance Babington Smith MBE, WAAF). *Below, left:* The heavy cruiser *Prinz Eugen*, with destroyers and auxiliary vessels, photographed at Kalvanes Bay in Norway by Pilot Officer Michael F. Suckling on 21 May 1941. *Below, right:* The battleship *Bismarck*, with attendant vessels, photographed at Grimstadtfjord in Norway by Pilot Officer Michael F. Suckling on 21 May 1941. (Both photos: Squadron leader P. Lamboit RAFVR)

become the Deputy Head of Photography at the Air Ministry and frequently lectured at Farnborough, also contributed to the design.

Britain entered 1942 with higher hopes for a successful conclusion to the war, with the entry of the USA into the conflict on 6 December 1941 and the knowledge that Germany was expending great efforts in the east after her attack on Russia on 22 June 1941. Nevertheless, there was national humiliation when the battleships *Scharnhorst* and *Gneisenau* with the cruiser *Prinz Eugen* left Brest on 12 February 1942 and made a successful dash through the English Channel to their home ports. However, the move gave the reconnaissance aircraft more opportunity to devote their growing resources to other tasks such as Bomber Command's requirements for bomb damage assessments. They also provided essential photographic information so that models could be made for the combined operation against St Nazaire on 28 March 1942, when the lock gates were blown up to destroy the only potential Atlantic anchorage for the huge battleship *Tirpitz*, as well as for the raid on Dieppe of 19 August 1942, when a rehearsal for an eventual invasion of France took place at the cost of very heavy casualties.

By this time, the Germans were able to put up effective resistance to RAF photo-reconnaissance aircraft. In November 1942 the RAF calculated that the chances of survival on a tour of operations in a fighter reconnaissance unit was no more than 31 per cent, compared with 44 per cent in a medium or heavy bomber squadron. The most dangerous squadrons for crews were those of Coastal Command equipped with strike aircraft, the survival rate being only $25\frac{1}{2}$ per cent in light bombers or merely $17\frac{1}{2}$ per cent in torpedo bombers.*

* See Public Record Office AIR 20/2859 Aircrew: Operational tours.

The near-destruction of Convoy PQ17, which sailed on 27 June 1942 from Iceland to Archangel in north Russia, created a major problem for the Allies. When it became known that the battleship *Tirpitz* and the cruisers *Hipper*, *Lützow* and *Scheer* had been sent northwards to Altenfjord, ready to fall on this convoy in the vicinity of Bear Island, the Admiralty ordered PQ17 to scatter. Only eleven of the original thirty-five merchant vessels reached Archangel, the remainder being picked off by U-boats and aircraft. Only 57,000 tons of supplies reached the Russians from the 156,000 tons carried. The disaster was one of the worst suffered by the Allies at sea.

Something had to be done to protect PQ18, which was scheduled to sail from Loch Ewe in September. Three squadrons of Coastal Command were ordered to fly to north Russia, consisting of the Hampdens of 144 and 455 (RAAF) Squadrons and the Catalinas of 210 Squadron. A daily watch on the German battle units in the Norwegian fjords was required, but the furthest radius of action for the Mosquitos based in Scotland was Narvik. It was decided to send a flight of Spitfire PR IDs to north Russia, to cover the fjords.

The RAF was not unfamiliar with north Russia. Some squadrons had operated from there after the First World War in support of the White Russians. From September to November 1941 a Hurricane wing had operated from Vaenga near Murmansk against the German Air Force, before handing its aircraft over to the Russians. On 7 July 1942, Flying Officer Keith H. Bayley flew from Scotland in Mosquito PR I serial W4054, photographing Altenfjord en route and then continuing to the airfield at Vaenga. After refuelling, he returned on the same day.

Much of the planning for the three Spitfires was carried out by Flight Lieutenant Len J. Cotton, the photographic officer at Benson. He was asked to find out the latest

Squadron Leader A.E. 'Tony' Hill DSO DFC was an audacious pilot who carried out many reconnaissance missions in unarmed Spitfires. Among these was the low-level photography of the German Würzburg radar station at St Bruneval on 5 December 1941. He was shot down on 20 October 1942 (the day after his appointment as commanding officer of the newly formed 543 Squadron) when trying to photograph the famous daylight raid by ninety-four Lancasters on the Schneider armaments factory at Le Creusot in central France. Although rescued from his burning Spitfire by the French, he died shortly afterwards. (Flight Officer Constance Babington Smith MBE, WAAF)

The German Würzburg radar at St Bruneval, near Cap d'Antifer, photographed on 5 December 1941 by Flight Lieutenant A.E. 'Tony' Hill of No 1 Photographic Reconnaissance Unit based at Benson in Oxfordshire, flying Spitfire VD (later designated PR IV) serial R7044. The building behind the radar dish was a sanitorium. From this and other photographs, the Model Section at Medmenham constructed an accurate model for study by paratroops, commandos, RAF aircrews and an RAF technician. (The late Squadron Leader J.E. Archbald)

date when photography was possible within the Arctic Circle, and calculated that results could be achieved provided the sun was at least fifteen degrees above the horizon. Thus operations could continue until mid-October, when there should be two hours a day available for photography. The ground party of fitters, riggers, electricians and photographers left by warship on 13 August. They took with them eight packing cases containing film, paper, processing tanks, chemicals, a printer and a drying drum.

The commander of the flight of Spitfires was Flight Lieutenant E.A. 'Tim' Fairhurst, the other two pilots being Flying Officer Donald R.M. Furniss and Pilot Officer G.W. 'Sleepy' Walker. Fairhurst was slightly disturbed to see that the only available maps of Russia contained large tracts marked 'uncharted territory', for they had no navigational aids in their Spitfires. They worked out a 'great circle' route from Sumburgh in the Shetlands to Kandalaska, near the White Sea. On 1 September they flew up to Sumburgh and then took off at five-minute intervals for north Russia. Then they flew in brilliant sunshine to Norway and through thick cloud over Sweden and Finland, in conditions the exact opposite of the meteorological forecast. Coming down though cloud over Russia, they picked up the coast of the White Sea and followed it to the camouflaged airfield of Afrikanda, where they landed after averaging flights of four and a half hours.

They were met by a pretty Russian girl in uniform who directed them in English to the officers' mess, where they were greeted by Flight Lieutenant G.V. Cottam, a language officer who had been born in Russia. Cottam told them that they would have to fly on to Vaenga, about 80 miles to the north-east, since German tanks sometimes attacked Afrikanda and flattened all the aircraft. Arriving at Vaenga the next day, they found

that it consisted of two airfields connected by a runway, set in a silver birch plantation. They were billeted in a red-brick country house overrun with mice. The roundels on their Spitfires were painted out and replaced with five-pointed Russian stars, which looked quite attractive against the PR blue. Relations with the Russians were a little strained, and the pressing need was for maps, for the only ones available were in Cyrillic script. However, the photographic officer Flying Officer Len Wager sent a set in a Catalina of 210 Squadron back to the UK, where they were immediately translated and returned.

Meanwhile, 144 and 455 Squadrons also arrived, having lost nine of their thirty-two Hampdens en route. One was shot down by a Russian fighter, while the others ran out of fuel or iced up and crashed. The unenviable role of the remainder, based at the other end of Vaenga, was to try to torpedo the German battle fleet if it put out to sea.

The Germans sighted convoy PQ18 on September 9 and trouble began. The PRU pilots were at lunch with the Russians when General Kusnetsov, their commanding officer, was informed that about twenty Ju88s were approaching from Norway. Kusnetsov did nothing for a while and then invited the RAF men to accompany him to the control tower. He looked at his watch and fired a signal pistol. Suddenly, Yaks, MiGs and even old biplanes emerged from their shelters in the trees and took off in all directions, flying through Russian flak to the attack. They claimed a victory afterwards, but the aircraft which were shot down appeared to be Russian. One of the Spitfires was riddled with bomb splinters and a replacement was flown out via Sumburgh by a New Zealander, Sergeant Donald R.I. Hardman.

On the following day, Fairhurst made the first photo-reconnaissance of Altenfjord, flying through flak at high level. The photographs revealed the presence of the

The F52 camera was an enlarged version of the F24, introduced in January 1942 for high altitude photo-reconnaissance. The format size was increased from 5-inch by 5-inch to 8½-inch by 7-inch, while long focus lenses of 14, 20 and 36 inches were provided. The magazine capacity was either 250 or 500 exposures. The camera continued in use with various modifications into the 1960s. This F52 camera, with a 20-inch lens and control attachments, was photographed at the Tangmere Military Aviation Museum, brought into the adjoining hangar from its normal display position. (B.M. Harris, courtesy Tangmere Military Aviation Museum)

An F52 camera with a 36-inch lens mounted vertically in a Mosquito, and an F24 with a 14-inch lens mounted obliquely to port. (Flight Lieutenant G.H. Parry RAF (Ret'd))

cruisers *Scheer*, *Hipper* and *Köln* with four destroyers, but *Tirpitz* was not there and could not be located anywhere. Every day when flying was possible, the pilots took turns to fly over the fjord, although the Russians did not approve, saying that sorties which did not include bombing were a waste of effort. Walker failed to return from a low-level sortie on 27 September, and it was believed that he had been shot down by flak.

PQ18 continued its journey, harried by the Luftwaffe and U-boats, but the German warships did not come out to attack. On 28 September, a PR Mosquito from Leuchars located *Tirpitz* in Narvik, where it had been out merely for sea trials. Nevertheless, only twenty-seven of PQ18's original forty merchant vessels reached Archangel.

By mid-October, the Hampdens were handed over to the Russians and the Catalinas returned to the UK with some of the airmen. Two of the Spitfires were still serviceable, the third having been used for spares. General Kusnetsov got into the cockpit of one and asked a series of questions through the girl interpreter. Then he taxied down to the runway and took to the air. Leaving their equipment behind, the aircrews and ground parties left for the UK by cruiser and arrived safely in mid-November. Future convoys to Russia would be able to sail under the cover of arctic darkness until the following spring.

On their return, the contingent from Benson found that No 1 Photographic Reconnaissance Unit no longer existed, for it had been broken up into five squadrons, as will be related in Chapter Eight.

The battleship *Tirpitz* photographed by a Mosquito of No 1 Photographic Reconnaissance Unit in February 1942 while sheltering in Aasfjord near Trondheim. Camouflage netting was draped between the port side of the ship and the shore in an attempt to break up the outline. (The late Squadron Leader J.E. Archbald)

CHAPTER SEVEN

AFRICA AND MALTA

When Italy entered the war on 10 June 1940, there was no photographic unit in Egypt comparable to that in the UK. The only aircraft capable of specialised long-distance work was the Lockheed Hudson which in its guise of the civil G-AGAR had been flown over Baku and Batum in the previous March and April. Repainted with RAF markings, this had arrived back in Heliopolis after leaving Heston on 4 June 1940, with Flying Officer R.G.M. 'Johnny' Walker as first pilot and Squadron Leader Hugh Macphail as second pilot. Photo-reconnaissance of the network of roads in both French and Italian Somaliland was required when Italy entered the war, and on 12 June 1940 the two RAF men flew the Hudson to Aden via Khartoum to begin the task, photographing en route the port of Assab and the airfields of Gura and Mindega. After completing their task from Aden, they returned to Heliopolis and then photographed the Italian-held islands of the Dodecanese on 28 June.

The Air Officer Commanding the Middle East, Air Chief Marshal Sir Arthur Longmore, was so impressed with the accomplishments of the Hudson that he retained the aircraft and its crew to supplement his very limited resources for aerial reconnaissance. At the same time he formed an Intelligence Photographic Flight to work directly under the Senior Intelligence Officer at Headquarters Middle East in Cairo, although no other suitable aircraft were available at this stage. Flight Lieutenant R. Idris Jones, who

had interpreted the photographs taken by the Hudson over Baku and Batum, was posted to Cairo to set up an Interpretation Section, this work having hitherto been carried out by NCOs. The creation of No 2 Photographic Reconnaissance Unit at Heliopolis was authorised in September 1940, but a ship which sailed the following January with a crated consignment of Martin Maryland reconnaissance aircraft was sunk. In the event, the new unit did not come into being until 17 March 1941.

Malta was the most vulnerable of the British bases overseas when Italy declared war. Less than seven hours after this declaration a tight formation of Italian bombers dropped bombs on Grand Harbour and the airfield of Hal Far. The only fighters capable of defending the island were four Gloster Gladiators which the RAF had acquired from the Fleet Air Arm and assembled from their packing cases. One of these was soon damaged beyond repair but the other three, nicknamed 'Faith, Hope and Charity' engaged the Italians in combat until Hurricanes began to arrive at the end of June.

The RAF's main photographic section in Malta was situated at the seaplane base of Kalafrana, where the NCO in charge, Flight Sergeant Geoffrey J. Buxton, had been responsible for processing the negatives taken during Sidney Cotton's clandestine flights of June 1939 in his Lockheed 12A. Other photographic work consisted mainly of processing films taken by 202 Squadron's

Wing Commander Geoffrey J. Buxton MBE, who served as an aircraftman photographer with J.H. Ross (Lawrence of Arabia) in 1922. As a flight sergeant in February 1939, he was in charge of the photographic section at Kalafrana in Malta. He commanded the RAF School of Photography in 1953/54. (The late Wing Commander G.J. Buxton MBE)

Sunderlands and some taken by Swordfish of the Fleet Air Arm or visiting RAF aircraft.

The Air Staff in London recognised that a more effective photographic capability was essential in the Mediterranean. On 6 September 1940 three Martin Marylands arrived at Malta, forming 431 General Reconnaissance Flight. The aircraft had been ordered originally from the USA by the French Air Force while the RAF crews had been trained on them when serving with 22 Squadron, a Beaufort squadron based at North Coates in Lincolnshire. The Marylands were capable of a radius of action of about 900 miles and had a service ceiling of 31,000 feet, their main role being to reconnoitre and photograph enemy ports and shipping movements in the Eastern Mediterranean. The Italian ports of Brindisi and Taranto were covered, as well as the Sicilian ports of Messina and Palermo and the Libyan ports of Tripoli and Benghazi.

In the autumn of 1940 Admiral Sir Andrew Cunningham, the C-in-C of the Mediterranean Fleet, decided to launch an attack with Swordfish torpedo bombers of HMS *Illustrious* against the Italian fleet at Taranto, and required photo-reconnaissance of this naval base. Two RAF men in Egypt were briefed to help while the aircraft carrier was at Alexandria. These were an Operations Officer from Headquarters Middle East, Wing Commander Cyril E.J. Baines, and the head of the Interpretation Section, Flight Lieutenant R. Idris Jones. Photography of Taranto was carried out by Marylands based at Malta and showed the unexpected hazard of a balloon barrage over the target.

One of the pilots of the Marylands was Pilot Officer Adrian Warburton, who had joined an Army Territorial Unit in 1937 and transferred to the RAF with a short-service commission in the autumn of 1938. He was so ham-fisted with his take-offs and landings that he had not been allowed to fly a Maryland to Malta but instead had navigated one of them. He was also an eccentric officer, contemptuous of many aspects of RAF authority, but he was to become one of the most renowned photo-reconnaissance pilots of the Second World War. Unknown to his flying assessors, he was a superb pilot once his machine was in the air and he seemed to be quite impervious to fear.

It was only illness of the other Maryland pilots which gave Warburton his chance to begin flying as a pilot. On 10 November 1940, he carried out one of the final flights over Taranto, flying twice round the harbour at extreme low level for preliminary photo-reconnaissances and then heading back for a third run in spite of heavy flak. His Maryland returned with a ship's aerial trailing from the tailwheel. The crew reported that the balloons were down and their photographs showed that 5 battleships, 14 cruisers and 27 destroyers were in the harbour. Many of these went to the bottom after the Swordfish attacked on the following day, giving the Royal Navy a great victory. The remainder of the Italian Navy retreated to safer anchorages.

While these events were taking place, photo-reconnaissance was also required in West Africa. After the fall of France in June 1940, an abortive attempt was made by British and Free French forces to land at Dakar in Senegal, in the hope that this French territory would abandon Vichy France and join the British cause. The expedition included French photographic personnel equipped with RAF apparatus, including F24 cameras and a J-type photographic trailer. Four French airmen photographers were collected at RAF Odiham in Hampshire under the command of a French pilot, Lieutenant de Thuisy. They joined the expedition on a Dutch boat, the *Pennland*, which left Liverpool on 30 August 1940, while General de Gaulle and his staff left on a sister ship, the *Westernland*.

However, the expedition failed in its purpose, following the resistance of the Vichy French at Dakar. The *Pennland* continued to

Nigeria, where the photographers transferred to the *Ektian* and on 8 October 1940 landed at Doula in the French Cameroons, a colony which had espoused the Free French and British cause. Air photography began soon afterwards, carried out by a French squadron, but processing of the negatives failed since the air conditioning in the trailer was unserviceable and the emulsion melted in the high temperatures. The photographer in charge, Bernard Lefebvre, was unfairly blamed by his commanding officer, but the air conditioning was never made serviceable.

It was considered necessary by the RAF to form a West African Command, partly since Takoradi on the Gold Coast possessed dock facilities and airfields which were vital for the assembly of crated aircraft and their flights across Africa to Egypt, and partly since strong elements of the Vichy French Fleet were docked at Dakar and constituted a threat to the Allies, if the Germans began to control them. There were also some thirty airfields or landing strips in the Vichy French colonies of the Ivory Coast, Guinea, Senegal and other parts of West Africa, from which there were other potential threats to the Allies. The new Command was not formed until October 1941, however, and for the time being the RAF had to reconnoitre a vast area of West Africa as best it could. Sunderlands of 95 Squadron arrived at Freetown in March 1941 and carried out convoy escort duties as well as some photo-reconnaissance flights. Marylands of No 1 Photographic Reconnaissance Unit at Heston were detached to Gibraltar to carry out other essential duties, covering the south of France and the west coast of Africa.

Back in Egypt, No 2 Photographic Reconnaissance Unit came into being on 17 March 1941 at Heliopolis under the command of Squadron Leader Hugh Macphail. Flight Lieutenant Paul Lamboit, who had spent a period with Bomber

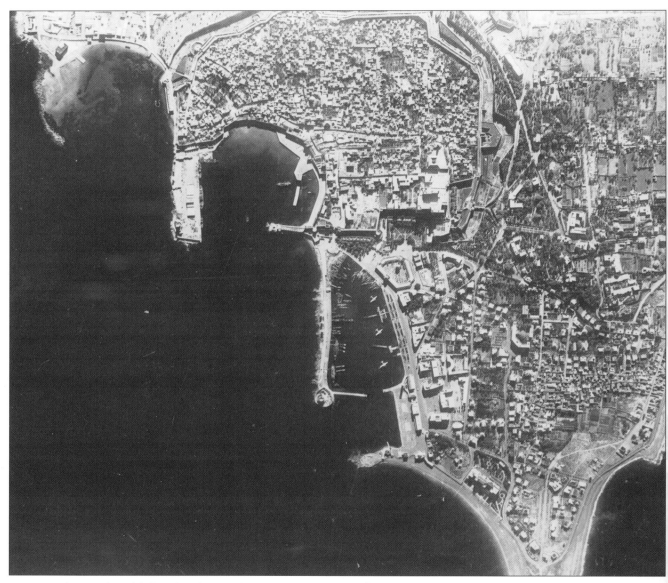

The town and port of Rhodes, with seaplanes in the harbour, taken by No 2 Photographic Reconnaissance Unit on 4 December 1942. (Squadron Leader P. Lamboit RAFVR)

Flight Lieutenant Gerard (Gerry) Glaister in a Spitfire of No 2 Photographic Reconnaissance Unit, still in the cockpit after landing from a reconnaissance mission. (Squadron Leader P. Lamboit RAFVR)

Command and had temporarily lost his acting rank of squadron leader, was appointed as Photographic Officer. Flight Lieutenant R. Idris Jones was appointed as Photo-Interpretation Officer. A consignment of Marylands arrived to equip the new unit, but these aircraft did not prove satisfactory and were transferred to 60 (SAAF) Squadron, a survey unit which had been engaged on work in East Africa with Avro Ansons. As an alternative, three Hurricanes were modified locally with extra fuel tanks in the wings and twin F24 cameras fitted vertically in the fuselages. The area the Hurricanes were expected to cover was vast, for it included airfields, ports, harbours and shipping in North Africa as far as Benghazi, as well as in the eastern Mediterranean.

The Hudson was placed on the strength of the new unit and on the day of its formation was flown to Heraklion in Crete by Flying Officer Johnny Walker, accompanied by one of the Hurricanes flown by a Kenyan, Flight Lieutenant A.C. 'Fatty' Pearson. Their targets for photography were three Italian airfields in Rhodes but soon after this was accomplished a flight of Italian Fiat CR42 biplanes attacked Heraklion. The Hurricane was hit by a single bullet and Pearson flew it back to Egypt. The Hudson was more seriously damaged and a few days later another Fiat CR42 came in so low that its undercarriage knocked 6 feet off the port wing. The Italian pilot flew off minus his undercarriage, leaving Johnny Walker to wonder what sort of landing he would make. After this, the Hudson was beyond repair and had to be written off. Walker got out of Crete in a Sunderland on 15 April 1941, before German airborne forces invaded and captured the island.

The Lockheed Hudson was replaced by a commercial Lockheed 10A Electra, one of three which had escaped from Yugoslavia when the Germans overran that country in May 1941. It was given the serial number AX701 and was

painted in PR blue, but it was not fitted with cameras since its role was to fly crews and equipment to the various operational bases. The controls were marked in Serbo-Croat, which caused the pilots some difficulty until they had discovered their use by trial and error.

The Lockheed Electra was flown to Iraq in the late spring of 1941, carrying a replacement for the Air Officer Commanding, who had been injured in a motor accident. From 30 July 1941 the Hurricanes also flew to Habbaniya and carried out photo-reconnaissance sorties, in case the Vichy French tried to occupy the area. Another detachment was sent to Shaibah in the Persian Gulf during August 1941, to cover part of Persia prior to the occupation of that country by the British. Other Hurricanes were detached from time to time to Cyprus and Palestine.

The second-in-command of No 2 Photographic Reconnaissance Unit was Flight Lieutenant A.M. 'Tony' Brown, who had previously flown with 208 Squadron, engaged on tactical reconnaissance with Hurricanes and Lysanders in the Middle East. He had the misfortune to become the first casualty of the unit. During a sortie to Benghazi on 2 October 1941, the fuel selection cock of his Hurricane froze up and he could not free it. Unable to switch tanks, he glided down and was captured by the German 21st Panzer Division. His place was taken by a Canadian, Flight Lieutenant J. Roger Whelan.

In Malta, the situation worsened with the arrival of about two hundred German aircraft on Sicilian airfields during January 1941. Bombing attacks against dock installations in Valletta and the airfields of Luqa, Hal Far and Takali were intensified and pressed home far more vigorously. The siege of Malta had begun. On 10 January 1942, 431 Flight was expanded into 69 Squadron, commanded by Squadron Leader E.A. 'Tich' Whiteley. The unit had been equipped with further

Bernard Lefebvre, a photographer with the Free French Forces, at Doula in the Cameroons, standing inside an RAF photographic trailer in late 1940. (Bernard Lefebvre, Photo Ellebé)

A Lysander of 'Arras' Squadron of the Free French Air Force at Pointe-Noir, on the coast of French Equatorial Africa, in 1942. The Free French established two reconnaissance squadrons in the country, the other being named 'Picardie' and based at Libreville. The two squadrons were part of the 'Artois' Group. (Bernard Lefebvre, Photo Ellebé)

Dakar harbour in Senegal, photographed in 1942. The warships *Richelieu*, *Gloire*, *Montcalm* and *Georges Leygues*, controlled by the Vichy Government, were picked out from this photograph, as well as anti-torpedo booms and nets. These warships were a constant worry to the Allies until the Anglo-American landings of November 1942 in North-West Africa, when a pact was made with the French authorities in the region. (Flight Lieutenant W.M. Hosman RAFVR)

consignments of Marylands, and two Hurricanes were added in April, being fitted with twin F24 cameras and used for shorter range sorties. Losses of reconnaissance aircraft continued but replacements arrived, as well as new aircrews.

The photographic section soon outgrew its resources at the seaplane base of Kalafrana. A new section was formed on 5 July 1941 at Valletta in the fortress of St John de Cavalier, which had been built centuries earlier with enormously thick walls and a strong roof. Geoffrey Buxton, by then commissioned as a flying officer, trained local photographers in the use of RAF equipment. The section continued to work throughout the continual bombing attacks, films taken by the Marylands and Hurricanes being rushed from Luqa by dispatch rider. After processing, they were interpreted by Flying Officers Howard Colvin and Ray Herschel.

In addition to the intelligence obtained from these photographs, there was a great advance in 1941 when the Government Code and Cypher School at Bletchley Park made a very important breakthrough. From May of that year, the RAF had been benefiting from the decryption of signals sent by the German Air Force but two months later the codes of the Italian Navy, which had been persuaded to adopt the German Enigma system, were also broken. From this time until Italy surrendered, the British knew the exact composition of the Axis convoys and dates of sailing to North Africa, as well as details of each cargo and its destination. British submarines were able to home in on the Axis convoys, which were tracked and photographed from high level by the Marylands, although for the remainder of 1941 the RAF in beleaguered Malta was able to muster only a few Blenheims to carry out anti-shipping attacks.

By the end of September 1941, Flying Officer Adrian Warburton had carried out 155 sorties in Marylands and Hurricanes from Malta, and had been awarded the DFC and bar. He had been in aerial combat on numerous occasions and he and his crew in Marylands had shot down several enemy aircraft and had even carried out bombing attacks. He was due for a rest and was posted as in instructor to 223 Squadron at Shandur in Egypt, a training unit which was occupied in converting crews to Marylands, Blenheims and Bostons. However, this posting was not to his liking and by early November he had contrived to join No 2 Photographic Reconnaissance Unit in Heliopolis.

In the previous September, two Mosquitos had been flown out from England to join this unit, but both had been damaged by enemy action when they reached Malta and thus were written off. Instead, the unit had acquired two Beaufighters, converting them for photographic work by removing the cannons and some armour plate and then installing three F24 cameras with lenses of 20-inch focal length. They formed a small flight under Flight Lieutenant Johnny Walker, who called for airmen photographers to volunteer as extra crew members. Operating from the forward airfield of Fuka, both Walker and Warburton flew with volunteers on photo-reconnaissance missions over the distant target of Crete, as well as other targets. Then a requirement came through for photographs of potential beach landing sites in Sicily, in anticipation of an eventual Allied invasion of the island, and the two Beaufighters were chosen for this purpose. It was obvious that they should operate from Malta and on 29 December 1941 Walker and Warburton flew the machines for refuelling purposes to Timini, west of Tobruk carrying another pilot, Flying Officer 'Benjie' White, and three airmen photographers. The weather ahead was bad but Warburton pressed on while Walker, who had never before flown to Malta, prudently delayed his flight for several days until the weather cleared.

Malta was undergoing its most intensive aerial bombardment when the Beaufighters arrived, and the men never began their survey of the Sicilian beaches. Instead they were waylaid by the Air Officer Commanding Malta Air Vice-Marshal Hugh Pughe Lloyd, and pressed into other reconnaissance duties. At the end of six weeks, Warburton had been awarded the DSO while two photographers, Corporal Norman Shirley and Leading Aircraftman Ron Hadden, had received DFMs. Shirley, who frequently flew with Warburton and became one of his friends, was wounded but pulled his pilot, Benjie White, from his burning and wrecked Beaufighter after returning to Luqa. The remaining Beaufighter was flown back to Heliopolis by Warburton.

More Hurricanes and Beaufighters had arrived at No 2 Photographic Reconnaissance Unit in Heliopolis, and in addition Spitfire PR IVs began to arrive in April 1942. These Spitfires were fitted with F52 cameras with lenses of either 20-inch or 36-inch focal lengths, but problems arose with the films for these had been stored in high temperatures during their long sea journey. This resulted in fogging of the emulsion, so that it was difficult to obtain clear prints. A remedy was found by adding a special chemical, known as an anti-fogging agent, to the developer. Fortunately humidity was low in the Middle East, so that there were no processing problems in the high temperatures, but there were difficulties when developing at advanced airfields, since sand could blow through the film dryer on to the negatives.

In June 1942 Squadron Leader Macphail was posted from the unit and his place was taken by Squadron Leader J. Roger Whelan. By then a Middle East Central Interpretation Unit, on the lines of the unit at Medmenham, had been set up at Heliopolis. It was commanded by Squadron Leader R. Idris Jones and included a number of WAAF officers. At the beginning of July, when Rommel had advanced so far in the Western Desert that his *Panzerarmee* was almost knocking on the doors of Cairo, the situation became so tense that an evacuation was ordered. The smell or burning papers pervaded Cairo but the orders for the photographic units to move eastwards were countermanded when the equipment was being loaded on to the transport vehicles.

A detachment of No 2 Photographic Reconnaissance Unit operated in the Western Desert but it was not the only unit of its type. The others were 1437 Flight, which carried out strategic reconnaissance with Martin Baltimores, 208 Squadron and 40 (SAAF) Squadron which were equipped with Hurricanes fitted with oblique cameras and engaged on close support work for the British 8th Army, and 60 (SAAF) Squadron employed on survey and mapping work with Marylands and Baltimores. Their diverse operations sometimes resulted in an overlap of photographic activities and caused problems for the interpreters. In July 1942 all these units were brought under 285 Wing, which was formed under Air Headquarters Middle East and co-ordinated the operations of the aircraft.

On the night of 29 July 1942 the airfield at Heliopolis was bombed for the first time, some aircraft and one of the hangars being damaged. Another attack followed two days later, when the German bombers were met by a box barrage and night-fighters. The airmen's quarters were hit, but the men had been evacuated to temporary accommodation. The Middle East Central Interpretation Unit was moved to the town of Heliopolis to be free of these attacks. In the following month Squadron Leader R. Idris Jones was posted to No 2 Section at Ras el Tin near Alexandria, and his place was taken by Wing Commander Eric L. Fuller.

Meanwhile, West African Command was set up in October 1941 at Freetown in Sierra

Casablanca harbour in the French Protectorate of Morocco, photographed before the Anglo-American landings in North-West Africa of November 1942. The battleship *Jean Bart* of 25,000 tons (bottom left, partly obscured by cloud) took part in opposing the landings but was put out of action by gunfire from British warships. (Flight Lieutenant W.M. Hodsman RAFVR)

Flight Lieutenant R. Idris Jones, Senior Photo-Interpretation Officer of
No 2 Photographic Reconnaissance Unit, at his desk in Heliopolis.
(Squadron Leader P. Lamboit RAFVR)

Airmen photographers laying mosaics at No 2 Photographic Reconnaissance Unit at Heliopolis on 10 September 1941. (The late Squadron Leader R.I. Jones)

Photo-interpreters at work at Heliopolis, probably in 1942. (Squadron Leader P. Lamboit RAFVR)

Members of No 2 Photographic Interpretation Unit, photographed at Heliopolis in 1942. Front row, left to right: Flight Lieutenant Paul Lamboit (Senior Photographic Officer), Squadron Leader J. Roger Whelan (Commanding Officer), Flight Lieutenant R. Idris Jones (Senior Photo-Interpretation Officer). (Squadron Leader P. Lamboit RAFVR)

Leone, under the command of Air Commodore Edward A.B. Rice. It comprised two Sunderland squadrons, No 95 at Fourah Bay near Freetown and No 204 at Half Die near Bathurst in the Gambia, as well as 200 Squadron equipped with Hudsons and based at Jeswang in the Gambia, and finally 128 Squadron equipped with Hurricanes and based at Hastings in Sierra Leone. Fortunately for the improvement of photo-reconnaissance, the post of Senior Air Staff Officer was filled by Group Captain Ronald H. Carter, who had previously commanded the Central Interpretation Unit in the UK and was thus able to form an effective intelligence and photographic organisation.

Carter requested special Hudsons from England to improve essential photo-reconnaissance but the machines were not immediately availabe. A Maryland from Benson arrived as an interim measure and carried out reconnaissance until it crashed on landing in March 1942. Two specially fitted Hudson IIIs arrived in the same month and were attached to 200 Squadron, which was already equipped with other Hudsons. Two Hurricanes of 128 Squadron were converted for photographic duties by fitting extra fuel tanks and F24 cameras, and also began work. The aircraft frequently encountered flak in their sorties and sometimes French fighters were sent up in attempts to intercept them.

Flight Lieutenant Bernard R. Catcheside was appointed as Command Photographic Officer and set up sections in Sierra Leone and the Gambia. Flight Lieutenant A. Macdonald and Flying Officers Jack E. Archbald, Fitzpatrick and Goodall arrived to begin work as photo-interpretation officers, followed by Pilot Officers Mike Hodsman and Fisher. They were dispersed to the airfields in Sierra Leone and the Gambia, as well as to Air Headquarters, and a more systematic photographic organisation began to operate. In addition to the ports and airfields controlled by Vichy France, discreet cover was also obtained of some of the offshore islands such as the barren coasts of the Portuguese Cape Verde Islands, in case German U-boats were using these as anchorages. On the ground, conditions for the photographers were extremely unpleasant, for they had to work in sweltering darkrooms without air conditioning and with 100 per cent humidity. The men were plagued by insects and there were always the dangers of malaria and yellow fever, although new drugs had been developed in the fight against these infections. Food was indifferent at best and there was little relief from monotony. Some men became lethargic, irritable and debilitated, but the work continued and excellent results were achieved.

An American Photographic Mission arrived at Freetown during April 1942, in the form of a single B–17 Flying Fortress accompanied by Major Elliot Roosevelt, one of the sons of the US President. The aircraft began to operate under conditions of secrecy over the Canary Islands, the Cape Verde Islands, Senegal and the Ivory Coast, continuing over these vast areas until it was damaged beyond repair. Numerous rolls of film were exposed and these were returned to the USA for processing. Copies of the photographs were eventually sent back to the RAF in West Africa but proved of little value for military purposes. However, it is probable that the Americans gained some useful experience in this type of flying and certainly Elliot Roosevelt soon became very prominent in the USAAF as a specialist photographic officer.

By August 1942 the plans for an Allied invasion of North-West Africa, code-named Operation 'Torch', had been crystallised and the small photographic unit in West Africa was given the task of continuous cover of Dakar and other targets. Two Spitfire PR IVs were allocated from a batch in transit at Takoradi and flown to Freetown, where cameras were fitted. The few aircraft

Above, left: Wing Commander Adrian Waburton DSO and bar, DFC and two bars, DFC (USA), who was one of the most daring and successful photo-reconnaissance pilots. He completed over three hundred operational sorties before his death in a Lockheed F-5B on 12 April 1944. In this photograph, he appears to be wearing wing commander tabs with a khaki background on his blue battledress. (Flight Officer Constance Babington Smith MBE, WAAF)

Above, right: Corporal Norman Shirley DFM, who flew as a cameraman with Adrian Warburton. (Corporal N. Shirley DFM, RAFVR)

The Martin Maryland was supplied from contracts placed by the French with the US and was used mainly by RAF and SAAF squadrons in the Mediterranean. It gave good service as a bomber but was also used for photo-reconnaissance. The Marylands of 12 (SAAF) Squadron in this photograph were taking off from a landing ground in the Western Desert. (SAAF Association)

available, two Hurricanes, a Hudson and the two Spitfires, were concentrated at Yundum, a newly completed airfield in the Gambia. The unit was supplied with its own Photographic Interpretation Section, under the main section at Air Headquarters at Freetown. By working intensively until the invasion began on 8 November 1942, the organisation built up an accurate picture of the French Navy and Air Force in West Africa, supplying target maps which could be used if necessary. On 23 November, however, the French in West Africa decided to join the Allied cause and the operations of the RAF photographic contingent ended a few months later.

In Egypt, a great deal of photographic reconnaissance was carried out before the battle of El Alamein began on 23 October 1942. A mosaic of the entire area was completed by 60 (SAAF) Squadron, and this proved of great use in planning the battle and also in the subsequent operations of the 8th Army. Adrian Warburton flew several photo-reconnaissance operations in this period, in Spitfires and Beaufighters, but on 11 August returned to Malta to take over command of 69 Squadron, with the rank of squadron leader. By then the squadron had acquired Martin Baltimores, machines developed from the Martin Maryland to meet the requirements of the RAF, having more powerful engines and better crew communication. The squadron had evolved into an unusual mixture of three flights. A Flight with Baltimores was used for collaboration with anti-shipping squadrons, B Flight employed Spitfire PR IVs on high-altitude photo-reconnaissance, while C Flight was equipped with the remaining Marylands as well as Wellingtons engaged in anti-shipping attacks at night.

Malta played a crucial role before, during and after the battle of El Alamein. Beaufort torpedo bombers had arrived during the previous June and were employed against Axis convoys and naval units while Beaufighters

provided their long-range fighter escorts. These operations were the most dangerous of all RAF activities, but numerous successes were scored at the expense of heavy casualties. On 20 August 1942, the surviving Beauforts of the various squadrons in Malta were grouped into 39 Squadron, providing a 'strike wing' in combination with the Beaufighters of 227 Squadron. The third component of this force was 69 Squadron, for the photo-reconnaissance aircraft identified the enemy convoys en route to North Africa after the Government Code and Cypher School had decrypted enemy signals and warned of their dates of leaving port. A Baltimore of 69 Squadron invariably accompanied the Beauforts and Beaufighters on their attacks from Malta and photographed the results from high altitude. This small RAF force was able to strike effectively at enemy supply ships in this critical period. In combination with the operations of British submarines, the RAF in Malta and Egypt ensured that almost every supply vessel destined for North Africa was sunk. With extended supply lines, the critical shortage for the German and Italian forces was fuel. According to the Germans after the war, lack of sufficient fuel for their armoured units was the major reason for their withdrawal from El Alamein and their retreat to Tunisia.

The invasion of Morocco and Algeria, code-named Operation 'Torch', which began on 8 November 1942, was preceded by intense photo-reconnaissance activity. Mosquitos from Benson were detached to Gibraltar and carried out special tasks in the Casablanca area, while other Mosquitos operated from Benson to keep watch on the French Fleet at Toulon, sometimes flying to Malta in the course of their operations. The Spitfires of 69 Squadron operated over ports in Sicily, southern Italy and the coast of North Africa as far west as Oran. The USA's Western Air Command was also provided with a photo-reconnaissance unit, the 3rd Photo Group under Lieutenant-

The Martin Baltimore was manufactured in the US to British specifications as an improvement on the Maryland, with more powerful engines and better crew communication. It served in the Mediterranean theatre from January 1942 onwards as a light bomber and a photo-reconnaissance aircraft in RAF, RAAF and SAAF squadrons. Here an RAF Baltimore IIIA, serial FA342, is shown taking off from Luqa to bomb enemy positions in Sicily. (SAAF Association)

Lieutenant-Colonel Elliot Roosevelt (left) and Lieutenant-Colonels Powers and Eldridge of the USAAF, with the commanding officer of 682 Squadron, Squadron Leader A.H.W. 'Freddie' Ball DFC (right) and his photographic officer Flight Lieutenant S.R. 'Wally' Walton (centre), photographed at Maison Blanche in Algeria in early 1943. (Warrant Officer J.H. Eggleston RAF (Ret'd))

On the night of 20 November 1942, a German bombing attack destroyed many Allied aircraft and installations at Maison Blanche in Algeria. The photographic section and a type-J trailer were also badly damaged and photographic equipment was destroyed. These items of processing equipment were improvised locally and used for the next few weeks by the photographic section at La Dersa. (All photos: Warrant Officer J.H. Eggleston RAF (Ret'd))

An improvised drying drum for up to 300 feet of F52 film, which was 9 inches wide.

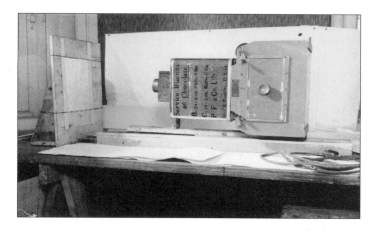

An improvised enlarger made from a biscuit tin and 5-inch by 5-inch contact printer.

An improvised contact printer for 9-inch square negatives.

Colonel Elliot Roosevelt. This was equipped with about twenty assorted aircraft, mostly F-4s, the photographic version of the Lockheed P-38 Lightning, but the crews were not experienced in their work and in any event operated independently from the RAF at this stage. From all the RAF photo-reconnaissance sorties, the Model Section at Medmenham made forty-six models of the landing beaches for the planners of Operation 'Torch', which was successfully executed by American troops in the western sector and the British 1st Army on the east.

On 15 November 1942 the newly formed No 4 Photographic Reconnaissance Unit arrived at Maison Blanche in Algeria, from Benson via Gibraltar. This consisted of six Spitfire PR IVs under Squadron Leader A.H.W. 'Freddy' Ball, under the RAFs new Eastern Air Command. The aircraft began to cover the area of Algiers and Oran, as well as the north-west coast of Africa as far as Casablanca. Five days after arriving, this unit lost several Spitfires and much photographic equipment in a very accurate air attack by the Luftwaffe on the airfield. Replacement aircraft soon arrived via Gibraltar, but the ground photographers had to improvise much of their equipment.

On 1 February 1943 the RAF's Photographic Reconnaissance Units in the Mediterranean theatre were disbanded and formed into squadrons, thus conforming with the arrangements at home. No 2 Photographic Reconnaissance Unit, which by then was based at LG219 near Heliopolis, became 680 Squadron commanded by Wing Commander Roger Whelan. No 4 Photographic Reconnaissance Unit at Maison Blanche became 682 Squadron under Squadron Leader A.H.W. Ball. In addition, B Flight of 69 Squadron in Malta became 683 Squadron under Wing Commander Adrian Warburton, while the other two flights remained in their old squadron, which was taken over the following month by Squadron Leader R.C.

MacKay. These new squadrons were equipped mainly with Spitfire PR IVs, which were becoming outmoded by comparison with the latest Me 109s, but the new Spitfire PR IXs did not begin to arrive for several months.

After their fighting retreat from the British 8th Army in the Western Desert, the Axis forces made a stand during February 1943 at the Mareth Line, built by the French as a fortification between Tunisia and Libya. This was flanked on both the east and the west by salt marshes, and mapping was essential for the attacking 8th Army. Two Mosquito PR IVs were sent out from England and allocated to 60 (SAAF) Squadron. They were fitted with American K–17 cameras, which were ideal for mapping purposes, and the work was carried out admirably before the defensive line was assaulted and breached.

During the Casablanca Conference between Franklin D. Roosevelt and Winston Churchill in mid-January 1943, it was considered essential to weld the USAAF and RAF operations in the Mediterranean under a single command. On 23 February 1943 the Mediterranean Air Command was formed, and within this organisation came the Northwest African Air Forces, which in turn controlled the North African Central Interpretation Unit, consisting of all the RAF photographic interpreters of the RAF's former Eastern Air Command and those of the USAAF's former Western Air Command. In the following month, the US 3rd Photographic Group and the RAF's 682 Squadron were combined into the North African Photographic Reconnaissance Wing under this new organisation, commanded by Lieutenant-General Elliot Roosevelt.

The Axis forces in Tunisia finally surrendered on 14 May 1943, clearing the way for the Allies to invade southern Europe via Sicily. Photographic reconnaissance played a major part in these campaigns, as will be seen in Chapter Nine.

CHAPTER EIGHT

THE NEW SQUADRONS

By the autumn of 1942, No 1 Photographic Reconnaissance Unit at Benson had grown to such a size that it had become administratively unwieldy. Some of its flights had expanded to the size of squadrons, and were considered as such within the unit. On 19 October 1942 it was disbanded and the parts formed into five new squadrons. The Mosquito PR IVs of H and L Flights became 540 Squadron at Leuchars, under the command of Wing Commander Michael J.B. Young, with the main duty of keeping watch on the movements of the German Navy along the coasts of Norway. B and F Flights at Benson became 541 Squadron, commanded by Squadron Leader Donald W. Steventon, and retained Spitfire PR IVs with the duty of covering enemy ports and areas of Germany, Denmark, Holland and Belgium, coupled with bombing assessment sorties. A and E Flights at Benson were formed into 542 Squadron under Squadron Leader David Salway, employing Spitfire PR IVs and operating mainly from nearby Mount Farm over ports in northern France as well as on bombing assessment sorties. No 543 Squadron was formed with Spitfire PR IVs at Benson under Squadron Leader Anthony E. Hill, with A Flight detached to St Eval to cover the west coast of France as well as fly on bomb damage sorties, and B Flight established at Mount Farm to train pilots going overseas. No 544 Squadron was formed at Benson under Squadron Leader William R. Acott, with A Flight at Benson flying Ansons and Wellingtons on experimental night photography sorties while B Flight was equipped with Spitfire PR IVs and based at Gibraltar.

Many of these duties were to some extent interchangeable, and they altered as the war progressed. In addition, 140 Squadron at Benson, equipped with Spitfire PR IVs, continued its Army co-operation work over northern France and the Dutch and Belgian coasts. Lastly, No 8 Operational Training Unit had been formed on 18 May 1942 at Fraserburgh in Aberdeenshire for training photo-reconnaissance pilots who served on home squadrons and overseas units, this work being supplemented by B Flight of 543 Squadron.

This photo-reconnaissance organisation was a far cry from the tiny unit of three years before, when Sidney Cotton had struggled to obtain suitable aircraft and recognition of its work. After the success of the Allied landings in north-west Africa, Air Vice-Marshal Charles E.H. Medhurst, the Vice-Chief of the Air Staff, stated in January 1943 that 'no Commander will now undertake an operation unless he has been completely equipped with air intelligence, not only with photographs and mosaics but also with models of the beaches he is to land on'. It was recommended that the squadrons should be given Group status, but this was not achieved until May 1944.

Operations by the RAF squadrons continued as before, but more intensively and over a wider range of targets. The Mosquito PR IV had joined the Mosquito PR I, slightly

A Consolidated Liberator I of 120 Squadron, based at Nutts Corner in Northern Ireland. This was the first version to reach the RAF, in June 1941. It carried a row of machine guns below the fuselage, operated manually, as well as 'Air to Surface Vessel' radar aerials mounted above the fuselage. With a range of about 2,400 miles, this was the first of Coastal Command's aircraft which helped to close the 'Atlantic Gap', where U-boats had hitherto been immune from attacks by shore-based aircraft. (The late Squadron Leader J.E. Archbald)

The unarmed Spitfire PR XI replaced the Spitfire PR IV from December 1942 onwards. It was fitted with the Merlin 61 series engine, giving a top speed of 422 mph, and production continued well into 1944. Some Spitfire PR XIs continued in service after the war, such as this serial PA888. (The late Squadron Leader J.E. Archbald)

The Lockheed F-4 and F-5 were photographic versions of the P-38 Lightning fighter employed by the USAAF. This photograph of F-5 serial 006, flown by Major Gerald M. Adams of the 14th Reconnaissance Squadron, 325th Reconnaissance Wing, was taken in late February 1945 from a Douglas B-26 Invader of the 7th Photo Reconnaissance Group based at Mount Farm in Oxfordshire, flown by Colonel George Humbrecht. (Dr E.V. Hawkinson USAF (Ret'd))

The K—20 was employed during the Second World War by the USAAF as a hand-held camera for day reconnaissance. Shutter speeds ranged between 1/25th and 1/250th of a second, while the lens was 6⅜-inch. The picture size was 4-inch by 5-inch, and the magazine gave 50 exposures. This camera was also used by the RAF. (J.K. Nesbit, courtesy RAF Cosford Museum)

modified with longer engine nacelles but still fitted with the twin Merlin XXIs of its predecessor, of which only ten were built. It was proposed to equip all squadrons with these long-range Mosquitos, partly on the grounds that the Spitfire PR IV was outclassed by the new Me109G. This was resisted by the pilots, who argued correctly that the Spitfire was far more manoeuvrable, much quieter, more suitable for low-level work, and possessed a much faster rate of climb than the Mosquito. Thus Spitfires were retained for the shorter range tasks, and a few of the new Mark IX fighters were adapted for photographic work and delivered to 541 Squadron in December 1942. The production version of this adaptation, known as the Spitfire PR XI, entered service with the same squadron the following month. It carried the same amount of fuel as the Spitfire PR IV but mounted a Merlin 61 engine of 1,560 hp with a two-speed, two-stage supercharger, replacing the Merlin 46 engine of its predecessor. This improved the top speed by 50 mph, attaining 422 mph. The new Spitfire PR XI also entered service with 542 Squadron in April 1943 and with 544 Squadron the following month. Some of these aircraft continued operating until the end of the war and beyond, even when new versions of PR Spitfires were introduced.

The squadrons achieved many successes in the last months of 1942 and throughout the following year. A continuous watch from Leuchars was kept on the heavy units of the Kriegsmarine in German ports and the Norwegian fjords as far north as Narvik. The German and Italian blockade runners, which had made audacious runs to the Far East and brought back vital supplies such as natural rubber, were located in the ports of western France and subjected to attacks by the RAF and the Royal Navy. By April 1943 all twenty-two of these vessels had been sunk or bottled up in ports.

The effects of bombing operations on Germany, northern Italy and occupied Europe were photographed assiduously and the results accurately interpreted. The famous attack by Lancasters of 617 Squadron on the night of 16/17 May 1943 on German dams in the Ruhr was preceded by very effective photo-reconnaissance and the results were accurately photographed during daylight. While the effects of the breaching of two dams on the German war economy may have been exaggerated at the time, the boost to the morale of the RAF and the British public generally was enormous. The effects of the huge raid by Bomber Command of 27/28 July 1943 on Hamburg, which created a firestorm and the deaths of about 40,000 people, was also photographed. This raid had been preceded by one of equivalent size on the night of 24/25 July and another by the US Eighth Air Force during daylight on 26 July. Bomber Command then continued these raids on Hamburg with another enormous attack on the night of 29/30 July, but by that time the majority of the inhabitants had fled the ruins of their city.

Of course, not all photographs taken by the RAF derived from the specialist photo-reconnaissance squadrons. All aircraft could carry cameras, some being installed forward-facing in the wings or mounted vertically in the fuselage, while others were hand-held by a crew member. Those taken by Bomber Command, mainly at night, are described in Chapter Eleven, but the daylight photographs taken from aircraft of Coastal Command often provided dramatic evidence for photo-interpreters. Some were taken from F24 cameras mounted vertically but fitted with mirrors angled backwards to record the effect of exploding bombs. G45 gun cameras mounted in the wings of aircraft such as the Beaufighter TFXs, carrying cannons, machine guns, torpedoes or rockets, provided action pictures of the final run-up at low level to

A Lockheed F-5 and a Spitfire, both serving with US reconnaissance units, photographed at a time of day when long shadows were cast. (Dr E.V. Hawkinson USAF (Ret'd))

Ground crew working on a Lockheed F-5 at Mount Farm in Oxfordshire, an airfield at which the 7th Photographic Group of the US Eighth Air Force was based. (Dr E.V. Hawkinson USAF (Ret'd))

This photograph of a PR Spitfire which came to grief on a runway was discovered by the Medmenham Club. It appears to have hit something hard with its starboard wing and then careered forward. There is no record of the date and place, but the tall and pointed rudder, doors for a retractable tailwheel and rounded windscreen indicate that it was not one of the PR I or PR IV variants. It seems to have been a Spitfire PR XI, of which 471 were built. The type 35 control on the pilot's instrument panel can be seen clearly on the original photograph; this provided a push button for single exposures and a knob for setting the time interval between successive exposures. (The Medmenham Club)

In early 1942 some Boeing B-17Fs were converted to photo-reconnaissance aircraft, designated F-9s, but it was soon discovered that they stood little chance against enemy fighters when operating in unescorted pairs during daylight. This photograph shows B-17Gs in the normal bomber role, part of the 447th Bomb Group of the US Eighth Air Force, based at Rattlesden in Suffolk. (The late Squadron Leader J.E. Archbald)

enemy convoys, while those taken with hand-held F24 cameras through the navigators' cupolas showed the effect of the attacks. Aircraft such as Liberators, hunting for submarines, sometimes brought back photographs showing the effect of depth charges or bombs on their targets, before they submerged or after being blown to the surface.

Meanwhile, the Americans had arrived in England. The US Eighth Air Force began daylight operations on 17 August 1942, although some of the American crews had flown in borrowed RAF aircraft from the previous June. Photographic units of the US Ninth Air Force followed in September 1942, but almost all their squadrons were drawn away a few weeks later to join the US Twelfth Air Force for the invasion of north-west Africa. One which remained was the 13th Photo-Reconnaissance Squadron, which moved to Mount Farm in February 1943, under Major James G. Hall, and began operations over France as part of the US Eighth Air Force. This squadron was equipped with Lockheed F–4s and F–5s, the photographic versions of the P–38 Lightning. The aircraft were fitted with K–17 cameras, the most widely used American camera of the Second World War. Unfortunately, the twin-engined Lockheeds did not possess sufficient speed or manoeuvrability to avoid German fighters, and the inexperienced American pilots suffered heavy losses in the first few weeks. The 14th Photo Reconnaissance Squadron, equipped with Spitfires, joined them in July 1943 to form the 7th Photo Recon Group. Commanded by James G. Hall, who was promoted to lieutenant-colonel, this Group formed the nucleus of a vast US photographic organisation which grew up in England.

American photo-interpreters had also begun to arrive in England, in the autumn of 1942, and joined the Central Interpretation Unit at Medmenham. In the spring of 1941 Lieutenant-Commander Robert S. Quackenbush Jr, of the US Navy's Bureau of Aeronautics Photographic Section, had been sent to the Central Interpretation Unit, together with two captains of the Marine Corps, to gain British experience. On their return to the USA they set up a photo-interpretation school at Anacosta Naval Air Station in Washington DC in order to train units for service on aircraft carriers and with amphibious forces in the Pacific. These three men had been followed at Medmenham by Captain Harvey C. Brown Jr of the US Air Corps. On Brown's return to the USA he set up a school at Harrisburg in Pennsylvania, where trainees who had already passed through the photography school at Lowry Field at Denver in Colorado received further instruction. Nevertheless, on arrival at Medmenham in 1942 these US photo-interpreters required practical experience under operational conditions. They began to acquire the skills necessary for the European theatre of war, and their co-operation with the RAF proved remarkably harmonious. All photographs which arrived at Medmenham received equal priority, whether originating from the RAF or the US Army Air Force (which supplanted the US Air Corps on 20 June 1941), and could be interpreted by officers of either country.

On 26 June 1943 No 106 (PR) Wing was formed, controlling the operations of all photo-reconnaissance units in Britain other than those allocated to the new Second Tactical Air Force, which was formed for the purpose of invading north-west Europe. This new Wing included the US 7th Photo-Reconnaissance Group as well as the RAF's 540, 541, 542, 543 and 544 Squadrons. In the following month, No 34 (PR) Wing was formed under the Second Tactical Air Force, with 140 and 16 Squadrons. The former was equipped with Spitfires and the latter with North American Mustang Is, converted for tactical photo-reconnaissance.

The Eder Dam photographed on 13 May 1943 byFllying Officer G.W. Puttick in Spitfire PR XI serial BS502 of 542 Squadron at Benson in Oxfordshire, with a spot of cloud covering the basin below. (*Aeroplane Monthly*)

An almost identical photograph of the Eder Dam on 18 May 1943, thirty hours after the attack by 617 Squadron, taken by Flying Officer D.G. Scott in Spitfire PR XI serial EN411 of 542 Squadron at Benson in Oxfordshire, showing water still pouring through the breach in the wall. (*Aeroplane Monthly*)

The Möhne Dam photographed by Flying Officer F.G. Fray in Spitfire PR XI serial EN343 of 542 Squadron a few hours after the attack by 617 Squadron on 16/17 May 1943, showing water still pouring through a breach over 200 feet wide and foam covering the remains of the power station. (*Aeroplane Monthly*)

On the night of 17/18 August 1943, the RAF's Bomber Command despatched 596 aircraft on a massive raid against the German rocket research establishment at Peenemünde on the Baltic coast, following extensive photo-reconnaissance and photo-interpretation. Forty bombers were lost, mainly as a result of the effectiveness of German nightfighters newly equipped with air interception radar and upward-firing cannons, but several scientists and numerous other workers were killed at the research station. It was estimated that the German rocket programme was set back by about two months and its scale considerably reduced.

The British Secret Intelligence Service had been aware for several years that the Germans were experimenting with rockets propelled by liquid fuel. From December 1942 reports from agents in neutral countries indicated that these experiments had reached the advanced stage of development at Peenemünde. Meanwhile, an airfield in the vicinity of this target had been photographed on 15 May 1942 by Flight Lieutenant Donald W. Steventon in a Spitfire of No 1 Photographic Reconnaissance Unit, who happened to notice it on the Baltic coast while en route to photograph Swinemünde. The results showed some puzzling circular objects in the nearby woods. The interpreters noted these as 'heavy constructional work' and the photographs were filed.

The Chiefs of Staff became increasingly perturbed by reports from agents of these German rockets, including information from the French Resistance of the construction near Calais of ramps pointed towards London. The Joint Parliamentary Secretary to the Ministry of Supply, Duncan Sandys, was appointed in April 1943 to take control of enquiries, while Wing Commander Hamshaw Thomas, who at the time was in charge of all 'third phase' work at Medmenham, controlled the photographic interpretation.

Peenemünde was photographed on several occasions, and certain earthworks were noted as possible stands for launching missiles. Then large rockets, some standing vertically and others lying horizontally, were identified from photographs taken in June by Mosquitos of 540 Squadron. These became known as V–2 rockets. From the photographs, Flight Officer Constance Babington Smith was also able to measure an aircraft which was later identified as the Me163 rocket fighter, which in May 1944 became the first jet-propelled aircraft to enter operational service anywhere in the world.

Photographs taken over northern France disclosed the existence of large concrete structures in the woods at Watten, near Calais, which were identified as possible launching ramps for rockets. On 27 August 1943, ten days after Bomber Command's night raid on Peenemünde, the US Eighth Air Force despatched 227 Boeing B–17 Flying Fortresses on a daylight raid to these targets, escorted by 137 Republic P–47 Thunderbolts. The sites, which were later known to have been constructed for V–1 flying bombs, were destroyed. The danger of rocket attacks against London seemed to have been forestalled for the time being.

In the late summer of 1943, another detachment of photo-reconnaissance aircraft was sent to north Russia, employing the older Spitfire PR IVs. Sea convoys to Russia had been suspended during the summer months but it was time for their resumption when daylight hours began to shorten. Three Spitfires of 543 Squadron, flown by Squadron Leader F.A. 'Tony' Robinson, Flying Officer B. Roy Kenwright and Flying Officer Johnny H. Dixon, took off on 3 September from Sumburgh in the Shetlands and flew direct to Vaenga. Kenwright's flight lasted five and a half hours and he ran out of petrol as he landed. Airmen photographers, with Corporal J.M. Davies in charge, left by

The pilot of a photo-reconnaissance Spitfire being debriefed by an intelligence officer in an Operations Room, after returning from a daylight sortie over Frankfurt in which he photographed the results of a raid by Bomber Command during the previous night. (*Aeroplane Monthly*)

Second phase interpretation being carried out on reconnaissance photographs by Z Section at Medmenham. The officer on the right was Lieutenant Xavier Alencio of the USAAF, who in civilian life was an animator of Disney Studios. (The Medmenham Club)

157

Mass production of town plans from aerial photographs at Medmenham, using a stylograph. (The Medmenham Club)

Captain L.E. Hollinger of the USAAF and Section Officer Kitty Sancto of the WAAF studying photographs of the Binnen Alsten in Hamburg, at the Allied Central Interpretation Unit at Medmenham. (The Medmenham Club)

Flight Sergeant Steve Waring working in the Model Section at Medmenham in 1943. The models were built up with the help of photographs taken by photo-reconnaissance aircraft. (The Medmenham Club)

sea, together with the language officer, Pilot Officer B. 'Booby' Trapp. Two photo-interpretation officers, Flying Officers R.R. Eyre and W.M. Hodsman, flew in a Catalina of 333 (Norwegian) Squadron from Sullom Voe in the Shetlands. A ridiculous episode occurred when the Russians impounded the aircrew's homing pigeons, which were used for conveying distress messages from men in dinghies, and kept the birds under armed guard in a shed until the Catalina departed.

On this occasion the RAF personnel were billeted in two flats on the top floor of a bomb-battered building in the nearby town of Grasnaya, where they lived mainly on tinned food left over from the 1942 detachment. A photographic processing vehicle which had been left in 1942 was pressed back into service, for the Russians had not discovered how to use the equipment. An efficient processing and printing section was set up, although the Russians were inclined to steal the liquid chemicals, under the impression that they were alcohol.

Once again, the pilots carried out their flights over the *Tirpitz* in Altenfjord, for their operations were associated with the forthcoming attack on the battleship by midget submarines of the Royal Navy. Excellent photographs were sent back to the UK, contributing to the attack of 22 September 1943 when the battleship was crippled. Their duties successfully completed, the detachment arrived back in the UK by destroyer on 11 November. The men found that 543 Squadron, which had been commanded for a year by Squadron Leader Gordon E. Hughes, had been disbanded three weeks before they landed, and its Spitfires and personnel distributed among the other photo-reconnaissance squadrons.

The Russians awarded Kenwright and Dixon their medal for Distinguished Battle Service, while Tony Robinson received the Order of the Patriotic War. The latter carried a pension of £1 a year, but this ceased after five years.

During the summer and early autumn of 1943, Spitfires of 541 Squadron continued to comb northern France for enemy positions, and certain installations of a new type began to show up on the photographs. At the end of September a report from the French Resistance gave the positions of 'secret weapon launching sites'. Photo-reconnaissance continued and about a hundred 'ski sites' were discovered from the Pas de Calais to Cherbourg, springing up at an alarming rate but cleverly camouflaged. From 5 December 1943, these were attacked relentlessly by Bomber Command, the US Eighth Air Force and the Second Tactical Air Force, and aerial photographs showed that the majority were destroyed or damaged. However, defensive precautions took place in England, in the form of massed anti-aircraft guns, balloon zones and fighter zones, against an assault by flying bombs and rockets which by then seemed inevitable. Meanwhile, the photo-reconnaissance squadrons in Britain, both RAF and USAAF, were presented with the additional task of preparing for the forthcoming invasion of Normandy.

The bomb-damaged barrack block at Grasnaya in north Russia which housed the RAF's photo-reconnaissance contingent during 1943 and 1944, when operating from Vaenga airfield. This photograph was taken in the autumn of 1943. (The late Squadron Leader J.E. Archbald)

The experimental rocket site on the island of Peenemünde on the Baltic coast. (Flight Officer Constance Babington Smith MBE, WAAF)

The V–2 rocket establishment at Peenemünde photographed in September 1944, showing the damage caused by Bomber Command's heavy raid of the night of 17/18 August 1943, after which much of the work on the site was moved to Blizna in Poland. The arrow marked 'A' indicated that light flak positions on the roof of the damaged building had been removed. (*Aeroplane Monthly*)

CHAPTER NINE

EUROPE'S UNDERBELLY

When the remaining Axis forces in Tunisia surrendered on 14 May 1943, the Allied forces poised to attack the 'soft underbelly of Europe', in the vivid phrase of Winston Churchill, included the North African Photographic Reconnaissance Wing of the Mediterranean Air Command. In July 1943 this Allied Wing was based at La Marsa in Tunisia and commanded by Lieutenant-Colonel Elliot Roosevelt. The RAF's contribution to the Wing consisted of the Spitfire PR IVs and PR XIs of 682 Squadron, based at La Marsa and commanded by Squadron Leader A.H.W. 'Freddie' Ball. The American contribution consisted of the 3rd Photo-Reconnaissance Group, with the Lockheed F–5s of the 5th and 12th Squadrons and the B–17 Fortresses of the 15th Squadron. It should be noted that an American Wing was in command of Groups, the reverse of the RAF's nomenclature.

The Wing also controlled the North African Central Intelligence Unit (NACIU), staffed by RAF photo-interpreters of the old Eastern Air Command and Americans of the US Twelfth Air Force. This became the centre in Tunisia for all Allied photographic interpretation and the resulting intelligence information. Three Mobile Photographic and Interpretation Units were preparing to participate in the invasion of southern Europe.

In addition, there were other RAF photo-reconnaissance squadrons further east in the Mediterranean. The Spitfire PR IVs and PR XIs of 683 Squadron remained at Luqa in Malta under the command of Wing Commander Adrian Warburton, while at the same base were the Baltimores of 69 Squadron, commanded by Wing Commander Terance M. Channon. Covering the eastern Mediterranean were the Spitfire PR IVs and PR IXs of 680 Squadron at LG219 near Heliopolis, commanded by Wing Commander J. Roger Whelan.

Demarcation lines were established for these photo-reconnaissance squadrons in Africa. The North African Photographic Reconnaissance Wing concentrated on the area to the west of longitude 12 degrees East, which included Sardinia and Corsica. The area to the east of 12 degrees East, including Sicily, Pantellaria and Italy, was covered by the RAF's 683 Squadron and 69 Squadron at Malta. From Headquarters Middle East, 680 Squadron covered the Mediterranean eastwards of the Greek island of Corfu.

In addition to these activities, which were primarily strategic, 285 Photographic Reconnaissance Wing, commanded by Group Captain Edward G.L. Millington at Sorman West in Libya, was allocated much of the shorter range tactical work for the invasion of Sicily. This Wing had already carried out skilled photo-reconnaissance work in the Western Desert in support of the British 8th Army. It now came under the North African Tactical Air Force, and consisted of 60 (SAAF) Squadron with Mosquito PR IVs and Baltimores commanded by Major Owen

A model of Palermo in Sicily, constructed from photography taken at 35,000 feet. (Squadron Leader P. Lamboit RAFVR)

Davies, 40 (SAAF) Squadron with Spitfire VBs and commanded by Lieutenant-Colonel J.P. Bleaaw, and 1437 Flight with six Mustang A–36s commanded by Squadron Leader S.G. Welshman. All these aircraft operated from Luqa prior to the invasion. The American contribution to this tactical reconnaissance section of the North African Tactical Air Force was the 111th Tactical Reconnaissance Squadron equipped with Mustang F–6s; this was part of the US Twlefth Support Command.

No 60 (SAAF) Squadron had become adept at mapping future battlegrounds and was equipped with the only Mosquito PR IVs available for photo-reconnaissance in the Mediterranean. The squadron had also managed to borrow from the UK a couple of the new Mosquito PR IXs, the high-altitude photo-reconnaissance version of the latest Mosquito bomber. Fitted with F52 cameras, the Mosquitos' surveys over Sicily were essential in planning the invasion. A detachment of Mosquitos from this squadron had also been sent to Tunisia, from where the aircraft surveyed the beaches of Sardinia, which had been considered as possible landing places, although the invasion of this Italian island was deferred in favour of Sicily. The Mustang A–36 was a development of the famous Mustang P–51 fighter, with two seats in tandem and two oblique cameras. The six Mustang A–36s flown by the RAF's 1437 Flight had been transferred from the US Twelfth Air Force.

There were three main objectives in the photo-reconnaissance operations. The first of these was to obtain vertical photography for large-scale mapping. The second was to take obliques of static positions such as beaches, defended river banks and other military objectives. The third was to discover the activity of the enemy by tactical reconnaissance over changing positions.

The shortage of suitable aircraft for the RAF photo-reconnaissance squadrons continued to give cause for concern. The older Spitfire PR IVs were outclassed by German fighters, especially the FW190, and only a handful of the new Spitfire PR XIs had become available. Mosquito PR IVs and PR IXs were demanded, but none could be supplied at this stage other than the few operated by 60 (SAAF) Squadron. This situation was not remedied satisfactorily for several months.

The joint Anglo-American invasion of Sicily, code-named Operation 'Husky', began on the night of 9/10 July 1943. Although some of the Allied airborne forces met with disaster when gliders were released prematurely by their tugs in adverse weather conditions, the invasion developed into a successful campaign. Meanwhile, the North African Photographic Reconnaissance Wing remained at La Marsa and its squadrons continued to operate from their North African bases. But some of the tactical photo-reconnaissance squadrons began to move to Sicily. The Spitfire VBs of 40 (SAAF) Squadron arrived at Pachino on 15 July. In addition a ground detachment was sent by ship from Bizerta in Tunisia to Syracuse in Sicily. This included photographers and one J-type trailer, together with tentage and equipment. From Syracuse, the detachment established itself at Lentini, south of Catania. The Spitfire VBs of 40 (SAAF) Squadron moved to this base on 27 July and it was also used by a detachment of Mosquitos from 60 (SAAF) Squadron, which by then was based at Sabratha in Libya, together with 285 Wing. The Mustang A–36s of 1437 Flight arrived at Francesco in Sicily on 31 July, but 285 Wing did not move to the island until early September.

The J-type trailer, which had been used by photographic personnel in France during 1939/40, was employed far more effectively in Sicily and later on the Italian mainland. It was a mobile darkroom designed for the hand processing and printing of films. Partly air-conditioned, it was divided into two compartments, a small processing room and a larger printing room. A generator set provided an independent power source in the field. Darkroom accommodation could be increased by the addition of a photographic tent which consisted of a steel framework on the ends of which were suspended one or more darkroom tents, the whole being covered by an outer waterproof canvas. This tent gave a central working space of 11 feet by 8 feet, with each adjoining darkroom section about 6 feet by 8 feet. In addition, a marquee was used to accommodate the washing, drying, numbering, finishing and sorting of the films and prints. The whole arrangement was not perfect, for there were difficulties in maintaining a strict black-out when working at night, and the detachment operated in an area subjected to several enemy air raids.

In addition to this detachment, No 3 Mobile Field Photographic Section (No 3 MFPS) under the command of Flight Lieutenant A. May arrived at Lentini, together with photographic semi-trailers, having left Africa on 19 July. These trailers, first introduced in 1942, provided accommodation for the processing, printing and duplication of films, on the same scale as a static section. A complete unit consisted of five semi-trailers, providing facilities for the continuous film-processing machine as well as the universal multi-printing machine and the enlarging-copying camera. The unit included lithotex print-drying equipment and could cope with contact printing, negative duplicating and film drying.

At Lentini, the photographic sections were set up about a mile from the airfield, adjacent to a stream which provided the nearest available water for washing films and prints. But film drying presented a real problem at first. Strange spectacles were sometimes presented by groups of airmen – photographers, electricians, instrument mechanics and transport drivers – strung out across the Sicilian airfield and holding long wet films, waving them gently in the breeze. Mosquitos stuck to the films like flies to sticky paper, moths settled on them affectionately, while wisps of vegetation draped themselves around them. Nevertheless, good results were achieved.

The Sicilian campaign was the beginning of the end for the Italians, who had entered the war at a time when Hitler had defeated the Anglo-French forces in Western Europe and felt that they could share in the spoils of the German victory. They had not anticipated their own defeats in Africa or the RAF's devastating attacks against their northern cities and ports further south, which were intensified in this period and the results photographed assiduously. By the end of August 1943 only a few Italian diehards had the stomach for further conflict. However, the Germans fought stubbornly and skilfully, eventually retreating in good order across the Straits of Messina to Italy.

The mainland was invaded on 3 September 1943 and Italy surrendered five days later, although the tough Wehrmacht and a few Italian fascist units continued a fierce resistance. No 285 Wing began to move to Sicily on 4 September and nine days later crossed over to Italy and eventually arrived at Foggia near the east coast. No 3 MFPS followed the British 8th Army to Reggio in the toe of Italy and then to a series of positions up the east coast. Flight Lieutenant May fell sick and was posted back to base, command passing to Flight Lieutenant T.J. Mathews, who had previously commanded No 2 MFPS at La Marsa. Both 40 (SAAF) Squadron and 1437 Flight also arrived at Foggia in early October, but 1437 Flight was disbanded on the 13th of that month and its

A group of senior officers examining a photographic mosaic at La Marsa in Tunisia. Left to right: unknown brigadier (British Army), Colonel Elliot Roosevelt (USAAF), General Sir Harold Alexander (Deputy Allied C-in-C North Theatre), unknown major-general (British Army), unknown US officer, Major-General Carl Spaatz (USAAF, C-in-C Northwest African Air Forces). The heavily fortified island of Pantellaria, on the wall map, surrendered to the British 3rd Infantry Brigade Group on 11 June 1943, after a heavy air raid and a bombardment from the sea. (Warrant Officer J.H. Eggleston RAF (Ret'd))

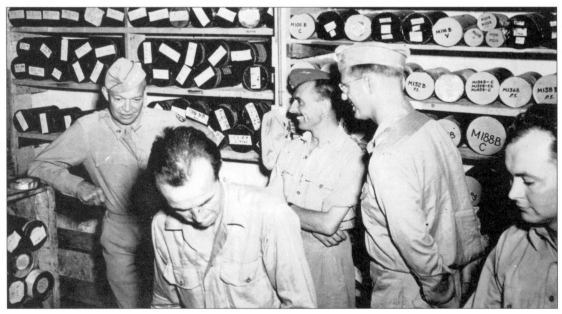

General Dwight D. Eisenhower (Allied C-in-C in the North-African theatre) at the air film negative library of the North African Photographic Reconnaissance Wing at La Marsa in Tunisia, with Squadron Leader S.R. 'Wally' Walton and Colonel Elliot Roosevelt smiling at him. (Warrant Officer J.H. Eggleston RAF (Ret'd))

Left to right: Air Chief Marshal Sir Arthur Tedder (Air C-in-C Mediterranean Air Command), Squadron Leader S.R. Walton (Photographic Officer), Brigadier-General Patrick W. Timberlake (Director of Operations, USAAF), Colonel Elliot Roosevelt (Commander of the North African Photographic Reconnaissance Wing). They were discussing photographs prior to the invasion of the Italian mainland in September 1943. (Warrant Officer J.H. Eggleston RAF (Ret'd))

place taken by 225 Squadron, equipped with Spitfire VCs, another tactical photo-reconnaissance squadron which had been working temporarily with the Allied Tactical Bomber Force.

The North African Photographic Reconnaissance Wing remained at La Marsa for several months after Sicily was invaded. Its commander, Elliot Roosevelt, has been accused of anglophobia and to some extent the allegation is justified. Certainly he resented any British domination of USAAF activities, either in the Mediterranean or in England, but at the operational level he was on cordial terms with RAF aircrews and ground personnel. Aged thirty-two, he had qualified as a civilian pilot before the war, although a minor problem with eyesight prevented his acceptance into the USAAF in that capacity. Instead, he had qualified as a navigator and frequently flew on operations, sometimes taking the controls. He was generous enough to use his B–17 Flying Fortress to carry what were regarded as luxury foodstuffs and even refrigerators to Malta, where shortages still existed in the RAF messes. At both Luqa and La Marsa, the Americans were particularly fascinated by Wing Commander Warburton's vast operational experience as well as his unconventional approach to life.

With the geographical changes in the Allied positions, the Mediterranean Air Command was again reorganised. On 30 October 1943 the new British 336 Wing was formed at La Marsa in Tunisia under the North African Photographic Reconnaissance Wing. This controlled 680 Squadron in Egypt and 682 Squadron at La Marsa, both by then equipped with Spitfire PR XIXs in addition to the older machines. Also, 683 Squadron in Malta came under the new Wing, equipped with Mosquito PR IVs and Spitfire PR IXs. Lastly, 60 (SAAF) Squadron, by then at Ariana in Tunisia and equipped with Mosquito PR VIs and PR IXs, was transferred to it from 285 Wing. This British Wing was responsible for the provision of photo-reconnaissance detachments to operate wherever required, either with the North African Tactical Air Force or under the control of the AOC-in-C Middle East.

The new 336 Wing was commanded by Wing Commander Adrian Warburton, who had handed over his 683 Squadron to Squadron Leader Harry S. Smith at the beginning of October 1943 and then spent a leave in England. Decorated with the DSO and bar and the DFC and two bars, Warburton had flown the astonishing total of 390 sorties and achieved the status of the premier photographic pilot of the war. He was also on terms of personal friendship with Lieutenant-Colonel Elliot Roosevelt. Unfortunately, the charmed life that he had enjoyed in the air did not continue on the ground. He had been presented with a personal jeep by Elliot Roosevelt and was involved in an accident on 26 November, which was sufficiently serious to put him into hospital at Algiers until late January 1944. His post was taken over temporarily by Wing Commander Freddie Ball.

In November 1943 a reorganisation of the American photo-reconnaissance units also took place when the 3rd Photo Group was joined by the 5th Photographic Group, consisting of two US squadrons. The Free French *Groupe de Reconnaissance* 2/33 was attached to these, but remained under French command. The 90th Photographic Wing was formed to control the 3rd and 5th Groups which, in addition to their other duties, provided photo-reconnaissance for the US Twelfth Air Force and the US Fifteenth Air Force, the latter having replaced the US Ninth Air Force, which had returned to England.

From LG219 near Heliopolis, the Spitfire PR IXs of 680 Squadron continued to cover

A photographic mosaic of the British 8th Army — the Desert Rats — invading the south-east corner of Sicily on 10 July 1943, in the Gulf of Noto. The United States 7th Army went ashore further to the west. The landings were successful everywhere. (The late Squadron Leader J.E. Archbald)

Receiving film magazines at a J-type processing trailer, at Lentini in Sicily in 1943. (Warrant Officer J.H. Eggleston RAF (Ret'd))

The water supply for washing photographic prints at Lentini in Sicily in 1943. (Warrant Officer J.H. Eggleston RAF (Ret'd))

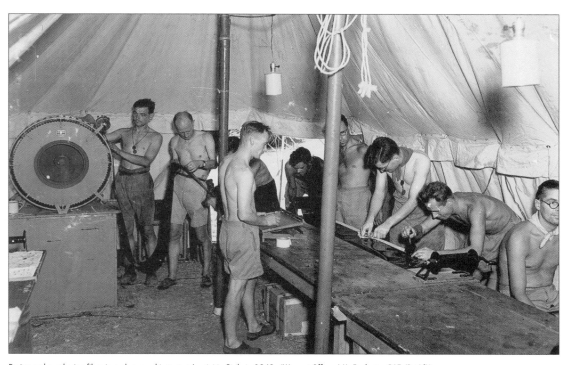

Drying and numbering films in a photographic tent at Lentini in Sicily in 1943. (Warrant Officer J.H. Eggleston RAF (Ret'd))

the eastern Mediterranean, but British military operations in this area suffered a severe setback. It had been decided to seize the Italian-held island of Rhodes in advance of an invasion of Greece and a possible link-up with the advancing Russians in south-east Europe. The island was garrisoned by the Germans. After extensive photographic cover by 680 Squadron, British troops landed by sea on 15 September 1943 on two other islands in the Italian Dodecanese, Cos and Leros, with the intention of cutting off Rhodes from the mainland. Further north, the island of Samos was invaded on the following day. As expected, the Italian garrisons surrendered, but the German reaction was surprisingly swift and effective. They withdrew aircraft from other spheres of operations and, with overwhelming strength and far shorter lines of communications, subjected the airfields on the islands to continual attack. Aided by dive-bombing Ju87s, German seaborne and airborne forces landed on Cos on 3 October and overcame the British. Leros followed on 12 November and Samos ten days later, the defenders becoming casualties or prisoners. Although the Germans also suffered heavy losses of ships, aircraft and troops, the British enterprise had to be classed as an expensive failure.

In December 1943, when the British 8th Army and the American 5th Army had fought their way beyond Naples, the North African Photographic Reconnaissance Wing transferred from La Marsa to San Severo, about 20 miles north-east of the Allied operational air bases around Foggia. Three squadrons of 336 Wing moved to this new base. These were 60 (SAAF), 682 and 683 Squadrons, while 680 Squadron remained in Egypt to cover the eastern Mediterranean. By then, this British Wing was commanded by Wing Commander Gordon E. Hughes, who had commanded 543 Squadron at Benson in

England for a year before its disbandment in October 1943.

There was yet another change in the command structure on 10 December 1943 when the Mediterranean Air Command and the North African Allied Air Forces were merged into the Mediterranean Allied Air Force. The North African Photographic Reconnaissance Wing was placed under the command of the new Allied Air Headquarters and renamed the Mediterranean Allied Photographic Reconnaissance Wing (MAPRW).

By this time the 'European underbelly' had proved far less soft than anticipated, for the Germans formed a very effective defensive line from coast to coast across Italy, backed by the heights around Monte Cassino and protecting the approaches to Rome. The Allied attempt to outflank this line by launching the seaborne landings at Anzio on 22 January 1944 were contained by the enemy. The bombing of the Monastery of Monte Cassino on 15 February, believed to be the hub of the German defences, had no effect. It was not until the opening of their spring offensive on 11 May 1944 that the Allies were able to make any considerable advances up the peninsula of Italy.

Meanwhile, on 25 January 1944, Colonel Elliot Roosevelt, who had been awarded a CBE by the British for his work in the Mediterranean, was recalled to England to take command of the strategic photo-reconnaissance units of the US Eighth Air Force. Command of his MAPRW in Italy was taken over by another American officer, Colonel Karl 'Pop' Polifka of the USAAF, an outstanding and popular pilot with much experience of flying the Lockheed F–5.

In England, Colonel Roosevelt began work on what became, in August 1944, the 325th Strategic Photographic Reconnaissance Wing. He asked for Adrian Warburton to be appointed as his deputy and the British pilot arrived at his headquarters at Mount Farm in Oxfordshire on 1 April 1944. By this time Warburton had been awarded the American DFC in addition to his other decorations. It is possible that he had not fully recovered from his injuries, and certainly he seemed to be suffering from depression. However, on 12 April 1944 he took off in a Lockheed F–5B of the USAAF, serial 42–67325, to photograph the ball-bearing plant at Schweinfurt, 100 miles north of Munich, which was due to be attacked by the US Eighth Air Force on that day. It was intended that he would then continue south and land at Alghero in Sardinia, which had been captured by the Allies. As it happened, the American bombers were forced to turn back owing to dense cloud over Germany, but the exact fate of Warburton remains a mystery, for he simply disappeared. It was thought that he might have hit a mountain somewhere high and inaccessible in the Swiss or Austrian Alps, but no trace of him or his aircraft was ever found. He was aged twenty-six and had become a legendary figure in the world of photo-reconnaissance, both British and American.

On 31 July 1944 another celebrated photo-reconnaissance pilot also lost his life, in the same type of machine as that flown by Warburton. This was Commandant (Major) Antoine de Saint-Exupéry, a 44-year-old Frenchman who had achieved fame as a pilot, a thinker, a novelist and an essayist. He had served in the French Air Force in the 1920s and then as a commercial pilot on African and South Atlantic routes. In spite of injuries sustained in crashes, he rejoined the French Air Force on the outbreak of war and became a photo-reconnaissance pilot. After the fall of France, he escaped to America and eventually joined the *1ère Escadrille* (1st Flight) of the *Groupe de Reconnaissance 2/33*, which was attached to the 23rd Squadron of the US 5th Photographic Group but remained under Free French command. He took off at dawn on 31 July 1944 from Bastia-Borgo in Corsica in a Lockheed F–5B serial 42–68223, bearing French markings. His duty was a reconnaissance over the Grenoble–Annecy area but, like Warburton, he disappeared and no satisfactory trace of his aircraft has ever been found. Some of his manuscripts and drawings were discovered in his effects and published posthumously.

The US 5th Photographic Group was engaged on reconnaissance of the south coast of France, preparatory to an invasion by the US 5th Army with the object of linking up with the Allied Armies which had already landed in Normandy. In this reconnaissance work it was assisted by several Spitfire PR IXs of 682 Squadron which were detached from San Severo to operate from Alghero in Sardinia. The invasion began on 14/15 August 1944 and the initial landings were almost unopposed.

Back in Italy, the Mediterranean Allied Photographic Reconnaissance Wing continued to operate from San Severo, although its US 3rd Photo Group was based at Naples until the end of the war. When the US operations began from Naples there were no American photographic ground personnel to support them and the work was undertaken by some of the RAF's No 2 Mobile Field Photographic Section, commanded by Flight Lieutenant White. This RAF section was posted away from Naples after a few months.

San Severo was a hive of activity during this period, with day and night shifts turning out prints by the thousand. From Foggia, Spitfire PR XIs and Mosquito PR IXs flew over everything of strategic interest between Munich in Germany and Ploesti in Romania, as well as over Yugoslavia and the south of France. The longest return flight in a single-engined aircraft was attained on 25 June by the commanding officer of 336 Wing, Wing

The town of San Severo, near Foggia in Italy, was the home of the Mediterranean Allied Photographic Reconnaissance Wing from the end of 1943. About a hundred RAF photographers were based in the headquarters, in addition to US personnel. The American units split away in October 1944, and henceforth RAF photography came under 336 Wing. This photograph was taken with an F24 camera in February 1945. (Flight Sergeant K. Loweth RAF (Ret'd))

Commander Gordon Hughes DSO DFC, when he flew in a Spitfire PR XI over Ulm, on the Danube in southern Germany. Although there were accepted limits to the sphere of operations, a Mosquito of 60 (SAAF) Squadron flew on a return flight as far as the southern outskirts of Berlin on one occasion. On other sorties, Mosquitos flew all the way to England in single hops, taking photographs en route and returning later on similar operations.

The Mediterranean Allied Photographic Reconnaissance Wing at San Severo included approximately a hundred RAF photographers. In addition there were the photographic personnel of 60 (SAAF) Squadron, while the American squadrons at San Severo had their own photographic personnel. There was also a USAAF photographic capability at Foggia. Co-ordination between the RAF and the USAAF was carried out by the RAF Senior Photographic Officer, Squadron Leader S.R. 'Wally' Walton, who was posted away later in 1944 and replaced by Squadron Leader B.K. Barber.

When the Allies reached Rome in June 1944, almost complete air supremacy was achieved in Italy, and this lasted until the end of the war. This was of great benefit to the photographic squadrons, and an enormous amount of tactical intelligence information was accumulated. One flight of either 682 Squadron or 683 Squadron operated alongside the tactical reconnaissance squadrons of 285 Wing. All these sorties served the American 5th Army and the British 8th Army by covering German positions and lines of communication. They were backed by the 'cab rank' system of RAF and USAAF fighters circling in the air until called upon to attack enemy positions as soon as located, either from the air or by the troops on the ground. The Allied Armies fought their way up the Italian peninsula with the aid of this method.

The Mobile Field Photographic Sections were also kept constantly busy, moving up with the advance from airstrip to airstrip. Flight Lieutenant White commanded No 2 MFPS on the west side of Italy while Flight Lieutenant Mathews commanded No 3 MFPs on the east. Each MFPS remained for about ten or fourteen days at each location, but was split into three parts to ensure mobility and to maintain continuous operations. On the first day of a move to a new location, an advance party moved up to the new area, to find suitable accommodation and facilities such as water and drainage. On the second day, the main party moved to the new site, and on the third day the rear party completed its work at the previous site and joined the new location.

At the beginning of September 1944, the USAAF decided that its Twelfth and Fifteenth Air Forces should have their own photographic Groups, preparatory to a possible move to another theatre of war, leaving the British photographic and intelligence organisations to meet the needs of the RAF and the 8th Army in Italy. Thus, on 1 October 1944, the Mediterranean Allied Photographic Reconnaissance Wing and the American 90th Photographic Wing were disbanded, and the American 3rd and 5th Photographic Groups were transferred to their Twelfth and Fifteenth Air Forces respectively. The RAF photographic squadrons in Italy were then controlled by their 336 Wing and 285 Wing until the end of the war.

On 29 April 1945 the German and Italian fascist units remaining in Italy, numbering almost a million men, surrendered to the Allies, the ceasefire becoming effective three days later. Among the victors, the RAF and USAAF photo-reconnaissance aircrews who served in Italy were all of high quality, as were their ground crews, not least among whom were the photographers. The

Continuous film processing machines being assembled at San Severo in Italy in early 1944. (Warrant Officer J.H. Eggleston RAF (Ret'd))

Print finishing in a school building at San Severo in Italy in early 1944. (Warrant Officer J.H. Eggleston RAF (Ret'd))

General Mark W. Clark, commander of the US 5th Army, arriving by Dakota at an airfield in Italy. An Auster light monoplane can be seen behind his tall figure. Together with Field Marshal Sir Harold Alexander, the Supreme Allied Commander in the Mediterranean, Clark accepted the unconditional surrender of the German forces in Italy on 29 April 1945, the cease-fire being ordered for 2 May. (Squadron Leader P. Lamboit RAFVR)

combination of strategic and tactical photo-reconnaissance squadrons working in concert with both static and mobile ground photographic sections, all responding to the requirements of the RAF and the Army, was proved correct. Even before the end of the war in Italy, these techniques were to prove invaluable during the invasion of Normandy and the subsequent drive towards the German homeland.

CHAPTER TEN

PHOTOGRAPHY AND THE INVASION

By the late autumn of 1943, the British had good grounds for believing that the war against Germany could be brought to a successful conclusion. The Axis forces had been cleared out of North Africa, Sicily was in Allied hands, the mainland of Italy had been invaded and the Italians had surrendered. The menace of U-boats was receding, following improved intelligence, the bombing of production plants in Germany and the closing of the 'Atlantic Gap' by long-distance aircraft fitted with new equipment. Germany itself was being subjected to 'round the clock' strategic bombing, by the USAAF in daylight and the RAF at night. In all these operations photo-reconnaissance played a prominent part and had become recognised by high-ranking Allied commanders as an essential instrument when making decisions. Further east, the German invasion of Russia had been halted and turned back, with terrible losses. It became evident to the British public that the Allies were preparing to invade western Europe and begin liberating the occupied countries.

Strategic reconnaissance continued under the RAF's No 106 (PR) Wing. By early 1944 this consisted of the RAF's 540, 541, 542 and 544 Squadrons, 543 Squadron having been disbanded in October 1943. These squadrons were equipped with either Mosquito PR IXs or Spitfire PR XIs, although the new

Mosquito PR XVI and Spitfire XIX, both with pressurised cabins and improved performance, were beginning to appear. In addition, the US Eighth Air Force made its contribution to strategic reconnaissance with the squadrons of its 7th and 25th Groups, equipped with Lightnings, together with Spitfires and Mosquitos borrowed from the RAF. Colonel Elliot Roosevelt was transferred to England in January 1944 to command these US Groups, which later became the 325th Reconnaissance Wing.

Relations between the RAF and USAAF units had been very harmonious in 1943, but in January 1944 Lieutenant-General James H. Doolittle, who had previously commanded the US Twelfth Air Force in the Mediterranean and now commanded the US Eighth Air Force, made it known that he would require independent control of his own photo-reconnaissance and photo-interpretation. This demand was strongly backed by Colonel Roosevelt, who acted as his advocate in the matter. Some difficult meetings and negotiations took place, but eventually it was decided to form No 106 (Photo-Reconnaissance) Group on 15 May 1944, to co-ordinate and control all USAAF and RAF strategic photo-intelligence work, other than the squadrons of the Allied Expeditionary Air Force set up in November 1943 for the invasion of Europe.

The Consolidated Liberator GRVI entered Coastal Command in the summer of 1944, joining the earlier versions of this highly successful 'very long range' aircraft. It was fitted with twin .50-inch machine guns in nose, dorsal and tail turrets as well as a single .50-inch in each waist position. This machine, photographed at St Eval in Cornwall, was also fitted with a Leigh Light under the starboard wing, for picking out U-boats at night. A church can be seen in the background of this photograph. This was originally built in Norman times and was within the boundary of the aerodrome during the Second World War. It has now reverted to its function as a parish church, but has been refurbished to commemorate the RAF and USAAF squadrons which served at St Eval. (Flight Lieutenant G.H. Parry RAF (Ret'd))

The Mosquito PR XVI was the first photo-reconnaissance variant to be fitted with a pressurised cabin for high-altitude work. It was adapted from the Mosquito XVI bomber and began to appear at the end of 1943. This photograph shows a Mark XVI painted in the invasion stripes. (*Aeroplane Monthly*)

The Hawker Typhoon IB is best remembered for its role as a rocket-firing fighter-bomber in the RAF's Second Tactical Air Force. The aircraft in this photograph, painted with invasion stripes, was fitted with four 20 mm cannons in the wings but there was provision for eight rockets or two 1,000 lb bombs. A G45 ciné camera was fitted in the nose. (*Aeroplane Monthly*)

Spring 1944 at Grasnaya, near Vaenga airfield in north Russia. Left to right: Flying Officer E.G. Searle (pilot), Flight Lieutenant Nicholas (equipment officer), Squadron Leader D.R.M. Furniss (pilot and commanding officer), Flight Lieutenant H.K. Pusey (photo-interpretation officer). (The late Squadron Leader J.E. Archbald)

This new 106 Group was commanded by Air Commodore John N. Boothman, who was promoted from his position as station commander of RAF Benson, with Group Captain Peter J.A. Riddell as his Senior Air Staff Officer. It remained under the control of Coastal Command but included a very strong American representation. The Central Interpretation Unit at Medmenham was given the prefix 'Allied' on the same date. Lastly, the Joint Photographic Reconnaissance Committee was set up to ensure that duties were equitably apportioned to the British and the Americans, and that all information was pooled.

Meanwhile, another photo-reconnaissance detachment was sent to north Russia, with the objective of keeping watch on the battleship *Tirpitz* in Altenfjord preparatory to an attack by Barracudas of the Fleet Air Arm from aircraft carriers. The ground party was assembled at Benson and left Scapa Flow by warship, together with a convoy, and arrived at Vaenga on 7 March 1944. It consisted of the photo-interpreters Flight Lieutenant H.K. Pusey and an Army officer, Lieutenant T.V. Newmark, together with Sergeant J.M. Davies, two airmen photographers, and other ground staff. Four of the older Spitfire PR IVs were fitted up at Benson with vertical and oblique cameras as well as long-distance fuel tanks. Three of these, flown by Squadron Leader Don Furniss, Flying Officer J.H. Dixon and Flying Officer E.G. Searle, took off on 7 March 1944 from Sumburgh in the Shetlands, heading for Vaenga. Dixon and Searle arrived safely but Furniss experienced carburettor trouble and was forced to descend to 2,000 feet over Norway, with his engine misfiring. He was shot at by the Germans and the Russians successively, until Russian fire hit the tail of his Spitfire. Nevertheless he landed at Afrikanda, left his damaged aircraft there and continued by train.

The detachment occupied the same quarters as during the previous year, but the photographic processing vehicle was found to be frozen up and took three days to thaw out. Vaenga airfield was kept reasonably clear by snow-scrapers and spiked rollers but there was a problem with slush on windscreens and camera lens windows when the thaw set in. Sorties began on 12 March and vertical photographs of *Tirpitz* were obtained from 20,000 feet, with obliques from 6,000 feet. On 2 April the Fleet Air Arm attacked and disabled the battleship, achieving complete surprise. The two Spitfires continued their work but were plagued with unserviceability. Flying Officer V.I. Gorrill of the RCAF set off from Sumburgh with the remaining Spitfire on 19 April. His gyro compass and other instruments went out of action and he crash-landed near the Finnish border, wrecking the Spitfire but emerging unscathed from deep snow. He was rescued by the Russians and flown to Vaenga, where he was put out of action when he scratched an eye in a snowball fight.

The detachment was recalled on 31 May and all the equipment and aircraft were handed over to the Russians. The ground party returned by warship but the pilots contrived a more circuitous route, by train to Moscow and then by civil aircraft to the Middle East, Gibraltar and home.

But the work of the strategic reconnaissance squadrons, which was mostly concerned with attacks by heavy bombers against Germany or targets in the occupied territories, represented only part of the photo-reconnaissance required for 1944. Experience in North Africa and Italy had confirmed that modern armies in the field needed to be supplied with a constant flow of tactical photographs of enemy forces, together with interpretations, if they were to win battles. Planning for the great enterprise of the invasion had begun as early as 1940,

The first North American Mustangs, such as serial AM148 of 26 Squadron in this photograph, were fitted with Allison engines and employed in the RAF on tactical fighter-reconnaissance from January 1942 onwards. Later Mustangs, fitted with the more powerful Merlin engines, became highly successful long-range escorts for bomber formations. (*Aeroplane Monthly*)

These three photographs of beach obstructions were taken about a month before D-Day by a Lockheed F–5 of the US Ninth Air Force, flying at 50 feet. The Germans believed that the Allies would land in this area, but in fact they arrived further west, on the beaches of Normandy.

These obstacles between Le Tréport and Perck-Plage (south of Le Touquet) were anti-tank obstructions about 5 feet high to which mines or explosive charges were fitted. (Squadron Leader P. Lamboit RAFVR)

Rows of stakes surrounding an old wreck along the beach between Dunkirk and Ostend. Some carried holders for explosive charges. (Squadron Leader P. Lamboit RAFVR)

'Hedgehog' obstacles further inland along the beach, with the stakes to seaward. (Squadron Leader P. Lamboit RAFVR)

after the fall of France. For the next three years, photo-reconnaissance took place in order to select the most suitable landing areas.

In 1942, an Army Photographic Interpretation section had been formed at the Central Interpretation Unit, with the task of examining all photographs taken of areas within 30 miles of the European coastline from Den Helder in Holland to the Spanish frontier. Located at Mount Farm in Oxfordshire, a satellite of Benson, 140 Squadron had been engaged for over two years on photographing all coastal defences and beach gradients between Calais and Cherbourg. By early 1944 this squadron was equipped with Mosquito PR IXs and PR XVIs as well as Spitfire PR XIs. The F–52 camera was adapted to take a strip of film which moved at a speed which compensated for image movement when the aircraft flew at low level. Other RAF squadrons allocated to reconnaissance Wings of the new Allied Expeditionary Air Force joined in this work, equipped with Spitfires and Mustangs.

American squadrons also joined in this activity from January 1944. The US Ninth Air Force had been transferred to England from the Mediterranean in the previous September. Its heavy bombers were then taken over by the US Eighth Air Force but the remaining tactical squadrons were built up to become part of the Allied Expeditionary Air Force. Of these, the 10th and 67th Groups, with eight squadrons equipped mainly with photo-reconnaissance Lightnings, combed the potential invasion beaches at the cost of considerable losses to aircraft and crews.

In this period, fighter squadrons of the RAF and USAAF carried out aggressive sorties to ensure that very few Luftwaffe aircraft were able to fly over these coastal areas. All the RAF and USAAF photographs were processed at Benson, and the negatives were then sent to Medmenham for selective

printing as needed. The task was immense, both for the photo-reconnaissance squadrons and the photographic interpreters.

The choice of the landing areas was obviously dependent on the suitability of beaches and the strength of enemy defences discovered in the aerial mosaics which were put together at Medmenham. The possible areas selected were the north coast of Brittany and the coast of Normandy between Cherbourg and Le Havre. Of these, Calvados Bay in Normandy proved the most interesting and was finally chosen. To confuse German Intelligence, numerous sorties were carried out over other areas, particularly in the Pas de Calais. A brilliant deception was devised around Dover, consisting of a concentration of troops in the harbour area, together with dummy barges and gliders. These were duly discovered by German photo-reconnaissance aircrews and helped to convince Feldmarschall Gerd von Rundstedt, the commander of Army Group West, that an area somewhere near Calais had been chosen for the Allied invasion.

In order to ensure the success of the enterprise it was essential that the Germans were kept in a state of ignorance as to the true landing places. It was therefore vitally important to eliminate the German radar stations along the coast from the Franco-Belgian border as far as Cap Fréhel in Brittany. Rocket-firing Typhoons and Spitfires made a series of low-level attacks for a period of three weeks from mid-May 1944, and in early June the German Signals Intelligence Unit near Cherbourg was blasted by a heavy bomber raid. However, a few radar stations around Cap d'Antifer and opposite Dover, were conveniently left unharmed.

The great invasion fleet of 6,500 ships and landing craft formed up on the night of 5/6 June 1944, off Littlehampton in Sussex, before setting off due south for the beaches of

Landing craft along Gold beach at Asnelles, photographed at 10.30 hours on D-Day, 6 June 1944. This was one of the beaches on which the British 2nd Army landed. The artificial 'Mulberry' harbour, named Port Winston, was built a short distance to the west of this position. (Squadron Leader P. Lamboit RAFVR)

The headquarters of the 325th Reconnaissance Wing of the US Eighth Air Force at High Wycombe in Buckinghamshire. (Dr E.V. Hawkinson USAF (Ret'd))

Normandy on Operation 'Overlord'. The enterprise had been postponed for twenty-four hours as a result of unseasonable bad weather, but further delays were not practicable even though weather conditions did not improve as much as hoped.

While the troops were afloat, Bomber Command carried out a remarkable series of operations, designed to confirm the German belief that the Allies intended to land further east, between Boulogne and Dieppe. Lancasters of 617 Squadron, the famous Dam Busters, flew between Dover and Fécamp, circling a number of small ships flying balloons fitted with reflectors which the German radar could pick up. These aircraft also dropped strips of aluminium foil 'Window', specially cut into shapes which simulated approaching ships on enemy radar screens. The whole procession moved towards the French coast at about 7 knots, giving the impression of a huge convoy. Meanwhile, the Stirlings of 218 Squadron carried out a similar operation further east, circling gradually towards Boulogne.

At the same time, Stirlings of 199 Squadron and B–17 Fortresses of the USAAF's 803rd Squadron used 'Mandrel' (Monitoring and Neutralising Defensive Radar Electronics) equipment to jam that part of the enemy's radar which might have picked up the true invasion fleet. Further to the west, Lancasters of 101 Squadron and RAF Fortresses of 214 Squadron patrolled between Beachy Head and Paris, jamming the enemy's nightfighter control system by the use of 'ABC' (Air Borne Cigar) equipment, while dropping 'Window' aluminium foil.

Halifaxes and Stirlings of 90, 138 and 149 Squadrons dropped dummy paratroops, fireworks and rifle-fire simulators over the village of Yvetot, north of Rouen, to deceive the Germans into believing that an airborne operation was taking place in that area. A German regiment in reserve was rushed to investigate these 'paratroops', but the true airborne landings were taking place elsewhere. These aircraft also dropped a few SAS troops north of Caen in this operation, to link up with the true airborne landings.

The exact effect of these deception operations is difficult to determine. They certainly confused the Germans and delayed the despatch of Panzers and other reinforcements to the correct landing places. The unfavourable weather also proved beneficial, for the Germans did not believe that any invasion fleet would sail in such rough seas or that airborne operations could take place in such strong winds. Field Marshal Erwin Rommel, the commander of Army Group B which defended the French coast, had even taken a short leave in Germany, while other senior German officers were also absent temporarily from their posts. The British and the Canadians had feared that their casualties might be as high as 30 per cent in the initial landings, but mercifully they were only 3 per cent.

The extent of support by the preliminary photo-reconnaissance to the invading troops proved most gratifying. Firstly, this photography assisted in the accuracy of the final navigation to the beaches. The coxswain of each landing craft was provided with a photograph of his allotted beaching point, taken about 1,500 yards from the shore by an aircraft skimming over the surface of the sea. Once ashore, the troops were able to pick up their bearings, for each infantry platoon commander was given an oblique photograph of the terrain inland from his landing area. It was said that never before in war had military commanders landed on a foreign shore so well equipped with detailed information of the defending troops, equipment and minefields facing them, or of the battlefield terrain beyond the landing beaches.

A vehicle of No 7 Mobile Field Photographic Section backing into Landing Craft T936 at Gosport in Hampshire on 30 August 1944, preparatory to making the crossing to Normandy. (The late Corporal C.E. Lloyd)

Vehicles of No 7 Mobile Field Photographic Section on a landing craft en route for Normandy in August 1944, where they joined No 34 Wing at the headquarters of the Second Tactical Air Force. (Squadron Leader P. Lamboit RAFVR)

A North American B-25 Mitchell of the RAF's 226 Squadron, based at Hartford Bridge in Hampshire, escorting a convoy carrying troops and supplies to the battle front in Normandy. (*Aeroplane Monthly*)

The seaborne forces which landed on the shores of Normandy on 6 June consisted of about 57,500 American troops of the US 1st Army, on Utah and Omaha Beaches, and about 75,000 British and Canadian troops of the British 2nd Army, on Gold, Juno and Sword Beaches. They were preceded by some 27,000 airborne troops who descended by parachutes or gliders, and they were followed by a stream of seaborne reinforcements. By 23 July sufficient Canadians had arrived to form the 1st Canadian Army.

These forces were supported by a massive naval and air effort which included the squadrons of the US Ninth Air Force and the RAF's Second Tactical Air Force. The latter consisted of a Headquarters Section as well as two Groups, No 83 which worked closely with the British 2nd Army and No 84 which supported the Canadian 1st Army.

In turn, the Headquarters Section of the Second Tactical Air Force and each of its two Groups controlled photo-reconnaissance Wings. Of these, No 34 Wing was attached to Headquarters and consisted of three squadrons. These were 16 Squadron equipped with Spitfire PR XIs and PR IXs, 140 Squadron with Mosquito PR IXs and PR XVIs, and 69 Squadron with Wellington XIIIs. The Spitfires had been employed identifying V–1 flying bomb sites in northern France and they continued daylight work at both high and low level, keeping watch on the movements of German reinforcements to the invasion beaches. Some of the sorties of the Mosquitos had already located possible positions for forward airfields, which were soon provided by the RAF's Construction Wings and Servicing Commandos, using portable runways, after the foot-holds had been won in France. The Mosquitos turned their attention to night photography, using K–19 night cameras with explosives triggered · by a series of photo-flashes to discover the movements of German military formations,

which were soon forced to move primarily in darkness. They were joined by 69 Squadron, which had returned from Malta in April 1944 and converted to Wellingtons equipped for night photography, becoming operational on D-Day.

No 39 (RCAF) Wing came under No 83 Group and consisted of 168 Squadron, 414 (RCAF) Squadron and 430 (RCAF) Squadron, all equipped with Mustang Is and IAs, and 400 (RCAF) Squadron with Spitfire PR XIs. No 35 Wing formed part of No 84 Group and consisted of 2 and 268 Squadrons equipped with Mustang IAs and IIs, and 4 Squadron with Spitfire PR XIs. The arrangement whereby an RAF Wing supported a Canadian Army while an RCAF Wing supported a British Army seems rather curious in retrospect, but in practice it worked well.

The P–51 Mustangs employed by these reconnaissance squadrons were powered by Allison 1,150-hp engines in the Mark Is and IAs, and Allison 1,120-hp engines in the Mark II. These versions of the American fighter had been the first to reach the UK, but the engines were found to be unsatisfactory at high level. Although they retained their armament of four .50-inch and four .30-inch guns in the Mark I and Mark II, or four 20-mm guns in the Mark IA, these Mustangs were employed by the RAF solely on low-level photographic work, being fitted with an F24 camera behind the pilot on the port side. The long-distance, high-level, versions of this famous aircraft, the Mustangs III and IV, were powered by 1,680-hp Merlin engines built in America and employed by the RAF purely in the fighter role.

RAF and RCAF photo-interpretation officers and men worked in the Army Photographic Interpretation Section (APIS) of all three reconnaissance Wings. One of these parties, attached to No 39 (RCAF) Wing which supported the British 2nd Army, sent its advance party from Odiham in Hampshire on 21 June and embarked on an American landing craft the following day. The craft sailed down the Thames Estuary and beached on the Normandy coast a day later. On 23 June the party arrived at Sommervieu airfield. With the exception of a few specialists, including two RAF photo-interpreters, all the personnel in this Wing were Canadians.

The three tactical reconnaissance Wings also controlled seven of the RAF's Mobile Field Photographic Sections (MFPSs), comprising vehicles with film-processing machines, multi-printers, copy enlargers, water bowsers, copy cameras, enlarging apparatus, generators and photostat machines. Each of these units, with a flight lieutenant commanding photographers and other personnel, had undergone pre-invasion exercises to ensure that they were brought to a high state of efficiency and mobility. Some modifications had been found necessary. Fordson tractors replaced Bedford tugs, 30 kilovolt diesel generators replaced petrol-driven generators, while water supplies were provided by 1,000-gallon bowsers with prime movers. To take an example of the pre-invasion exercises of these mobile units, No 4 MFPS found itself in North Yorkshire before the end of September 1943, training with No 84 Group. During the following winter, motor transport and other personnel went down to Southampton to study methods of loading and off-loading vehicles with the invasion landing craft. The men also learnt how to waterproof vehicles so that neither these nor their contents became water-logged when driven off a ramp into 3 or 4 feet of water and then up a beach to dry land.

Nine MFPSs were in service by D-Day, numbered consecutively. Nos 2 and 3 were in Italy, but the remaining seven were sent to France. Nos 1, 7 and 9 accompanied No 34 Wing and the headquarters of the Second Tactical Air Force, Nos 4 and 8 formed part of No 35 Wing and No 84 Group, while Nos 5 (RCAF) and 6 (RCAF) were allocated to No 39 (RCAF) Wing and 83 Group.

During the first weeks of Operation 'Overlord', the three reconnaissance Wings remained in England, while prefabricated 'Mulberry' harbours were towed across the Channel and moved into positions off the invasion coast to enable the off-loading of armour, artillery, ammunition and other essential supplies. At the end of June, No 39 (RCAF) Wing moved over to Normandy to support the British 2nd Army, together with Nos 5 (RCAF) and 6 (RCAF) MFPS. These two mobile photographic sections went into production within hours of their arrival at Sommervieu airfield. By the end of July, No 5 (RCAF) MFPS alone is recorded as having produced the astonishing total of 302,000 prints, enlargements, mosaics and plots, far more than in the whole of the previous seven months.

Next to follow was the advanced headquarters of No 35 Wing, which flew on 30 July to Plumetot airfield, about 10 miles from Caen, to take up its appointed tactical role with the Canadian 1st Army. The rear echelon of the Wing remained in England a little longer but came over to France in mid-August. No 8 MFPS landed on Juno beach on 13 August 1944, en route to join this Wing. It then drove to airfield B4 at Beny-sur-Mer, about 4 miles to the south, and became operational six hours after landing. Its sister unit, No 4 MFPS, followed on 18 August and became operational at the same airfield five hours after landing. Work had accumulated during the transit periods and the two units jointly produced as many as 30,000 prints in their first twenty-four hours of operation.

The mobile photographic units often worked in pairs, one processing negatives from the sorties on continuous processing machines and multi-printers, with the other producing reprint orders. Photostat machines

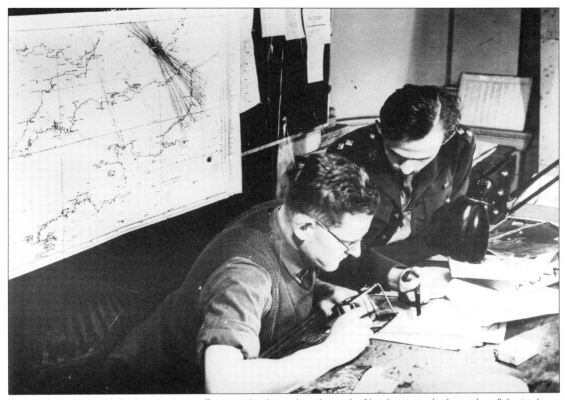

The battle against the V-1 flying bombs, with two Army officers at Medmenham studying photographs of launching sites and a chart on the wall showing the plotted tracks of the bombs. (The Medmenham Club)

RAF officers examining the wreckage of one of the first V-1 flying bombs shot down by fighters over southern England in June 1944. (*Aeroplane Monthly*)

Preparing master cover traces at Medmenham for maps of the Arnhem operation in September 1944, from aerial photographs. The officer on the left was Flight Lieutenant Julian Phipps. (The Medmenham Club)

The Production Control Section of the Allied Central Interpretation Unit at Medmenham, staffed by RAF, WAAF and USAAF personnel. (The Medmenham Club)

were also employed, so great was the demand. Tactical requirements were normally met by photographs from oblique cameras facing forward, port or starboard, mostly taken by Mustangs at low level. However, the work often included the preparation of mosaics from vertical photographs, as well as photographs taken by G45 ciné cameras fitted in fighter aircraft.

Nos 35 Wing and 39 (RCAF) Wing supplied close tactical support for the two Armies while they were still in their Normandy bridgeheads. In the weeks before the invasion, much of the railway system of northern France had been reduced to a tangle of twisted wreckage by RAF and USAAF bombing attacks. The Armies placed great store on last-minute cover of pinpoint targets. Requests were often received from Army Liaison Officers, and the pilots of the photo-reconnaissance aircraft were briefed with the intelligence information available for a particular area. Sorties were usually of short duration and the pilots gave R/T reports while in the air, followed by immediate interrogation on landing. Their photographs were rapidly printed by an MFPS and photocopies were circulated to the troops, even down to platoon level.

As soon as enemy forces were identified on roads or fields, rocket-firing Typhoons and Spitfires of the Second Tactical Air Force, flying in the 'cab rank' system developed in Italy, swooped down on them like avenging demons, blasting tanks, artillery and infantry. The Germans soon learnt to detest these aircraft, for their own fighters had been swept out of the sky. They named them '*schreckliche Jabos*' (terrifying fighter-bombers). Rommel himself was wounded in one of these attacks, while in his staff car on 17 July, and replaced in his command. However, the German troops continued to fight with their usual courage and tenacity.

No 34 Wing came over to France at the end of August, together with Nos 1, 7 and 9 MFPSs, to join the headquarters of the Second Tactical Air Force, after experiencing two days of very rough crossing. By this time the British and Canadian Armies had broken out of their bridgeheads and begun to fight their way towards the Rhine. The ability of all the mobile photographic units to continue functioning while moving rapidly was severely tested in this period.

As an example of these movements, No 4 MFPS left Beny-sur-Mer airfield on 1 September and travelled through France on the heels of the 1st Canadian Army to airfields at Boisney, Fresnoy Folny, Fort Rouge and St Denis-Vestrem, staying only a few days at each airfield. On 11 October 1944 the unit crossed the Belgian border and reached Antwerp/Deurne, where it operated until late November. It then moved off once more and after a three-hour trip reached Gilze Rizen in Holland, where it caught up with No 8 MFPS and stayed for three and a half months. From Gilze Rizen, both MFPS moved to Mill and from there to Enschede, which proved to be their last wartime location before Germany surrendered. The units sometimes managed to borrow Canadian soldiers who were resting for short periods away from the front line. These men washed, dried and sorted the prints and helped with other duties while the photographers concentrated on the more technical aspects of production.

Meanwhile No 7 MFPS, which had driven with the headquarters of No 34 Wing from Belleroy via Amiens and arrived at Melsbroek near Brussels, suffered casualties when a flying bomb exploded nearby on 22 October. However, the MFPS personnel captured four German soldiers at a farm in Perck on 21 November. The photographic units at Melsbroek suffered a setback on 1 January 1945 when the Luftwaffe made its last great

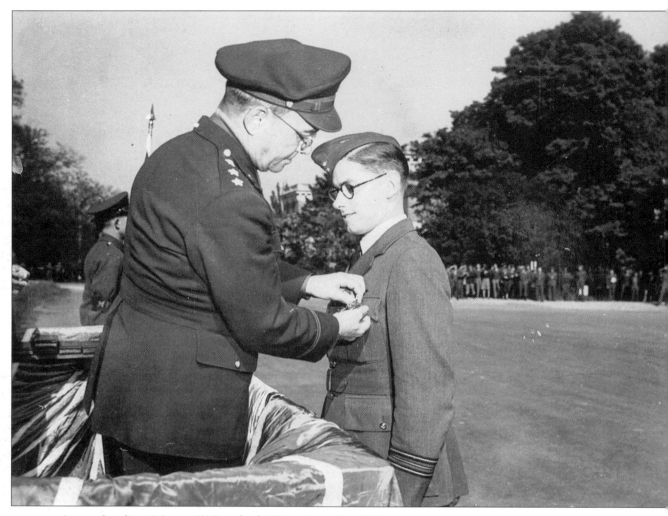

Lieutenant-General Lewis H. Brereton, USAAF, awarding the US Bronze Star on 20 April 1945 to Squadron Leader R. Idris Jones, at Maison Lafitte near Paris. Jones, an RAF photo-interpretation officer, had been seconded to the Allied Airborne Army. (The late Squadron Leader R.I. Jones)

offensive of the war. Six Mosquitos, six Spitfires and eleven Wellingtons of No 34 Wing were destroyed on the ground in this attack.

As an example of the intense work of the mobile units, during the campaign from 6 June 1944 to VE-Day on 8 May 1945, the two MFPSs of No 35 Wing produced about 500,000 exposures, resulting in the production of 4,500,000 prints for the Canadian 1st Army. This enormous effort involved the production of 73,000 feet of ciné film and the use of 60,000 gallons of developer and 51 tons of hypo fixer. This was a very high production rate for the period, especially under such difficult conditions. Equivalent figures for the other units are not available, but there is no reason to suppose that they contributed less to the total effect of the mobile units.

While these events were taking place, the strategic photo-reconnaissance squadrons continued their work from Britain. Some of the aircraft joined in tactical work when the first V–1 flying bombs were launched against London on 12 June 1944. Most of the launching sites had been built underground to avoid detection from the air, and Mosquitos made very dangerous sorties at extreme low level to bring back photographs. Thereafter, the only danger from V–1s occurred when they were launched from He111s over the North Sea, although the results were very inaccurate. A far greater threat was the long-range V–2 rocket, which was first fired on 8 September 1944. Since these rockets stood vertically and needed no launching ramp, they were far more difficult to detect from the air. They remained effective until the last was fired on 27 March 1945.

The watch on the battleship *Tirpitz* in Norway was maintained until, on 12 November 1944, Lancasters of 617 Squadron dropped 12,000-lb 'Tallboy' bombs which capsized the vessel and removed a major threat to Allied shipping. Other photographs, taken over German ports, verified that U-boats were being assembled from pre-fabricated components built elsewhere. This information resulted in heavy bomber attacks against manufacturing bases and assembly yards. Photographs taken over the Augsburg area showed that Me262 jets were being constructed, and in fact a Mosquito of 544 Squadron evaded one of these fighters over Munich on 25 July 1944.

From July 1944 the greater part of the effort of Bomber Command and the US Eighth Air Force was concentrated on oil installations, for by then the advancing Russians were at the point of capturing the Romanian fields, leaving the Germans almost entirely dependent on their manufacture of synthetic oil. Transportation within Germany also received much attention in the closing stages of the war. Strategic reconnaissance aircraft faithfully identified targets and the results of bombing attacks.

The defeat of the German Armies was an achievement in which all branches of the Allied forces can claim a share. There were many reasons for the victory, but the fact that the Allied forces were able to obtain a continuous and clear picture of the enemy's strength and intentions was due in no small measure to the photo-reconnaissance pilots, the intelligence staffs and the photographers of the Mobile Field Photographic Sections.

CHAPTER ELEVEN

NIGHT BOMBING AND PHOTOGRAPHY

On the outbreak of the Second World War, the RAF relied on gun turrets for protecting its bomber squadrons when operating in close formation during daylight, each aircraft covered by cross-fire from the combined turrets. These power-operated turrets, each fitted with up to four .303-inch Browning machine guns, were considered to be so effective that any enemy fighters which approached would find the defences too formidable. This faith was shattered in the first few weeks of the war when Wellington bombers, often riddled with bullet and cannon shell holes from Messerschmitt fighters, returned from daylight attacks on German warships, leaving many of their number at the bottom of the North Sea. In the absence of suitable long-range fighters for escort duties, it became apparent that strategic bombing would have to be carried out mainly at night, with consequent difficulties in both navigation and air photography. These two problems were not fully overcome in Bomber Command for almost three years.

The use of night photography from aircraft was not new, for experiments over the Western Front during the First World War had been quite successful. The techniques which originated in those days were continued in Bomber Command's night offensive against Germany after the fall of France, when F24

cameras were carried in some aircraft and used in combination with photographic flash-bombs. However, Bomber Command's objective was to carry a camera in every operational aircraft, in order to study the results of each sortie on return and check that the targets had been reached. This became imperative when D.M.B. Butt, who was secretary to Lord Cherwell, Winston Churchill's 'one-man brain's trust', reported in August 1941 that, from an analysis of 650 photographs taken at night between 2 June and 25 July, only one aircraft in three had succeeded in dropping its bombs within a radius of 5 miles of its intended target. The whole future of Bomber Command's strategic bombing campaign was thrown temporarily into doubt.

One immediate result of this disclosure was to accelerate the development of additional navigational aids to be carried in bombers. The first of these was Gee, which came into general use in March 1942. This consisted of a radio receiver fitted in the aircraft, which enabled the navigator to see the difference in time signals from synchronised pulses sent out from three separate ground stations in Britain. The results were then plotted on a special Gee chart, so that the intersection of the three lines determined the aircraft's position with considerable accuracy. Owing to the

The Vickers Wellington, such as this example on the strength of 75 Squadron, was the mainstay of Bomber Command from before the outbreak of the Second World War until late 1942. Some Wellingtons continued in front-line service with Bomber Command squadrons until October 1943. (*Aeroplane Monthly*)

The Short Stirling was the first four-engined bomber to be used operationally by Bomber Command in the Second World War, entering service in August 1940. This Stirling I of 149 Squadron was photographed while being bombed up preparatory to a raid. Stirlings continued in service with Bomber Command until September 1944, while others were employed on supply-dropping, transport work and glider-towing. (*Aeroplane Monthly*)

curvature of the earth, the range was usually confined to about 400 miles, but Gee enabled high-flying aircraft to identify targets in the industrial heartland of the Ruhr, before the Germans began jamming the transmissions towards the end of 1942. It was with the aid of this system that Air Chief Marshal Sir Arthur T. Harris, the newly appointed C-in-C of Bomber Command, was able to launch the first 1,000 bomber raid, against Cologne on the night of 30/31 May 1942. The accurate results of this enormous attack, photographed later in daylight by photo-reconnaissance aircraft, were greeted with elation by the British public and convinced some military experts that Bomber Command was developing the ability to destroy the German war economy almost unaided.

The second of these navigational aids was Oboe, introduced in late 1942. This employed two transmitters in England, one of which sent out a series of radar pulses which the aircraft amplified and returned, so that the transmitter station could tell if the aircraft was to the right or left of its track, and gave instructions accordingly. The second transmitter could tell when the aircraft had reached its target and also gave instructions. Oboe was very accurate, although its range was as limited as Gee's and it could only handle one aircraft at a time. Its main use was to enable a few bombers to drop target indicator markers over the target. An adaptation of Oboe was later introduced under the name of GH. With this, the interrogation and display equipment was fitted in the aircraft itself, so that many aircraft could use the system at the same time. It was not until early 1944 that the Germans were able to introduce counter-measures against Oboe or GH but, thanks to the ingenuity of A.H. Reeves and the scientists at the Telecommunication Research Establishment, the squadrons of Bomber Command were usually able to keep one jump ahead of the enemy with their night-bombing operations.

The third navigational aid was self-contained, of unlimited range and could not be jammed by the enemy. Code-named H_2S, it was first used operationally by the Pathfinder Force at the end of January 1943. The system consisted of a small transmitter in the aircraft, which emitted a radar signal to the ground beneath. This was reflected back and displayed on the screen of a cathode ray tube of about 5 inches in diameter, around which a trace revolved once a second. The image from the trace gave a rough picture of the ground, although sometimes this was not easy to read. However, an operator could usually pick up a distinctive landmark such as a coastline or a river. Most important of all, it operated above cloud. The great raids against Hamburg of July 1943, resulting in enormous devastation, were carried out with the aid of this instrument together with the dropping of 'Window', streams of small aluminium strips which when falling blotted out the display screens of German radar. An American-built version of H_2S, named H_2X, was employed by the USAAF and enabled their Fortresses and Liberators to bomb targets from high altitude above cloud during the latter stages of the massive daylight bombing campaign which developed from small beginnings in June 1942.

All these devices increased the effectiveness of the strategic bombing campaign at a time when heavy four-engined bombers such as the Stirling, the Halifax and the Lancaster were coming off the production lines, with the capacity to strike hard at German industrial centres. In addition, the twin-engined Mosquito was becoming available as a light bomber and photo-reconnaissance aircraft.

However, it was the setting up of the Pathfinder Force which heralded the great improvement in accuracy of the RAF's night bombing operations. In spite of initial opposition from Sir Arthur Harris, this was formed in August 1942 under the command

The Handley Page Halifax was the second four-engined bomber to enter service with Bomber Command during the Second World War, in November 1940. Various marks then continued until VE-Day. This photograph is of a Halifax II serial HR926 of 35 Squadron. (The late Squadron Leader J.E. Archbald)

An F24 camera installed in a Halifax. (Flight Lieutenant G.H. Parry RAF (Ret'd))

The twin-engined Avro Manchester did not fulfil expectations after it entered service with Bomber Command in November 1940, for the engines proved unreliable and under-powered. It was withdrawn at the end of June 1942. The Manchester Ia serial L7427 in this photograph was on the strength of 83 Squadron, which was equipped with these machines from December 1941 to May 1942 before converting to Lancasters and joining the Pathfinder Force. (*Aeroplane Monthly*)

of a dynamic Australian, Group Captain (later Air Vice-Marshal) Don C.T. Bennett. Composed initially of four squadrons, equipped with Stirlings, Halifaxes, Lancasters and Wellingtons, it was formed under No 3 Group and developed steadily into an elite corps, eventually attaining its own Group status.

At first, the Pathfinder method consisted of marking the target with sticks of flares and then dropping showers of incendiaries, slightly in advance of the main bomber stream. After the introduction of Oboe and the acquisition of Mosquito aircraft, this progressed to putting down lines of yellow target indicator (TI) flares along the line of approach and then marking the target itself with a series of coloured target indicators during the period of the attack. This marking was backed up by other Mosquitos dropping target indicators of a different colour, together with high-explosive bombs, while yet more Pathfinder aircraft led the main bomber force to deliver their heavy cargoes of bombs and incendiaries. Very precise planning within Bomber Command resulted in cities and towns in Germany suffering enormous casualties and devastation, bringing disruption to the German war effort.

The results of these attacks were photographed assiduously by high-flying Mosquitos and Spitfires of the photo-reconnaissance squadrons, operating mainly in daylight, and enabled photo-interpreters to make assessments of the damage. But Bomber Command required more than this. Each bomber was required to carry a camera and to operate it simultaneously with the release of the bombs, in order to bring back evidence of an accurate attack. This procedure was intricate as well as far more difficult on operational sorties than during training in the UK, where the bombers flew over blacked-out ranges without interference.

To provide the illumination for the exposure, a photo-flash cylinder of about 30 inches in length and $4^{1}/_{2}$ inches in diameter was employed. This was filled with a special mixture of flash powder which, if wrongly handled, was enough to blow the aircraft apart. The blunt-nosed cylinder was fitted at the tail with a small propeller which was prevented from rotating prematurely by a steel pin through the shaft. During the run-up to the target, it was the duty of the wireless operator to attach a lanyard to this pin so that, when the flash-bomb was launched from the flare chute in the fuselage, it was pulled out of the shaft. It was also the duty of the wireless operator to bring this pin back for interrogation during debriefing, as proof that the photo-flash had been dropped 'live'.

Simultaneous with the release of the flash-bomb together with the high-explosive bombs or target indicators, an electric current was passed to a timing device known as a Type 35 Control, which had been pre-set to the bombing altitude. This control ticked off the predicted time of fall of the flash-bomb to 0.6 of the altitude of the aircraft less four seconds, and then opened the camera shutter for a period of eight seconds, ready for the explosion of the flash. During this crucial eight seconds the pilot was required to keep the aircraft straight and level, regardless of flak and searchlights, so that the resulting photograph would show the position marked or bombed.

The objective of fitting and using a camera in every bomber was not fully attained until the end of 1943, but meanwhile their introduction was certainly not popular among the aircrews. The reasons for the dislike were simple. Firstly, the photographs could determine whether the crew had dropped the bombs over the wrong target or had been guilty of 'creep-back' over the correct target; this was the name used to describe the release of the bombs before the

In February 1943 Bomber Command decided that all its aircraft engaged on night bombing should be fitted with a camera and take at least one photograph to synchronise with a photo-flash released with the first bomb, or with the target indicator flare in the case of Pathfinder aircraft. This objective was achieved by the end of the year. This photograph is of Lancaster I of 83 Squadron, which formed part of the Pathfinder Force from 15 August 1942 and then carried out target-marking for the main bomber streams until the end of the war. (The late Squadron Leader J.E. Archbald)

A typical photograph of the heavily defended target of Berlin, taken from 10,000 feet on the night of 29/30 March 1943, before the introduction of the 'master and slave' twin camera system invented by Squadron Leader Howard W. Lees of the Pathfinder Force. Ground details were obscured by the tracks of target indicators, searchlights and flak, all further confused by the evasive action of the aircraft. Such photographs, although dramatic, were of little use to photo-interpreters. (Squadron Leader H.W. Lees RAFVR)

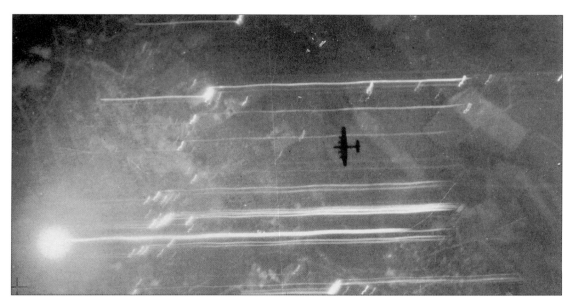

The first heavy attack against the Barmen district of Wuppertal in the Ruhr was made on the night of 29/30 May 1943, when 719 aircraft were despatched and 33 were lost. The target was accurately marked and devastation was complete, with about 3,000 people killed. Interpreters of this photograph could pick out a Lancaster flying north towards a cloud of smoke as well as the round light of a target indicator. The streaks on the picture were caused by a technical fault, the film winding on before being completely protected by the capping blind. (The late Squadron Leader J.E. Archbald)

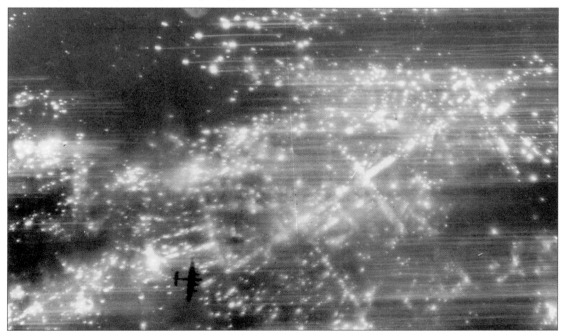

Hannover photographed on the night of 8/9 October 1943, when Bomber Command despatched 504 aircraft and lost 27. Photo-interpreters were able to pick out a four-engined bomber flying over a mass of incendiary fires to the south-south-west of the railway station, while the broad white ribbon running from the nose of the aircraft to the top right of the photograph was the Sallestrasse. The raid resulted in the destruction of almost 4,000 buildings with over 30,000 damaged, as well as the deaths of 1,200 people and 3,345 injuires. (The late Squadron Leader J.E. Archbald)

aiming point had been reached. If there was no satisfactory explanation for such errors, the sortie might be deleted from the build-up to the thirty which each Bomber Command flyer was required to complete in an operational tour. Secondly, photography required the crew to fly directly towards the target for the period between releasing the bombs and the explosion of the flash-bomb, and then to fly straight and level for another eight seconds while the film was being exposed. This long exposure was necessary since an instantaneous exposure would almost certainly miss the brief illumination of the flash, which lasted for a peak of only 1/60th of a second and tailed for a total of 1/10th of a second. It was accepted at first that the long exposure caused 'fire tracks' on the picture from the 'stretched' recordings of light sources such as ground fires and searchlights while the aircraft was moving.

The total period of straight and level flight usually lasted for only about half a minute, but that was a very long time when searchlights were probing and the flak was intense. It is true that more bombers fell to the guns of night-fighters on the outward or return flights than to flak, but the fiery spectacle over the target was often enough to test the courage of the most determined of men.

There were, of course, valid reasons why crews sometimes brought back unsatisfactory photographs. There could be cloud over the target and very occasionally there were mechanical, electrical or flash failures. In addition, another problem arose, for it had not been foreseen that bombing would develop into the saturation of targets by incendiaries dropped by numerous aircraft. With the camera shutter open for eight seconds, the movement of the aircraft over a blazing target resulted in numerous fire tracks on the ground being recorded as irregular traces on the film, thus obliterating other details.

Before the end of the war, Bomber Command had built up to eleven Groups, including No 8 (Pathfinder Force) Group. Each Group appointed its own Photographic Officer, but it was the Pathfinder Force which led the way in the improvements in night photography, just as it led the way in marking the targets. The Group Photographic Officer for this force was Squadron Leader Howard W. Lees, who was posted as a Flight Lieutenant to RAF Wyton in Huntingdonshire during January 1943 and was among the nucleus of the new unit when it attained Group status a few weeks later. Shortly after his arrival, while the new formation was still a lodger unit at Wyton and under the control of No 3 Group, it received a visit from Group Captain F.C. Sturgiss OBE, the Photographic Officer of Bomber Command. Sturgiss asked Lees if he had any suggestions for overcoming the problem of fire tracks which were obscuring much of the evidence that the bomber offensive was improving its accuracy.

Lees immediately came up with the idea of fitting two films and two shutters in the same camera, geared to expose alternately, so that the period of 'standby duty' for each film would be limited to about one second. During one of those periods the vital 1/60th of a second of flash illumination would be recorded. Thus each ground fire would appear only as a fairly small point of light instead of a track, and moreover the photo-interpreters would be able to locate its position.

It was not feasible to design and produce such a camera within a short space of time, although the idea eventually came into being in the shape of the F97 camera shortly after the war. As a more practicable alternative, Lees had two F24 cameras installed in the same aircraft. He modified the camera gear boxes and electrical circuits so that while one camera – the Master – was exposing, the

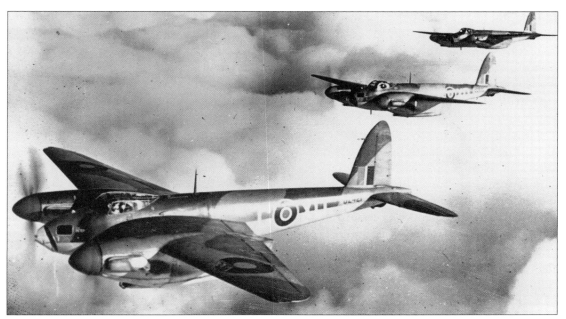

De Havilland Mosquito IV bombers, such as these on the strength of 139 Squadron, formed part of No 8 (Pathfinder Force) Group. They were employed in dropping target indicators for the main bomber stream. (*Aeroplane Monthly*)

Squadron Leader Howard W. Lees, the Group Photographic Officer of No 8 (Pathfinder Force) Group, standing by the turret of a Lancaster. His inventions led to great improvements in the quality of night photographs taken from aircraft of Bomber Command and were adopted in post-war cameras. (Squadron Leader H.W. Lees RAFVR)

other – the Slave – was rewinding. Having rewound, the Slave shutter re-opened and simultaneously energised the solenoid of the Master, so that this rewound in turn. By this means the exposure time was reduced from eight seconds to little more than 1.6 seconds required for the rewinding cycle.

Thus the 'Master and Slave' camera was born, resulting in a great improvement in the clarity of the night photographs. The system was introduced into the Groups of Bomber Command from the spring of 1943 onwards. The clarity of photographs improved further when the American K–24 camera was issued in February of the following year, for this was made with a high-speed gearbox which reduced the exposure time from the 1.6 seconds of the F24 to .33 of a second.

However, there was an associated problem which Lees was anxious to solve. Many of the night photographs gave evidence of having been taken while the aircraft was banking, usually during avoiding action against enemy defences. Lees thought it was unfair to expect aircrews to fly straight and level after continuing to the centre of the target. It troubled him especially since he had to brief aircrews to do this, when he was not subjected to such hazards himself. Staff officers were not permitted to fly on operations, lest they be taken prisoner and interrogated, although he did manage to go on one sortie.

The flash-bomb in use was blunt-nosed and trailed behind other bombs during descent, so that the flash illumination was outside the area of the photograph when it was taken. Lees thought that it would be better to design one which kept pace with the bombs and burst closer to the ground. Thus the flash itself would appear in the picture and be plotted as the position bombed, subject to parallax error wherever it appeared off-centre in the photograph. It was calculated that this would allow the pilot to take evasive action

up to seventeen degrees of bank and still record the flash within the frame.

By hanging with his head out of the entrance door of a Halifax over the bombing range at Rushford in Suffolk, Lees was able to witness the erratic behaviour of the 4½-inch flash-bomb after it had been launched sideways from the flare chute. It was seen to cartwheel, which not only retarded its forward velocity but also must have caused the propeller to rotate in opposite directions and thus delay the release of the firing mechanism and the flash burst.

The flash that Lees had in mind was one which would have the same ballistics and terminal velocity as the bombs, and be dropped from the bomb bay. But he knew that no substitution of bombs would be authorised, for every bomb hook was required for weapons of destruction or target markers. Thus he proposed combining the flash with a target indicator, which was a 250-lb bomb casing filled with about sixty coloured 'Roman candles'. These candles were ejected by a small explosive charge, detonated by a reliable barometric fuse, and cascaded out over the target at a low altitude. Twenty of these candles were removed to make room for a 4½-inch flash, enabling the target to be marked with the remaining forty and to be photographed at the same time. This occurred at 0.2 of the aircraft's altitude instead of the 0.6 previously used. The resulting flash would be seen as a circle of light in the photograph but was unlikely to handicap the photo-interpreters.

Air Vice-Marshal Bennett wasted no time in having a prototype prepared and ordered Lees to collect his 'toy' from the bomb dump at RAF Wyton and take it in his car to the Bomb Development Unit at RAF Feltwell in Norfolk. It was tested successfully from there over Rushford Bombing Range and put into production as the 'TI Flash'. However, it was not used by the heavy bombers, as Lees had

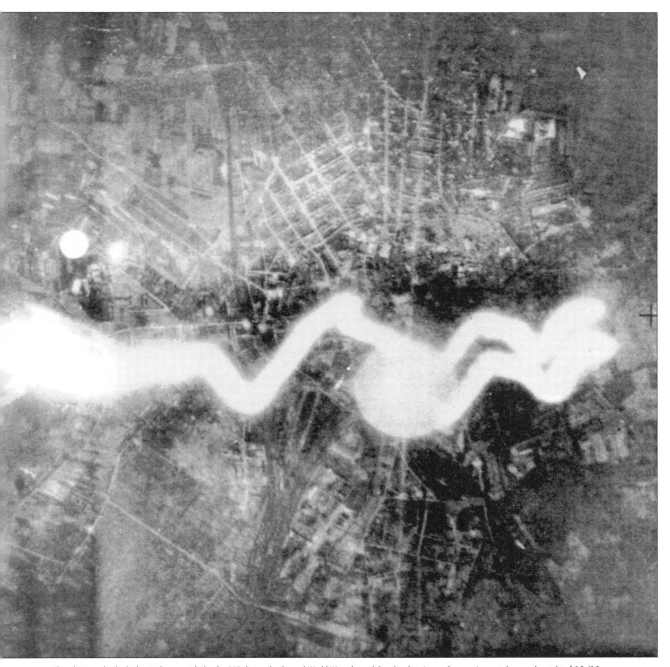

This photograph, the highest taken at night by the RAF during the Second World War, showed Osnabruck in Lower Saxony. It was taken on the night of 18/19 April 1944 from 36,000 feet by Mosquito IX serial ML923 flown by Flight Lieutenant J.W. Jordan of 105 Squadron, part of No 8 (Pathfinder Force) Group, based at Bourn in Cambridgeshire. It was a purely experimental photograph, using a combined indicator and photo-flash devised by Squadron Leader Howard W. Lees, during which the shutter was open for 30 seconds and recorded the progress of a target indicator dropped by another Mosquito. Jordan also dropped one target indicator and red photo-flash as well as three 500-lb bombs, but there was no attack by the main bomber force on Osnabruck on that night. (Squadron Leader H.W. Lees RAFVR)

originally intended. Instead, it was realised that the invention provided the means for Mosquitos, which were not fitted with flare chutes and so far had been unable to take night photographs, to bring back evidence of their success in the bombing war. It was first used by Group Captain Charles E. Slee of 139 Squadron on 8/9 October 1943 to check the accuracy of the GH radar navigational aid, and produced an excellent photograph of Düren in Germany from 25,000 feet.

Thereafter the TI Flash was used almost exclusively by target-marking Mosquitos, dropped with three 500-lb bombs, and unfailingly ensured night photographs of good quality from high altitudes. This was particularly true of those taken over Berlin, while the highest night photograph of the war was taken over Osnabruck from 36,000 feet. These photographers gave support for Air Vice-Marshal Bennett's drive for more Mosquito squadrons in his Light Night Striking Force, which was harassing the enemy while suffering minimal losses. However, production of the TI Flash was never sufficient to supply the heavy bomber squadrons and thus put to the test Lees' contention that it would enable the crews to take evasive action and save lives, as well as providing a more accurate assessment of bombing and target marking.

Another of Lees' inventions was related to the H_2S radar screen. It was decided to photograph this screen over the target at the time the target indicators were released, or at a turning point sharply before. The Radar Officer of the Pathfinder Group had been trying, in utmost secrecy, to obtain photographs of the image on the screen with a Leica 35-mm camera fitted with a close-focusing device but, since anything closer than $17\frac{1}{2}$ inches was out of focus, he was unsuccessful and asked for advice. After being sworn to secrecy and told not even to mention this matter to the Photographic

Section of Bomber Command, Lees was shown the new and highly secret H_2S set. He arranged for Wyton workshops to make some 11.7-mm extension rings, which were then fitted to all the Leica cameras which could be bought from dealers, and in turn these were fitted to lightweight copying stands. The navigator operating the set was required to hold one of these over the H_2S screen and depress the shutter level for one second, the time of the sweep of the trace.

The first results were obtained on the night of 2 October 1943, when the navigator of a Lancaster of 83 Squadron took a very clear photograph of the screen showing Friedrichshafen on the shore of Lake Constance. Leipzig was also recorded by the same squadron in early December, but the main venture in risking this secret took place over Berlin on the night of 1 January 1944, when forty-one successful pictures were taken by eight cameras. Lees had earlier asked Bomber Command to issue a 35-mm enlarger for printing the negatives but this request was refused since he was not allowed to state its purpose. However, he used his own enlarger and developing tanks, installing them in an unventilated cellar at Station Headquarters. Seven enlargements were required from each negative, together with three rows of contact titling information on each print. Thus it was a great relief when secrecy was eventually relaxed and he was able to arrange for processing under normal conditions at Station Headquarters. When the USAAF joined in the battle against Berlin in March 1944, these early H_2S photographs were included in a booklet which was issued to the H_2X operators, to show them what to expect on their screens in the run-up to the target.

However, the results of this rather make-shift method of photography of the H_2S display began to deteriorate when handled in the photographic sections of the various

The Kodak 'Bantam' camera, with a 1-inch lens, was used to photograph the display screen of the H_2S radar set when over the target. It was mounted on a hinged bracket so that it could be kept clear of the set when this was being viewed by the operator. However, when the bombardier called 'Bombs gone!' it was swung into position to record the effect of the bombs. The shutter release was held down for one second for each exposure, this being the length of time the radar trace described a full circle. After landing, the camera assembly was removed and handed to the duty photographer for film processing. (Squadron leader H.W. Lees RAFVR)

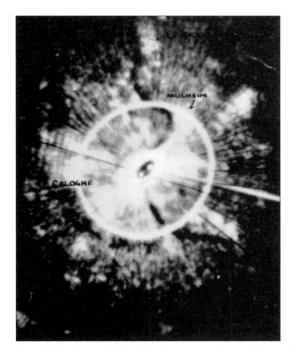

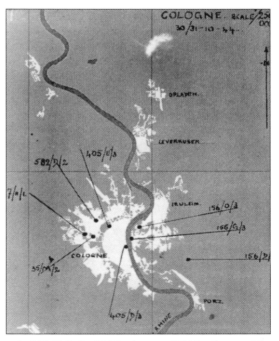

Above, left: This photograph of an H_2S radar screen was taken over Cologne on the night of 30/31 October 1944 by a Lancaster of 156 Squadron, part of No 8 (Pathfinder Force) Group, based at Wyton in Huntingdonshire. The photo-interpreters were able to relate this and other photographs to the ground positions, from which the diagram (*above right*) was constructed. The main bomber force of 905 aircraft caused enormous damage to Cologne on that night, without loss of aircraft. (Squadron leader H.W. Lees RAFVR)

WAAF personnel registering films of night photographs in the negative library at Medmenham. (The Medmenham Club)

Identification of night photographs being carried out at Medmenham, by comparison with large-scale maps of photographs prepared with the aid of aerial mosaics. (The Medmenham Club)

Pathfinder stations. In November 1944 Howard Lees collected 200 Kodak Bantam 35-mm cameras from the Maintenance Unit at Stafford. These had been specially designed in America and fitted with a 1-inch Dallmeyer lens, which enabled the distance from lens to image to be halved. Lees then designed a hinged bracket so that the camera could be swung firmly into position, already correctly focused and aligned, when the photograph was required. This device is now in the RAF Museum at Hendon. By this time an improved version of H_2S had been developed, and the results obtained were excellent. Lees then modified a 16-mm Eyemo ciné camera to take one-second exposures every alternate second, which provided a 'moving picture' of the run-up to Berlin from the Tegel See. In a way, this was a primitive forerunner of the modern video.

Bomber Command also employed colour photography, towards the end of the war. This was required since the Germans, with characteristic resourcefulness, began to light decoy fires in places where bombing could do no harm, together with fake target indicators, to fool the main bomber stream. The Pathfinder Force began to vary the colour of its target indicators, and Bomber Command wished to verify if each bomber had attacked those of the correct colour. In May 1943 attempts at using Kodachrome colour film were made over the bombing range, but the ground detail was poor. Within a few months, a supply of Kodacolour film arrived from the USA, but results were still inadequate.

In early 1944 the Group Photographic Officer of No 5 Group, Squadron Leader Len A. Eades, experimented with laying the Kodacolour film in front of the usual high-speed night film, so that the light of the flash affected both. This worked well, although the colour film showed only the colours of the target indicators. However, the system was introduced gradually until, by the end of the war, over 80 per cent of the bomber force were using this composite film.

While these immense night attacks against the German heartland and targets in the occupied territories were taking place, Bomber Command carried out several daylight raids. The majority of these were short-range sorties made by medium bombers against targets in occupied territories, usually with the escort of swarms of Spitfires. After the invasion of Normandy and the establishment of air superiority over German skies in the summer of 1944, however, Bomber Command resumed daylight attacks against targets in Germany. The heavy bombers flew in close formation, in accordance with the pre-war conception, but with an escort of P-51 Mustang long-range fighters carrying drop-tanks. In these daylight attacks, photographs were taken in the usual way. But the main burden of daylight attacks against Germany and occupied Europe was carried by the USAAF from bases in England and Italy, escorted by their long-distance fighters.

The RAF made night sorties over Germany from the beginning of January 1940 onwards, the final attack taking place on the night of 2/3 May 1945 against Kiel by Mosquitos of the Pathfinder Force. Bomber Command's last effort in the European war was a great errand of mercy. Much of western Holland was still occupied by the Germans and the population was starving. By arrangement with the local German commander a truce was organised, and between 26 April and 7 May 1945, Bomber Command flew nearly 3,000 sorties in daylight to drop food supplies for these civilians, under Operation 'Manna'. Bombers of the US Eighth Air Force joined in this effort, under Operation 'Chowhound'. Thus the Allied Air Forces not only played an enormous part in the liberation of Europe but saved civilian lives towards the end of the war.

CHAPTER TWELVE

SOUTH-EAST ASIA

When the Japanese landed at Khota Bharu on the east coast of the Malayan Peninsula on 8 December 1941, there was a woeful lack of RAF strategic photo-reconnaissance aircraft in the area. Long-range Hurricanes had been requested, but these were not available, for at the time the British were far more intent on supplying aircraft to the Russians than building up the RAF in South-East Asia. Two Brewster Buffalos had been stripped of armament and non-essential equipment so that, fitted with two F24 cameras, their range was considerably increased. There was also a solitary Bristol Beaufort II, one of six built in Australia which had arrived in Singapore shortly before the invasion in order to replace the obsolescent Vildebeest torpedo bombers of 36 and 100 Squadrons. Without trained crews, the Beauforts were not considered suitable for operations but one, serial T9543, was retained for reconnaissance purposes.

Most of the RAF squadrons in Malaya were equipped with aircraft which were at the end of their usefulness for front-line operations. Moreover, the gathering of signals and other intelligence, under the Far East Combined Bureau in Singapore, was in the hands of the Royal Navy and thus biased towards the requirements of that service. There was almost no knowledge about the disposition of the Japanese Air Force which was to play such a crucial role in the forthcoming conflict, and very little information on the performance of its aircraft. Instead, there was a general belief that the Japanese armed forces were inferior in equipment and fighting ability to those of their Western opponents.

The small flight of RAF photo-reconnaissance aircraft, under the command of Squadron Leader C.G.R. Lewis, was based at Seletar in Singapore, where it was known locally as No 4 Photographic Reconnaissance Unit. Of course, it was unable to keep watch on the movements of Japanese forces from their bases in Indo-China or Siam, whereas numbers of the Mitsubishi Ki 46-II 'Dinah' flew regular reconnaissance missions over Malaya, at altitudes which the RAF fighters could not reach.

On the day of the landings in east Malaya, the Beaufort flew into the small RAF airfield near Khota Bharu, carrying films of the Japanese disembarking from troopships at Singora and Pattani in Siam. The machine had been damaged in combat and caught fire when it tried to take off again. It was written off, but the films were processed in a wooden hut by Leading Aircraftman Stan Lewis, using inadequate equipment and guesswork, while the airfield was being strafed by Japanese fighters. They were then flown to Seletar by a Buffalo. Shortly afterwards, the airfield buildings were set on fire and the base was abandoned.

One of a flight of Catalina flying boats present in the area had been shot down a day before the Japanese landed in Malaya. Attempts by RAAF Hudsons and RAF

The RAF's Brewster Buffalo, the equivalent of the US Navy's F2A-2, was rejected as a front-line fighter when it arrived in England during July 1940. As with other machines and equipment which were considered inferior at home, all Buffalos were sent to the Far East where they were allocated to five RAF and one RAAF fighter squadrons as well as to No 4 Photographic Reconnaissance Unit. Although these machines were outclassed by Japanese fighters, the pilots achieved remarkable results. (*Aeroplane Monthly*)

The bridge over the Sittang River, east of Rangoon, after the central spans had been blown up by the retreating British while some of their men were still on the Japanese side. These men had to use improvised rafts or swim to safety, to avoid capture. (Squadron Leader J.D. Braithwaite RAFVR)

The RAF's photographic section in retreat over the Irrawaddy north of Rangoon in early April 1942. The oil fields at Yennangyaung, in the background, were destroyed by the British shortly before they were occupied by the Japanese 33rd Division. (Corporal A. Fox DFM, RAFVR)

The bridge over the Irrawaddy at Ava, near Mandalay, which was blown up by the British on 30 April 1942 to impede the advancing Japanese. Two spans fell in the river and created a sandbank. (Squadron Leader J.D. Braithwaite RAFVR)

Vildebeests based at Khota Bharu to attack the Japanese invasion fleet were partially successful but did not stop the landings. In later attempts to attack Japanese transports, the Vildebeests were almost wiped out.

As the Japanese advanced down the Malayan Peninsula, squadrons of RAF Blenheims, operating from northern airfields which lacked sufficient anti-aircraft defences or radar coverage, were gradually whittled down to a handful of survivors. The Buffalos of RAF, RAAF and RNZAF squadrons suffered in combat against the superior Japanese fighters. During these events the reconnaissance Buffalos flew over 100 sorties and, amazingly, they were not shot down although they frequently returned full of holes. The pilots relied on manoeuvrability to escape the Japanese fighters. Two more were converted and joined in the sorties. But the end came when the Buffalos were destroyed or damaged on the ground in an air attack on 7 February.

Only a handful of Hudsons, Vildebeests, Buffalos and Blenheims remained when the retreating Commonwealth forces reached Singapore. A consignment of Hurricanes arrived in crates and their RAF pilots shot down numerous Japanese bombers, but these machines were also outclassed by the Japanese fighters and the numbers were steadily depleted. When the fall of Singapore became imminent, five officers and twenty-eight other ranks of the photographic sections had gathered on the island. All managed to escape by various means, some experiencing astonishing adventures, and arrived in Palembang in Sumatra. After their departure and that of the surviving aircraft, the surrender of Singapore on 15 February 1942 was undoubtedly the most humiliating defeat suffered by British arms in the war. Inadequate aerial reconnaissance and the failure of intelligence had been among the main reasons for this débâcle.

The British hoped to retain Sumatra, with the help of the Dutch, but the chances of defending an island 1,000 miles long with their depleted forces were nil. On the day before the fall of Singapore, one of the RAAF Hudsons which had flown to Sumatra spotted a Japanese invasion fleet sailing in the direction of the island. The enemy transports were then mauled by Hudsons and Blenheims, but the remaining ships continued their journey. Meanwhile, Japanese paratroops landed on the fighter airfield at Palembang and overcame the defences. The invasion fleet was again attacked by the defending aircraft, supported by Hurricanes which had previously arrived from an aircraft carrier, and the transports and landing barges were almost wiped out. But more Japanese paratroops were dropped and the British, by then desperately short of supplies, were ordered to retreat to Java. The few remaining RAF and RAAF aircraft were flown to the airfield at Semplak in the west of this island, while the ground personnel were evacuated by boat on 18 February, amid scenes of great confusion. The men of the photographic section accompanied them.

By then, the military situation in the Dutch East Indies had become hopeless, with the civilians demoralised by the defeats of the British and Dutch. Nevertheless, the handful of Blenheims, Hudsons and Vildebeests returned to the attack, suffering further losses. It was not long before the relentless Japanese attacked again, beginning their landings on 1 March. A few days later, the evacuation of Java began. The surviving handful of RAF and Dutch aircraft were either destroyed or flown to Australia, while some of the personnel left by boat from the south of the island. Priority was given to aircrews and technical staff, but three photographic men were captured, including Stan Lewis. Another fell sick and was taken off by a destroyer. The remainder were evacuated in various vessels, mostly in the Dutch freighter *Kota Gede* of 7,800 tons, and were lucky enough to reach Colombo in Ceylon. No preparations had been made for their arrival, but local civilians rallied round to help with accommodation.

Meanwhile, Siam had surrendered without resistance to the Japanese and the country was used as a base for the assault on Burma, which began on 23 December 1941 with an air attack on Rangoon. This and subsequent raids caused many civilian deaths and casualties, so that streams of panic-stricken refugees poured out of the capital. Japanese troops crossed the Burmese border on 15 January 1942, and the British forces began a long retreat.

The RAF in Burma had built a chain of excellent airfields and landing fields, but as with Malaya these lacked sufficient anti-aircraft guns or radar warning facilities. Moreover, there were very few aircraft, even counting those types which were regarded as obsolescent in Britain. There were a few squadrons of RAF Buffalos, one squadron of RAF Lysanders and another of the Indian Air Force, while shortly after Christmas a squadron of Hurricanes and about thirty Blenheims arrived. In addition, there were three squadrons of the American Volunteer Group which, equipped with P–40 Warhawks, had flown from China to Mingaladon near Rangoon. Opposed to this force, the Japanese could mount about 400 modern aircraft. Nevertheless, the P–40s and Buffalos attacked the Japanese bombers so effectively that they were forced, at least for the time being, to discontinue daylight raids.

Facilities for strategic photographic coverage in Burma were at first almost non-existent. Some topographic mapping had taken place during 1940 under the direction of Lieutenant-Colonel W. Westland Wright, using the services of the Air India Survey and

Transport Company based in Calcutta. Part of the probable invasion route had been mapped during these surveys. A Blenheim I of 60 Squadron had been converted for photographic work and began strategic reconnaissance over Siam. When the Japanese attacked, one Buffalo of 67 Squadron and one P–40 Warhawk were modified for photography. These carried out tactical reconnaissance, and later two Hurricane IIBs of 17 Squadron were also converted for this purpose. The two Lysander squadrons did their best to carry out Army co-operation duties, but were hopelessly outclassed by the Japanese Air Force.

On 25 January two photo-reconnaissance Hurricane IIBs were flown from the Middle East to Mingaladon by Flying Officers F.D. Procter and K.A. Perkin. They began strategic reconnaissance three days later, the pilots covering targets as far afield as Bangkok and Chiengmai in Siam and Tavoy and Moulmein in southern Burma. As the Japanese approached Rangoon on 21 February, these two Hurricanes were withdrawn to Magwe, 300 miles to the north. The ground party of photographers followed with a mobile darkroom and three large trucks, mostly containing supplies abandoned by fleeing shopkeepers.

The photo-reconnaissance Blenheim was destroyed in an air raid on 21 February but other Blenheims of 60 Squadron carried out some photographic sorties. Meanwhile the defending RAF aircraft were steadily being whittled down, although they inflicted heavy casualties on the Japanese aircraft, both in the air and on the ground. Flying Officer Perkin was shot down on 21 March by Japanese fighters. He landed his Hurricane in a lake near the oil wells at Yenangyaung, but skidded to the bank and suffered nothing worse than a cut eyebrow. The other Hurricane was written off after a bombing attack.

The North American B-25C Mitchell II was mainly employed by the RAF as a bomber but also used by No 3 Photographic Reconnaissance Unit for photo-reconnaissance in the Far East theatre. This unit became 681 Squadron in January 1943 but the twin-engined aircraft were transferred to the new 684 Squadron the following September. This B-25C of 684 Squadron was photographed in 1944 at Comilla in India. It was probably N5-145 of the Military Aviation Arm of the Royal Netherlands–Indies Army, one of five which were transferred to the RAF and employed in this role. (F.W. Guy via G.J. Thomas)

Ground crews of No 3 Photographic Reconnaissance Unit (India) in front of one of the North American B-25C Mitchells acquired from the Military Arm of the Royal Netherlands Indies Army. The photograph was taken in May 1941 at Pendevesvar in India. (Corporal A. Fox DFM, RAFVR)

Group Captain S.G. Wise, who arrived as a wing commander in India during May 1942 to command the Photographic Reconnaissance Unit. He had previously flown as a pilot with No 1 Photographic Reconnaissance Unit in the UK and had also commanded 248 Squadron, a strike squadron of Coastal Command equipped with Beaufighters. (The late Group Captain S.G. Wise CBE, DFC*)

Hurricane PR IIC serial BN125, which arrived in October 1942 from the Middle East to join No 3 Photographic Reconnaissance Unit at Dum-Dum, India. The fairing beneath the fuselage enclosed the cameras. The machine was painted in royal blue, with wing and tail markings outlined in yellow, but with the fuselage roundels painted over. (The late Wing Commander F.D. Procter DFC via G.J. Thomas)

All the time the Japanese continued their advance, apparently invincible. Magwe was evacuated and the RAF retreated once more, this time to Akyab, which immediately came under air attack. The photographic ground party set off again, taking the road past Mandalay and Maymyo towards the mountains around Lashio on the route to China. However, they were ordered to return as far as Swebo, where they were picked up by a Dakota and flown to India. By then, the few surviving RAF aircraft had also flown to India, while the ground staff made their way over the hills to Bengal. The surviving P–40s withdrew to China, and almost the whole of Burma fell into Japanese hands.

India seemed to be as vulnerable as Burma, but the Japanese were halted by the onset of the summer monsoon and the mountainous terrain which separated them from their next objective. This breathing space was a godsend to the RAF, which needed to rebuild its shattered squadrons. It was also recognised that strategic photo-reconnaissance was essential, although these had been almost unknown in India before the war with Japan. Some coverage of the military zone on the North-West Frontier had taken place by Army co-operation and bomber squadrons, with interpretation carried out locally by air intelligence liaison officers, but otherwise air photography had been undertaken only for a survey of India.

In January 1942 the Air Staff had agreed that a Far Eastern Photographic Intelligence Unit should be sent to Singapore. Fortunately, the party travelled only as far as India, where in March it was formed into three sections – a School of Photographic Interpretation, a Central Interpretation Section, and a Photographic Library. These were commanded by Squadron Leader J.D. Braithwaite, a pilot who had served with the Burma Volunteer Air Force which carried out liaison duties during the Japanese invasion.

Earlier, he had fitted a camera in a Puss Moth and made a survey of the oil installations south of Rangoon.

After the photographic parties from Singapore and Burma had linked up with these sections, a new unit was formed on 10 April 1942 and given the title of No 5 Photographic Reconnaissance Unit. It came under 221 Group and was commanded temporarily by Squadron Leader A.C. 'Fatty' Pearson, who had arrived from No 2 Photographic Reconnaissance Unit in Egypt. The unit acquired five North American B–25C Mitchells which had been stranded in India when en route to join the Military Aviation Arm of the Royal Netherlands Indies Army, at the time when Java surrendered. These aircraft were converted at Karachi for strategic photography by removing their armament and installing three F24 cameras in the ventral gun position, an F52 camera in the tail, and an extra fuel tank in the bomb bay. On 13 May they were flown to Pandeveswar in Bengal, where the Dutch crews helped the RAF pilots to convert on to them. The unit was renumbered No 3 Photographic Reconnaissance Unit (India) on this date, to follow consecutively after No 1 in the UK and No 2 in the Middle East.

On 16 May Wing Commander S.G. 'Bill' Wise arrived to command the unit. He had flown with No 1 Photographic Reconnaissance Unit in Britain and during the previous year had commanded 248 Squadron, a strike squadron of Coastal Command which was equipped with Beaufighters. During May, three Hurricane IIBs arrived from the Middle East to join the new unit at Pandeveswar. This base was a singularly unattractive place, situated in a sand-blown open plain which was churned into mud when the rains came. Maintenance was difficult and the men suffered from poor food and heat exhaustion. The aircraft carried out photographic missions over

Burma, concentrating on enemy airfields and lines of communication, but the monsoon restricted these operations for several weeks.

At the end of June the unit began to move to Dum-Dum, near Calcutta, a permanent station which was far more suited to their requirements. One B–25C was lost in an accident but more Hurricanes arrived, so that by the end of September the unit had on charge four B–25Cs and six Hurricane IIBs. Three camera mountings for F24s were installed in the latter machines, two forward and one in the rear fuselage, while additional internal fuel tanks increased the range to about 1,100 miles.

The films were taken to nearby Barrackpore for processing and interpretation. Squadron Leader G.J. Craig, who in civilian life had worked for Kodak in London, was posted to Barrackpore as Senior Photographic Officer, while Squadron Leader G.D. Parke took over as Interpretation Officer. At first the sections operated from a trailer, but they soon moved to Tagore Palace, a residence of the Maharajah of Tagore, with their various messes in huts nearby. The effectiveness of the unit increased rapidly, both in terms of the photographic coverage and the work on the ground. There was a great demand by the Army and the RAF for these photographs.

In the extreme heat and humidity, problems arose with the cameras, which were mostly an assortment of F24s with 5-inch, 14-inch and 20-inch lenses. The glass covering the camera portholes of the aircraft was of a lower standard than that used in the UK and gave optical distortion. Fortunately, after some experiments, it was found that this glass was unnecessary in the prevailing hot climate and the covers were removed. Photographic sharpness was also reduced since condensation formed in the lenses of cameras fitted in the Hurricanes, caused by warm air flow from the aircraft radiator

during flight. This problem was overcome by placing the lenses into the Kodak cold store in Calcutta for two days, after which they were filled with dry air and sealed. Camera vibration in the mountings, which also reduced photographic quality, was associated with worn and faulty rubber suspension, and this could be only partially corrected. During film processing, temperature differences between the solutions and the wash water caused 'reticulation', or crinkling of the gelatin emulsion of the negatives. This was corrected by ensuring uniform liquid temperatures during processing. In printing, the photographs often lacked sharpness, resulting from poor contact between the printer pressure pad and the negative, but this was eventually corrected by modifying the pad.

Wing Commander Wise called for volunteers among the ground photographers to fly in the B–25C Mitchells. One of those who put his name forward was Leading Aircraftman Alan Fox, who had been in Mingaladon when the Japanese attacked and taken part in the evacuation from Burma. The other crew members were the pilot, the second pilot and the navigator. The operating altitude was 26,000 to 30,000 feet and Fox found the aircraft freezing cold. His job was responsibility for the cameras, replacing the film magazines and attending to stoppages, but in addition he kept watch from the astrodome for any dot in the sky which might turn out to be a Japanese fighter. Some interceptions were made and the usual method of escape was to build up speed by putting the Mitchell into a steep dive. Fox eventually flew on seventy-five sorties, to targets such as the airfield at Myitkyina in Burma, the docks at Rangoon, the airfield at Chiengmai in Siam, the Andaman Islands and the new Burma–Siam railway which was being built by thousands of British and Commonwealth prisoners. He was awarded a

The main airfield at Toungoo in Burma, photographed in early 1943 after it had been developed by the Japanese. (Squadron Leader J.D. Braithwaite RAFVR)

Spitfire PR XI serial PL773 of 681 Squadron in India. This mark of aircraft replaced the Spitfire PR IV in the UK photo-reconnaissance squadrons towards the end of 1942 but did not appear in India until October 1943. It was powered by a Merlin 61 engine which gave a top speed of 417 mph. Two vertical cameras were installed in the rear fuselage, sometimes with the addition of an oblique. These Spitfires were painted in 'special blue'. (The late Group Captain S.G. Wise CBE, DFC)

Flying Officer F.D. Procter standing in front of a Spitfire PR IV at Dum-Dum. This was one of the first two Spitfires to arrive at No 3 Photographic Reconnaissance Unit (India), ferried from the Middle East in October 1942. After the unit became 681 Squadron on 25 January 1943, Procter commanded the squadron from December 1943 to April 1945. (The late Wing Commander F.D. Procter DFC via G.J. Thomas)

Spitfire PR XI serial PL776 photographed at Alipore, where 681 Squadron was based from May 1944 to June 1945. This aircraft was flown by Wing Commander F.D. Procter from July 1944 to April 1945, during part of the period when he commanded the squadron. (The late Wing Commander F.D. Procter DFC via G.J. Thomas)

A Spitfire PR XI of 681 Squadron being serviced at Chandina in India, an airstrip constructed in 1943 on paddy fields as a satellite to Comilla, near the Burmese border. It was built without runways, hard-standings or permanent buildings. The squadron was based there from 9 December 1943 to 30 January 1944, returning to Dum-Dum when the surface became unusable with the onset of the winter monsoon. (Squadron Leader T.N. Rosser OBE, DFC, RAFVR)

DFM, and was believed to be one of only three airmen photographers to receive this decoration.

On 10 October 1942 two Spitfire PR IVs were ferried from the Middle East to India, thus improving still further the effectiveness of the unit, and two more arrived within that month. The new aircraft were fitted with pre-war F8 cameras, used for high-altitude photography, and at first these had to be removed until suitable processing equipment became available. In the following month, No 3 Photographic Reconnaissance Unit called for additional volunteers from pilots in the Hurricane squadrons who had had experience in Spitfires, to join those who were already flying the Hurricane IIBs. One who came forward from 72 Squadron was Flying Officer Tom N. Rosser, who then flew on numerous photo-reconnaissance sorties until May 1944, becoming a flight commander and earning a DFC.

The Hurricane and Spitfire pilots carried out extensive strategic sorties over Burma, usually taking in several targets during flights of over four hours. Airfields and railways were of special interest, as were the tracks leading to the Arakan. The aircraft often flew to the limits of their range and the pilots feared engine failure and the violence of the monsoon more than pursuit by enemy aircraft. Tom Rosser recollects that there were no navigation aids, apart from the R/T in the Spitfire. Compass courses were flown over the jungle-clad Arakan range, and then pinpoints were usually made by map-reading over the Chindwin river and then the Irrawaddy. If there was cloud on the return journey, Rosser normally made a generous time allowance over the hills and then let down over the flat ground beyond, hoping to pick up a visual pinpoint.

Unlike the Spitfire PR IV, the Hurricanes IIA and IIB were not designed as long-range reconnaissance aircraft. They were fighters with the guns removed, an assortment of tanks in the wings and no heating. The pilot usually supervised the complex business of filling the tanks, while squatting on a metal wing which was blazing hot. Then he donned a heavy sweater, woollen socks, fleece-lined boots, overalls and gloves. Soaked with sweat, he ascended into the bitter cold of high altitude in order to fly above Japanese fighters and anti-aircraft fire.

While the RAF was carrying out its sorties, the British Army built up its forces and in December 1942 began a gradual thrust down the Arakan with the intention of recapturing Akyab. Tactical photographic support for the ground forces was carried out by Lysanders of 20 Squadron and Hurricanes of 28 Squadron. The objective of taking Akyab was not achieved on this occasion, since the landing craft were not available, but the assault demonstrated the importance of close collaboration with the RAF, both in terms of tactical reconnaissance and supply from the air.

On 25 January 1943 No 3 Photographic Reconnaissance Unit was renumbered 681 Squadron, in common with the policy of giving squadron numbers to all such units. In the same month Squadron Leader Craig was sent to Ceylon to work on camera installations for the B–24 Liberators of 160 Squadron, which by the following May began to supplement the work of 681 Squadron by covering the Andaman Islands, southern Malaya and northern Sumatra.

Early in February, General Wingate began his famous Chindit operations behind the Chindwin river to disrupt Japanese communications, and in the following month was supported by some of the Hurricanes of 28 Squadron and 1 (India) Squadron in the tactical reconnaissance role, the aircraft being fitted with long-range tanks.

By May, only two B–25C Mitchells remained with 681 Squadron, through unserviceability and the loss of aircraft on an operation on 13 February. Help was requested from the US Tenth Air Force in India, and two aircraft were converted and collected by pilots of 681 Squadron in June.

A major hazard in these PR operations was the weather, especially in the monsoon period when close-set pillars of cumulo-nimbus cloud towered from a few feet above the ground to 40,000 feet or more, the tops giving the appearance of boiling steam. On 8 June 1943 Warrant Officer F.D.C. Brown in a Spitfire of 681 Squadron was faced with a wall of these clouds when returning to Chittagong from a sortie. He had insufficient fuel to fly round it and dived straight ahead. His Spitfire went into a spin and he pushed the stick forward and then blacked out. When he came to, he was falling through the air with bits of his aircraft fluttering around him while the main part of the fuselage, minus the engine, wings and tail, was falling several hundred feet below. He pulled his parachute ripcord and landed in a paddy field in the mouth of the Ganges river, where he was dragged along the ground by the strong wind. Some Bengali villagers found him and took him on a twenty-hour journey by sampan and bullock cart to safety, where he eventually recovered from his injuries.

Following the reduction in 681 Squadron's capacity to carry out very long-range reconnaissance, it was decided to supply the squadron with Mosquitos. Two PR IVs arrived on 9 August 1943 and others followed, including Mosquito PR IXs. In addition, two more B–25 Mitchells were supplied by the USAAF in the same month. The operational capacity of the squadron was thus greatly extended, but losses continued. The fates of those who failed to return were not usually known in the squadron, although one Spitfire pilot was led out of Japanese-occupied territory by friendly Burmese. Another Spitfire pilot who was captured by the Japanese is known to have been hideously tortured to death, and it is possible that the same fate befell others.

On 29 September 1943 all the twin-engined aircraft in 681 Squadron were transferred to the newly created 684 Squadron, also based at Dum-Dum and commanded by Squadron Leader Basil S. Jones. In the following December, with the improvement in the weather, both squadrons moved east over the Brahmaputra River, 684 Squadron to Comilla and 681 Squadron to its satellite Chandina. The photographic section was set up near a dirt road, where dust proved a major problem when drying the negatives, but good results were still achieved. At the same time there was another administrative change with the creation of No 171 Photographic Reconnaissance Wing, controlling both squadrons. Wing Commander Wise was given command of the new Wing while Squadron Leader Paul Lamboit, who had arrived in 681 Squadron the previous summer, became the Photographic Officer. Squadron Leader Freddie D. Procter, one of the two pilots who had flown the Hurricanes in Burma, took over command of 681 Squadron. The strength of the single-engined aircraft in this squadron had been augmented by the arrival of Spitfire PR XIs to supplement the Spitfire PR IVs and the Hurricane IIBs, although losses continued in both squadrons, which were flying intensively on operations.

The arrival of the Mosquitos enabled 684 Squadron to increase the range of its sorties. On 15 December Squadron Leader Jones covered the distant target of Bangkok for the first time, a feat for which he and his navigator were awarded immediate DFCs. Jones left the squadron in the same month and his place was taken by Wing Commander W.B. Murray. In early 1944 Mosquito PR XVIs began to arrive and, with their pressurised cabins, improved further the

Above, left: Squadron Leader Jack E. Archbald was one of the first professional photographers to join the RAFVR after the outbreak of the Second World War. He was posted to No 2 Camouflage Unit (later the Photographic Development Unit and then No 1 Photographic Reconnaissance Unit) at RAF Heston. Later in 1940 he joined Bomber Command, where he was employed training aircrews on photographic procedures. He was posted to South East Asia Command in 1944, where he was employed for a while as Deputy Command Photographic Officer for the Near and the Far East. (Mrs Ann Archbald) *Above, right:* Leading Aircraftman Alan Fox DFM, holding an F24 camera, at Dum-Dum airfield in Bengal in 1944. (A. Fox DFM, RAFVR)

A Consolidated Liberator III of 354 Squadron, based at Cuttack in India during 1944. These 'very long range' aircraft were fitted with extra fuel tanks and employed on general reconnaissance and photographic work, but they also attacked shipping off Burma and carried out anti-submarine patrols. (Wing Commander G.J. Craig RAFVR)

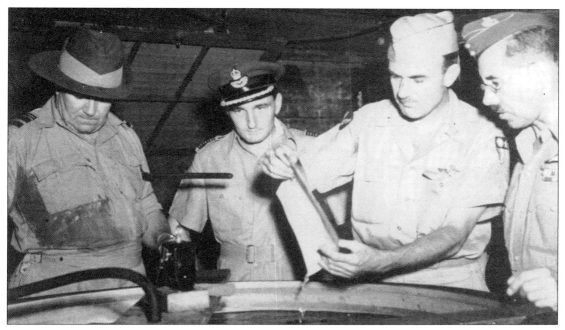

The USAAF Photographic Section at Bally in India, photographed in 1944. Left to right: Air Vice-Marshal T.M. Williams (Assistant to the Air Officer of Eastern Air Command), Group Captain S.G. Wise (Officer Commanding Photographic Reconnaissance Wing), Colonel Milton Kaye (Officer Commanding USAAF Photographic Wing), Air Vice-Marshal R.V. Goddard (on visit from the UK). (Wing Commander G.J. Craig RAFVR)

Commanders of the Eastern Air Command, photographed in May 1944. Left to right: Group Captain S.G. 'Bill' Wise (commanding 171 Photographic Force), Air Marshal Sir Richard Peirse (Allied Air C-in-C), Major-General George E. Stratemeyer, USAAF (Second-in-Command to Sir Richard). (Wing Commander G.J. Craig RAFVR)

A Spitfire PR XI of 681 Squadron, with M. 'Bluey' George of the RAAF in the cockpit, possibly photographed at Dum-Dum. George began flying with the squadron as a flight sergeant and was commissioned by early 1945. The cameras were F8s, used by the RAF in the 1930s for high-altitude photography. These had been withdrawn generally with the introduction of the F52 camera, but several were purchased from the Indian Government for use over Burma. (The Medmenham Club)

effectiveness of the twin-engined aircraft in the squadron. With the approach of the monsoon season in January 1944, the two photo-reconnaissance squadrons returned to Dum-Dum.

The Allies planned advances into Burma in early 1944, the British and Indian 14th Army from the west, the Chinese and Americans from the north, while Wingate's Chindits penetrated behind Japanese lines and harassed their lines of communications. Survey photography of Burma began, so that accurate maps could be constructed for these advances. Yet another administrative change took place in February 1944, when No 171 Photographic Reconnaissance Wing was renamed No 171 Photographic Reconnaissance Force and incorporated into Eastern Air Command. In turn, this was part of Air Command, South-East Asia, which was formed by the amalgamation of the RAF in the area with the US Tenth Air Force. The US 8th Photo-Reconnaissance Group joined this Force, consisting of three squadrons equipped with Lockheed F–5s, P–40 Warhawks and F–7A Liberators, all initially under the command of Group Captain Wise. However, no arrangements were made for a headquarters organisation at this stage, and the RAF and USAAF continued to operate independently although in collaboration.

As it happened, the Japanese commander decided to attack first, in the Arakan during early February 1944, followed by advances further north at Imphal and Kohima during the following month. But by then the Allies had achieved air superiority with their fighter, bomber and reconnaissance squadrons, and above all with their ability to supply their ground forces from the air. Tactical reconnaissance was carried out by the Hurricanes of 28 Squadron as well as those of 1 and 6 (India) Squadrons. After weeks of fighting, during which their lines of supply were cut by Allied air attacks and many of

their aircraft destroyed, the Japanese were repulsed with heavy losses and forced to retreat. At the same time, their reconnaissance 'Dinahs', which hitherto had been immune from air attack, began to fall victim to Spitfire V fighters which had arrived in India.

Paul Lamboit was posted back to the UK in March 1944 and his place was taken once more by Gordon Craig, who had finished his work of equipping 160 Squadron with cameras. The two RAF reconnaissance squadrons moved to Alipore the following month and operations continued at an intense pace.

By May the survey of the battle area had been completed, amounting to 57 per cent of all Burma, an area about three times the size of England. Among many other matters, this survey enabled photographic interpreters to identify jungle clearings formed by former rice fields, where rats carrying the scourge of scrub typhus fed; these were to be avoided by the Allied troops. Holes in landing strips were also identified, dug by the Japanese with the intention of placing a man with a 500–lb bomb in each of them, ready to blow up landing aircraft in kamikaze fashion.

The Allied ground offensive could not be renewed intensively until the end of the monsoon season in October. During the intervening period a detachment of Mosquitos from 684 Squadron was sent to Yelahanka near Madras to help in aerial surveys of southern India. Another detachment was sent in August to China Bay in Ceylon, where it was joined by the first detachment and both were engaged on a survey of northern Sumatra in preparation for an eventual invasion of that island. These detachments returned to Alipore when the major offensive developed on all fronts in Burma, leaving 160 Squadron to continue reconnaissance from Ceylon.

The Japanese evacuated Rangoon towards the end of April 1945 but the British did not realise this until an RAF pilot read messages written by PoWs on the roof of the gaol: 'BRITISH HERE', 'JAPS GONE'. The inmates had painted these partly to avoid the possibility of being bombed by the RAF. (Squadron Leader J.D. Braithwaite RAFVR)

The PoWs in Rangoon gaol added 'EXTRACT DIGIT' to their roof notices, which was an unmistakably RAF expression. An RAF pilot landed at nearby Mingaladon airfield on 2 May 1945 and walked to meet the senior officer of the gaol, an RAAF wing commander. (Squadron Leader J.D. Braithwaite RAFVR)

The Mitsubishi Ki-46-III, known to the Allies as the 'Dinah', was one of the most successful reconnaissance aircraft employed by the Japanese during the Second World War. On the Burma front, it was able to fly above the ceiling of RAF fighters until the Spitfire arrived in the area. This captured Dinah was evaluated by the Allied Tactical Air Intelligence Unit of the South East Asia Air Command after the Japanese capitulation. (J.M. Bruce/G.S. Leslie Collection)

A Japanese mechanic working on an engine at RAF Mingaladon in Burma, photographed by the author soon after the capitulation. The Japanese worked hard and efficiently for the Allies after they had been ordered to surrender by Emperor Hirohito. (R.C. Nesbit)

Life returning to Hiroshima, photographed in January 1947. This shows the mainstreet with the telephone exchange still standing, although the interior of the building was gutted by the heatwave of the atom bomb dropped on 6 August 1945. (Sergeant J. Muncie RAF (Ret'd))

The rebuilding of the Christian church in Hiroshima, 1947. (Sergeant J. Muncie RAF (Ret'd))

The Allies began their advances in northern Burma, supplied from the air. Wing Commander W.E.M. Lowry took over 684 Squadron in November 1944, but unfortunately the Mosquitos had to be withdrawn in that month since defects in their wooden structure had developed in the steamy tropical climate, caused partly by faulty bonding of glue. With the few remaining Mitchells in the squadron well past their prime, the function of very long-range reconnaissance was thus performed mainly by the USAAF during this period, but the Spitfires of 681 Squadron continued flying.

By 2 January 1945 the Japanese had been forced back from many of their positions in northern Burma, and had also evacuated Akyab. They fought to the death when they could not extricate themselves, including those in the garrison of Ramree Island to the south of Akyab, which was reoccupied in March. In the same month, Mandalay fell to the 14th Army after an intense bombardment from the air, and the way to Rangoon down the Irrawaddy was opened.

The formal structure of No 171 Photographic Reconnaissance Force was finally resolved on 9 January with the appointment of Colonel Milton W. Kaye of the USAAF as commander, with Group Captain Bill Wise as his deputy while retaining command of the RAF's squadrons. By then, four American squadrons were engaged on photo-reconnaissance. The Warhawks of one of these squadrons had been replaced with North American P–51C Mustangs, modified with cameras as F–6C Mustangs, and these were engaged mainly on support for the Chinese and American forces advancing from the north.

The Mosquitos of 684 Squadron came back up to strength by the end of February. From advanced bases, the whole of Burma could be covered by both RAF reconnaissance squadrons, while the Mosquitos could also cover the north of Siam and Malaya. The remaining B–25C Mitchells were relegated to courier duties, mainly flying between Alipore and Ceylon, where a detachment of the Mosquitos of 684 Squadron was engaged on reconnaissance of the Nicobar Islands, southern Malaya and northern Sumatra. In the same month, the Spitfires of 681 Squadron flew intensively over southern Burma from advanced bases. There was a change of command when Squadron Leader D.B. Pearson, one of the pilots who had flown the reconnaissance Buffalos in Malaya, took over from Wing Commander F.D. Procter. At the end of March, the Hurricane IICs of 7 (India) Squadron joined in tactical reconnaissance for the 14th Army.

A combined assault on Rangoon, code-named Operation 'Dracula', began in early May 1945, but it became clear from aerial photographs that the Japanese had abandoned the capital before the troops landed. Signs on a jail known to contain PoWs which read JAPS GONE and EXTRACT DIGIT were so unmistakably British that Wing Commander A.E. Saunders landed his Mosquito VI of 110 Bomber Squadron at Mingaladon and walked into Rangoon, where he was met by the senior officer of the PoWs.

Following these victories, the Americans and the Chinese departed from this theatre of war to reinforce their armies in China, leaving the forces controlled by the British to finish off the Japanese in Burma. By this time there remained only about 17,500 Japanese troops, in the district of Pegu. These were intent on crossing the Sittang river into Siam but were bombed mercilessly by the RAF and cut down by guerilla forces, leaving only a few starving and ragged remnants. The British began making arrangements to recapture Malaya, in a combined operation code-named Operation 'Zipper'.

Meanwhile No 171 Photographic Reconnaissance Force was disbanded. Group Captain Wise departed for the UK and the two RAF squadrons then came under No 347 Photographic Wing. This was commanded by Group Captain C.E. St J. Beamish, who had previously commanded RAF Benson. The first Mosquito PR 34s arrived in 684 Squadron during July 1945 and were detached to the Cocos Islands, where a new airfield had been built to give access to southern Malaya and Sumatra. One of the achievements of this long-distance reconnaissance squadron was the identification of the PoW camps where the inmates were living in appalling conditions of brutality. In August 681 Squadron received Spitfire PR XIXs, so that at last the two squadrons were equipped with the most advanced reconnaissance aircraft in existence. But the end of the war came when the Japanese surrendered unconditionally on 14 August 1945, after the atomic bombs had been dropped on Hiroshima and Nagasaki.

CHAPTER THIRTEEN

BEHIND THE IRON CURTAIN

When the Americans in the Allied Central Interpretation Unit (ACIU) returned home with the US Eighth and Ninth Air Forces in August 1945, the unit lost the 'Allied' part of its title and was placed under the control of the newly created Central Photographic Establishment, part of Coastal Command, while 106 Group was disbanded. In August 1947 the CIU was renamed the Joint Air Photographic Interpretation Centre (UK), known as JAPIC (UK). Of course, by this time many of the staff had been demobilised to resume their civilian careers, and the establishment was rapidly whittled down from about 1,700 during wartime to 350 personnel. The majority of these were based at Nuneham Park, near Oxford, which had been used as an overflow section during the war, leaving only the Model Section and the Print Library at Medmenham. Meanwhile the School of Photography at Farnborough, which had trained 6,510 photographers during the war, with the temporary aid of a second school in Blackpool, moved into improvised quarters at Farnham in Surrey, where it remained until a second move during 1948 to Wellesbourne Mountford in Warwickshire.

Some of the RAF's photo-interpreters had been sent to Paris before the end of the European war, as part of the British Bombing Survey Unit, to assess the damage and disruption caused by Allied bombing. After VE-Day, personnel were also sent to Germany, to collect and record those enemy photographs which had not been destroyed. Those of European Russia were of particular interest, although not considered adequate for updated mapping or accurate knowledge of the military and industrial capacity of that vast country. While there, the RAF team was able to gain further information of the German photo-reconnaissance organisation, which had been partly assessed by British Intelligence during the war.

There is no doubt that the Germans appreciated the value of photo-reconnaissance before the war, perhaps to a greater extent than the RAF and British Intelligence. However, the service was designed to conform with the structure of the Luftwaffe, being split among the various Luftflotten (Air Forces) which supported the Armies on the various fronts, with specialised squadrons and mobile field photographic units, somewhat on the lines of the RAF's Reconnaissance Wings which formed part of the Second Tactical Air Force. Thus the work was concentrated on tactical reconnaissance, and light aircraft such as the Henschel 126 and the Focke Wulf 189 produced good results in the early years of the war, during the period when German Armies conquered much of Europe under cover of their air superiority.

Each Luftflotte was also equipped with strategic reconnaissance aircraft, such as the Dornier 17–E which could outfly at high altitude any RAF fighter aircraft at the beginning of the war. However, no competent

The Spitfire PR XIX was the last of the photo-reconnaissance versions of this famous aircraft, replacing the Spitfire PR XI soon after the war. The main production aircraft was powered by a Rolls-Royce Griffon 66 engine and fitted with wing tanks with a capacity of 172 gallons. It was unarmed and employed mainly for strategic work at high altitude. The last operational flight made by any Spitfire was in one of these machines over Malaya on 1 April 1954. This photograph is of serial PM631. (The late Squadron Leader J.E. Archbald)

Fitting an F24 camera in the oblique position of a Spitfire. (*Aeroplane Monthly*)

A Mosquito PR XVI, serial RG116, in post-war markings. A very long-range version of this mark of Mosquito, known as the PR 34, carried 200-gallon drop-tanks under each wing as well as extra tanks in the bomb bay, giving a range of about 2,500 miles (*Aeroplane Monthly*)

organisation such as the Central Interpretation Unit at Medmenham was ever set up in Germany to assess the photographic results. Although a department in the German Air Ministry, known as Air Photos of the Air Inspectorate for Reconnaissance, was formed in 1942, it was given a very low priority and indeed the majority of the photo-interpreters remained NCOs and their work was seldom used for the systematic gathering of intelligence or for high-level military decisions.

In addition, the equivalents of the unarmed and high-performance photo-reconnaissance Spitfire and Mosquito were not developed in Germany. The German cameras were of excellent quality but were too heavy for very high-altitude work, and the aircraft which carried them were eventually outclassed by the new Allied fighters. In short, German strategic reconnaissance and photo-interpretation became little short of disastrous, and the words of General Werner Freiherr von Fritsch, who had said in 1938 'The military organization which has the best photographic intelligence will win the next war', were proved correct.

Even before the war in Europe came to an end, the RAF's strategic photo-reconnaissance squadrons began some peaceful operations. On 21 March 1945 the Secretary of State for Air announced that they would undertake aerial survey work on behalf of Government departments and the Colonial Office. Eight days after this announcement, the Mosquitos of 540 Squadron moved from Benson to Coulommiers, east of Paris, to begin a survey of France. This task was completed by the following November, when the squadron moved back to Benson and began work in Britain on behalf of Ordnance Survey, in order to help update maps. The F49 survey camera had been developed for this work, which was also aided by new equipment such as the Decca Navigator, which provided an accurate position from radio beams.

The survey of Britain produced some unexpected benefits to such experts as the archaeological officer of Ordnance Survey, the former RFC air observer Osbert G.S. Crawford, since the photographs sometimes showed outlines of ancient settlements which were indistinguishable from the ground. Dr Glyn Daniels, a former photo-interpreter at Medmenham who became a well-known TV personality, wrote 'The interpretation of air photographs and visual air reconnaissance has become one of the major instruments of archaeological research'. This survey work was continued for several years, 540 Squadron being renumbered 58 Squadron on 30 September 1946 when it was equipped with the latest Mosquito PR 34 as well as the Anson C19, a version of the venerable aircraft which was particularly suitable for medium-altitude photography.

Requests for overseas surveys proved overwhelming, to the surprise of the Secretary of State for Air. No 541 Squadron was reorganised, with A Flight operating Spitfire PR XIXs while B Flight received Lancasters converted for survey work as PR 1s. In March 1946 the Lancasters were sent to Takoradi for a survey of the Gold Coast, but on their return the following September the squadron was disbanded, B Flight becoming 82 Squadron. These Lancasters were then detached to West Africa and Kenya, in order to carry out further surveys, the tasks not being completed until October 1952.

The other RAF photo-reconnaissance squadrons in Britain did not last long after the war. The strategic 542 Squadron was disbanded on 27 August 1945, followed by 544 Squadron on 13 October 1945. Drastic reductions also took place within the RAF based in Germany. On 14 July 1945 the Second Tactical Air Force was renamed the British Air Force of Occupation (BAFO) and rapidly reduced in strength. By the end of 1947 it had been reduced to ten squadrons,

The destruction of the buildings around Cologne Cathedral, with the Rhine in the top left. This city was the target of the RAF's first 1,000 bomber raid, on 30 May 1942. (Corporal L. Jewitt RAF (Ret'd))

The city of Wiesbaden, with the Rhine bottom left, showing pedestrians and motor vehicles. Some of the buildings seem to have escaped the effect of Allied bombing, although many others are gutted. (Corporal L. Jewitt RAF (Ret'd))

with only 2 Squadron, by then equipped with Spitfire PR XIXs, engaged on tactical photo-reconnaissance work.

Events were to demonstrate that these reductions were unwise, for the uneasy wartime alliance between the Western Allies and the Soviet Union soon deteriorated into hostility. Winston Churchill, who had lost the British election at the end of the war, stated during a speech at Fulton in the USA on 5 March 1946 'From Stettin on the Baltic to Trieste on the Adriatic an Iron Curtain has descended across the Continent'. On the eastern side of this physical barrier, the Soviet Union and the countries dominated by it faced the Anglo-Americans.

One effect of this hostility was the re-formation of two strategic photo-reconnaissance squadrons at Benson, No 541 with Spitfire PR XIXs on 1 November 1947 and No 540 with Mosquito PR 34s exactly a month later. Any hopes that a peaceful co-existence might be resumed were shattered when, on 24 June 1948, the Soviet Union refused to allow further communication by land between West Germany and the sectors of Berlin controlled by the Western Powers, in spite of an international agreement. The result was the Berlin Airlift, carried out by the Americans and the British until September 1949, four months after the Russians lifted their blockade. American squadrons also returned to Britain in 1948 as part of the United States Air Force (USAF), an independent body which had been created on 18 September 1947 on terms of equality with the US Army and Navy.

The appalling threat of nuclear warfare prompted the West into further rearmament. The North Atlantic Treaty Organisation (Nato), consisting initially of the USA, Canada, Britain and nine other European countries, came into effect on 24 August 1949. A formidable bloc was thus formed against Soviet Russia and within this the RAF

was built up again, in spite of the impoverished state of the British post-war economy. It was known that Russian scientists had developed a nuclear bomb in that year and had thus broken the monopoly held by America. The Western powers feared that such terrible weapons might be delivered either by long-distance Russian bombers or as warheads of missiles.

On 1 March 1950 a further reorganisation took place in the RAF, when the Central Photographic Establishment of Coastal Command was disbanded and the photo-reconnaissance squadrons, together with JAPIC (UK), were transferred to No 3 Group of Bomber Command. By then the photo-reconnaissance activities of the RAF were linked with those of the USAF, and in particular its Strategic Air Command. In December of the same year a major conference was held at RAF Benson to discuss the objectives to be attained. This was attended by numerous representatives of the Air Ministry, Bomber Command, the Admiralty, the War Office, the USAF, the RCAF, the US Navy, BAFO, JAPIC, the School of Photography and officers of the various photo-reconnaissance squadrons. It was stated that the primary tasks were to provide photographic evidence of the ability of Soviet long-range aircraft to mount attacks against the UK, the ability of Soviet submarines to attack sea communications, and any movements of Russian troops westwards through Europe. The other tasks were to provide cover of the internal and industrial capacity of the Soviet Union, to carry out general surveys to correct out-of-date maps, as well as reconnaissance for damage assessment and the production of target maps.

There was another aerial reconnaissance objective which was discussed at this conference and which began to assume prime importance. It had become necessary to assess

The Lancaster PR 1 was a version of the famous bomber, with the turrets faired over, employed after the war on photo-reconnaissance duties. During the period it was equipped with this aircraft, from October 1946 to December 1953, 82 Squadron carried out photographic surveys of Nigeria, the Gold Coast, Sierra Leone, the Gambia and Kenya, parts of which were not mapped at the time. Other Lancaster PR 1s were employed by 683 Squadron from November 1950 to November 1953 over Arabia and Africa. This Lancaster PR 1 serial TW904 of 82 Squadron was photographed over a Kenyan game reserve in 1949. (C.F. Scandrett via Flight Lieutenant A.S. Thomas)

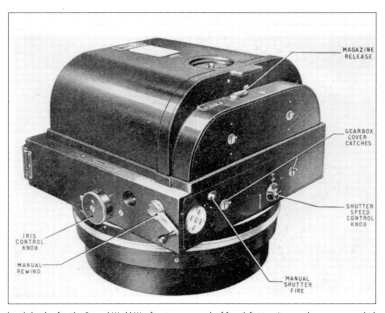

The F49 camera was introduced shortly after the Second World War for air survey work of fine definition. It was a heavy camera which, when loaded with a film and fitted with a 20-inch lens, weighed nearly 87 lb. The Mark I and Mark III had shutter speeds between 1/150th and 1/200th of a second, and the magazine held 200 exposures of 9-inch by 9-inch. The camera could be operated electrically or manually. (Flight Lieutenant G.H. Parry RAF (Ret'd))

The Gloster Meteor FR 9 was introduced into RAF service with 2 Squadron in Germany during December 1950, replacing the Spitfire PR XIX for tactical photo-reconnaissance. It was armed with four 20-mm cannons and employed mainly on low-level work, with a nose camera mounted either obliquely or straight ahead. These machines also served in the Middle East. This photograph of Meteor FR 9 serial VZ602 of 226 Operational Conversion Unit was taken in 1951. (Flight Lieutenant A.S. Thomas RAF)

The Gloster Meteor PR 10 first entered RAF service with 541 Squadron in January 1951. It was unarmed and mounted vertical cameras as well as a nose camera, replacing the Spitfire PR 19 for strategic reconnaissance at high altitudes. This photograph of Meteor PR 10 serial WB!65 of 81 Squadron was taken on 17 December 1959, when the squadron was based at Tengah in Singapore. (Flight Lieutenant A.S. Thomas RAF)

Fitting an F24 camera into the nose of a Gloster Meteor FR 9. (*Aeroplane Monthly*)

This North American RB-45C was a test-bed machine with an engine bolted underneath the fuselage. It was a photo-reconnaissance version of the four-jet bomber and first flew in April 1950. The nose was adapted for a ciné or an oblique camera, and there was provision for up to ten cameras in all. It was unarmed and could carry a crew of up to five. The maximum speed was 370 mph, the ceiling 37,550 feet and the range 3,450 feet with in-flight refuelling. (*Aeroplane Monthly*)

RAF aircrew, dressed in tropical kit, in front of a North American RB-45C Tornado photo-reconnaissance aircraft, during training in the USA. (P. Lashmar)

any development of radar defences in the Soviet Union, which had been inadequate during the war, so as to provide American and British scientists with information necessary to develop RCM (radio counter-measures), or jamming equipment. This type of work, known as electronic intelligence or 'Elint', had been carried out by the RAF's 100 Group during the war, employing trained radar operators in specialised aircraft fitted up for this purpose. In April 1946, 90 (Signals) Group was formed to take over this work. Aircraft named 'ferrets', equipped with electronic search equipment, cruised the borders of the Soviet Union. They occasionally made passes as though they intended to intrude and thus activated the Russian radar defences, for assessment. This procedure could be highly dangerous if MiG fighters were in the vicinity and the Russian pilots were not too worried about crossing their borders. By 1952 only one squadron of the RAF was engaged on this work, 192 Squadron equipped with Boeing B-29A Washingtons and based at Watton in Norfolk.

To accomplish the photographic objectives, reconnaissance aircraft would need to continue infringing Soviet airspace, and both the USA and Britain were prepared to contravene international law in order to acquire intelligence considered essential for the defence of their countries. From the beginning of 1951 such penetrations were carried out far more intensively. Details of the RAF operations have not yet been released in Britain, but both the USA and Russia have been more forthcoming. Some information has appeared in books published in America and Britain, and a television programme on the subject was shown by BBC TV 'Timewatch' on 16 February 1994.

From the end of the war some British and American photo-reconnaissance aircraft, including Mosquitos from Benson, had

'inadvertently' crossed the Iron Curtain as a result of 'navigation errors'. These aircraft suffered their first casualty on 8 April 1950 when a Consolidated PB4Y-2 Privateer (a version of the famous Liberator) of the US Navy was shot down over Latvia by a Lovochkin LA-11 fighter, resulting in the deaths of all ten crew members. This was the first of a series of losses. However, President Harry S. Truman authorised the establishment of US spy-plane units in England. Among these were the 72nd Strategic Reconnaissance Squadron, equipped with Boeing RB-50 Superfortresses, and a detachment of the 91st Strategic Reconnaissance Group, equipped with North American RB-45C Tornados.

The Tornados were based at RAF Sculthorpe in Norfolk. This American aircraft, powered by four turbo-jet engines, possessed considerable advantages over the RAF's piston-engined Mosquito PR 34. The maximum speed of the Tornado was 570 mph compared with the 425 mph of the Mosquito. There was provision for ten cameras and a crew of up to five, while the Mosquito usually carried three cameras and a crew of two. At 37,550 feet, the ceiling of the Tornado was about 1,500 feet higher than that of the Mosquito, almost beyond the reach of Russian fighters and over the limit of Russian flak. Moreover, the Tornado was equipped with facilities for radar photography, using the technique of photographing H_2S (H_2X in American aircraft) developed by Squadron Leader Howard Lees of the Pathfinder Force during the war, whereas the smaller and cramped Mosquito did not normally carry this instrument. Although 2 Squadron had received the RAF's first jet reconnaissance aircraft in December 1950, in the form of the Gloster Meteor FR 9, this single-seat aircraft had a range of 1,400 miles and could be used only for tactical work. It was employed in

This prototype English Electric Canberra PR 3, serial VX181, first flew on 19 March 1950. It was adapted from the Canberra B2 light bomber as a replacement for the Mosquito PR 34. The first squadron to be equipped with these machines was 540 Squadron, in December 1952. (*Aeroplane Monthly*)

Senior Aircraftman Colin Saunders (left) and Senior Aircraftman Herbert Hinman about to fit an F52 camera with a 36-inch lens in a Canberra, in March 1955. (*Aeroplane Monthly*)

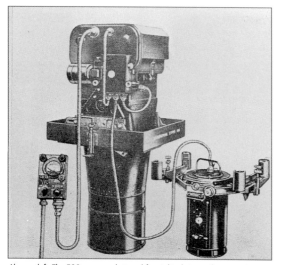

Above, left: The F89 camera, designed for night photography, came into use soon after the Second World War. The Mark 2 (shown here) operated electrically, with a moving film which gave 165 exposures of 7-inches by 8½-inches. Lenses were 20-inch and 36-inch. *Above, right*: The F97 camera was developed after the Second World War for night photography at levels between 500 feet and 3,000 feet and at speeds between 300 knots and 600 knots, using photo-flash cartridges. The camera contained two 5-inch lenses which operated alternately, and it carried a moving film which gave 480 overlapping exposures of 5-inch by 4½-inch. (Both photos: Flight Lieutenant G.H. Parry RAF (Ret'd))

The F95 camera was developed for oblique photography in daylight, at low level and high speed, and was usually mounted on a pod beneath the aircraft. The lenses were 4-inch or 12-inch while the shutter speeds were 1/1,000th of a second at four pictures a second or 1/2,000th of a second at eight pictures a second. The picture size was 2¼-inch by 2¼-inch while the film magazine of the Mark 2 (shown here) gave 500 exposures. (Flight Lieutenant G.H. Parry RAF (Ret'd))

The F96 camera was designed for day reconnaissance at high altitude. The picture size was 9-inch by 9-inch and the film in the magazine ranged from 250 feet to 1,000 feet. Shutter speeds of the Mark 1 were 1/125th, 1/250th of a second, while the lenses ranged from 6-inch to 48-inch telephoto. The camera was the largest employed by the RAF, as can be seen from this example with a 48-inch lens and young WRAF servicewoman 5 feet 3 inches in height. (Sergeant D. Jenkins RAF (Ret'd), courtesy RAF Cosford Museum)

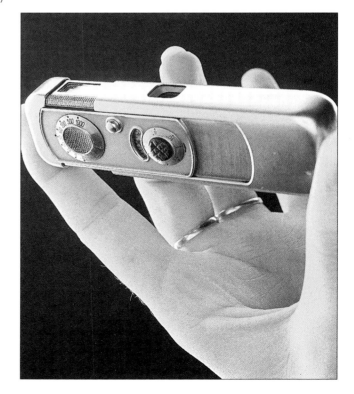

One of the smallest cameras was the ultra-miniature Minox, well-loved by makers of spy movies. It had a lens with a focal length of 15 mm and used a film with a width of 9.5 mm, giving a picture size of 11 mm by 8 mm. (Sergeant D. Jenkins RAF (Ret'd), courtesy RAF Cosford Museum)

Germany where, in September 1951, BAFO had resumed the title of Second Tactical Air Force, to emphasise that the RAF would soon serve alongside that country as an ally instead of as part of an occupying power.

At this stage in early 1951, President Truman had banned further USAF flights over the Soviet Union as too provocative, especially when his country was embroiled in the Korean War. Thus it seemed that the RAF would need to undertake the special photographic tasks with the USAF Tornado. The Strategic Air Command of the USAF approached the Joint Chiefs of Staff of Nato for permission, and agreement was reached with Clement Attlee. This was endorsed by Winston Churchill when he resumed the Premiership in October 1951. A special RAF unit was formed at Sculthorpe by the Vice Chief of Air Staff, Sir Ralph Cochrane, under the command of Squadron Leader H.B. 'Mickey' Martin, one of the pilots who had flown on the famous Dam Buster raid of 1943. When it was found that Martin was medically unfit to fly at such high altitudes, command was passed to Squadron Leader John Crampton of 101 Squadron, who was already experienced with jets, his squadron having been the first to receive the new English Electric Canberra bomber in May 1951.

The first RAF crews went to America in September 1951, where they trained at the Air Force bases of Langley, Barksdale and Lockbourne, gaining experience of flying the Tornado as well as knowledge of the targets required by the Strategic Air Force of the USAF. They returned to Sculthorpe in December 1951 and continued training for a while, flying with crews of three – pilot, co-pilot, and navigator/radar operator. The first mission took place on 21 March 1952, when a single aircraft flew up and down the Berlin air corridor at high speed and maximum altitude, to test the reaction of the Russians. The next operational flights took place on 17 April 1952 when three Tornados, with USAF insignia removed and replaced with RAF roundels, refuelled from Boeing KC-29 tankers and then penetrated Russian air space. One flew to Murmansk, another to the environs south of Moscow, and the third through central Russia. All returned safely with radar photographs of key targets, in spite of flak, and were refuelled over Western Germany on the way out. The success of the missions delighted General Curtis LeMay, who commanded the USAF.

The RAF crews than returned to their normal units and, although other missions were planned, nothing took place until 24 April 1954 when three Tornados were again employed. One flew north of Moscow, another south of Moscow, and the other through central Russia as far as the Ukraine. Once again, all returned safely. Unknown to the crews, the Russian MiG pilots, who had no radar equipment at this stage, had been ordered to ram the intruders, somewhat in the fashion of the Japanese kamikaze pilots but not head-on so as to give them the chance of baling out. However, the Russian pilots were unable to find the reconnaissance aircraft in the dark.

On 8 May 1954, another mission took place when a Boeing RB-47 Stratojet of the USAF took off from Fairford in Gloucestershire, without the authority of the US President, and penetrated Soviet airspace south of Murmansk, photographing airfields. It was attacked by several MiG-15s but these were unable to maintain altitude and the turbo-jet bomber returned safely. Tornados carried out other missions in 1954, without loss. For instance, a flight with RAF crews flew over Moscow on 29 April. However, by then there had been further major developments.

Britain had exploded its first atomic bomb, in Australia on 3 October 1952. The Americans had exploded a hydrogen bomb in the Pacific the following month. This was

The Canberra PR 7 followed the Canberra PR 3 in May 1954, with engines of 7,500 lb thrust compared with the 6,500 lb thrust of its predecessor. The camera ports can be seen in this photograph of serial WJ819. (*Aeroplane Monthly*)

One of the first Canberra PR 9s received by 58 Squadron at RAF Wyton in 1960, undergoing pre-flight checks. The navigator, Flight Lieutenant Peter Thompson, is checking his equipment in the nose. The pilot, Flight Lieutenant Fred Hoskins, is standing on the ladder while a fitter is checking his ejector seat. (Short Bros & Harland)

The Canberra PR 9 began to succeed the PR 7 in January 1960, with engines of 11,250-lb thrust instead of the 7,500-lb thrust of the PR 7. These PR 9s of 59 Squadron were lined up at RAF Wyton, with the two nearest visible as serials XH164 and XH136. (Short Bros & Harland)

followed by a report of the explosion of a hydrogen bomb by the Russians in August 1953. The prospect of nuclear war seemed to be looming even larger. It was known that Russia had been experimenting with nuclear bombs in Novaya Zemlya inside the Arctic Circle, but the US Central Intelligence Agency had received information of long-range missile testing at Kapustin Yar, east of Stalingrad, and photographic cover of the site was urgently required. However, Dwight D. Eisenhower, who had been sworn in as President of the USA on 20 January 1953, also refused permission for overflights by the USAF.

By the end of 1954, ten US aircraft of various types had been shot down around the borders of the Soviet Union on ferret missions. An RAF aircraft had also been lost, an Avro Lincoln serial RF531 from the Central Gunnery School at Leconfield in Yorkshire, shot down on 12 March 1953 by MiG fighters near Lüneburg. In this instance, the aircraft seems to have strayed over the border by accident, when on a training flight. There were no survivors from the crew of seven, five of whom fell in the Russian zone, their bodies being returned later.

At this time, photo-reconnaissance versions of the Canberra had been developed. The first was the Canberra PR 3, which entered service with 540 Squadron in December 1952. It was followed by the Canberra PR 7, which first went to 542 Squadron at Wyton in Cambridgeshire, where the former Spitfire squadron re-formed on 17 May 1954. The range of this machine was no better than the Tornado but it possessed the great advantage of a maximum speed of about 600 mph and an altitude of over 50,000 feet. It could thus fly above the ceiling of Russian fighters and flak as well as above the levels at which condensation trails might form and give away its position. With a crew of two, pilot and navigator/ radar operator, it could carry up to

six F52 cameras for daylight work. Alternatively, it could be fitted with two F97 cameras for night photography at low level, or two F89 cameras for night photography at high level, or two F95 cameras for daylight oblique photography at low level, or one F49 camera for survey work. Although it was not normally equipped for radar photography, the new Canberra PR 7 was otherwise ideal for reconnaissance over Kapustin Yar.

One of these machines was especially adapted but details of its flights have never been released, although they are reported to have been approved by Winston Churchill. They were code-named Operation 'Robin' and the Canberra is believed to have borne the serial WH726 and to have been fitted with a 100-inch camera specially made in America. It flew from Giebelstadt in the eastern part of West Germany on daylight operations over the Soviet Union and landed in Iran. A MiG pilot who was ordered to intercept one of these flights, Mikhail Shulga, described on the BBC TV programme how he managed to climb to 48,500 feet and could see a Canberra shining in the sunlight, several thousand feet above. His efforts to reach it became fruitless when the MiG stalled several times. The Canberra always completed its missions successfully. The Russians were understandably furious at these incursions but could not protest too vociferously since they did not wish to confess to the world the inadequacy of their defences.

In May 1955 the military alliance of the Warsaw Pact was formed, consisting of the communist countries of East Europe under the leadership of the Soviet Union, in response to the formation of Nato. Aware of Anglo-American superiority with reconnaissance aircraft but at the same time anxious to reduce international tension, President Eisenhower proposed at a summit meeting in Geneva on 19 July 1955 an 'Open Skies' policy in which both sides would have the right to reconnoitre the other's territory. But Nikita Khrushchev, the leader of the Soviet Union, turned down the proposal, probably since his aircraft could not match the performance of the Americans and the British. Instead, the Russians accelerated development of surface-to-air missiles and brought out fighters with better performance, such as the near-supersonic MiG-17 (Nato code-name Fresco). At a Red Air Force Day display of 24 June 1956, Khrushchev was able to warn General Twining of the USAF that any Canberras which entered Russian airspace in the future were 'flying coffins' and would be shot down.

By this time, however, the Americans had developed a most unusual aircraft which was capable of flying even higher than the Canberra. This was the Lockheed U-2A, a single-engined aircraft with an enormous wingspan. It cruised rather slowly, at about 250 mph, and its range was about 2,200 miles, but it was capable of flying at over 72,000 feet. It was fitted with electronic sensors and a panoramic strip camera named the Hycon-B, which weighed about 500 lb and contained a special lens system. This system, when used with a film of high resolution, gave 60 line pairs per millimetre, about five times that of the cameras used in the Second World War. A special thin film was developed by Eastman Kodak which enabled the camera to carry over 10,000 feet.

The U-2A could cover a wide photographic swathe across the Soviet Union. It was financed by the Central Intelligence Agency and thus its development was conveniently independent of the USAF. The unit was given the cover title of the 1st Weather Reconnaissance Squadron, Provisional (WRSP-1) and the first machines were airlifted to the US airfield at Lakenheath in Suffolk, where they were reassembled and test-flown. Permission to operate from Britain was withdrawn, however, and the first flight over the Soviet Union took place from Wiesbaden in Germany on 4 July 1956, sanctioned by the US President and supported by the German Chancellor, Dr Konrad Adenauer.

The results of these flights showed that the 'bomber gap' – a belief that bombers of the Soviet Air Force were far more numerous than those of the Strategic Air Force – did not exist. However, they did show that the Russians had made considerable progress in developing strategic missiles, which caused the Americans to divert part of their programme away from their bomber force and on to 'Minuteman' inter-continental ballistic missiles.

The confidence of the Western Allies in their technical superiority suffered a severe shock when the Russian launched their 'Sputnik 1' satellite into orbit in October 1957, thus narrowly beating the United States in the race to develop this new form of reconnaissance. Nevertheless, overflights by U-2s continued. American records show that six RAF pilots also qualified in this machine from June 1958 onwards, at Laughlin Air Force Base in Texas, while another was killed in training. Two RAF navigators and a flight surgeon were also trained in the programme. Operations took place from January 1959 from Incirlik in Turkey, the RAF men being given the cover of employees of the Meteorological Office. Although precise details have not yet been released, it is probable that about eighteen U-2 flights took place over Russia, while others took place over Egypt, Syria and Israel. It would be naive to believe that the RAF pilots did not carry out some of these missions and instead devoted their efforts to sampling the air in the upper atmosphere.

The U-2 flights over Russia came to an abrupt end on 1 May 1960 when a SA-2 surface-to-air missile exploded near one of the machines at an altitude of 68,000 feet

The Supermarine Swift FR 5 was the fighter-reconnaissance version of the earlier Swift interceptors, first entering RAF service in February 1956. The nose was lengthened to include three cameras but it retained its armament of two 30 mm Aden guns. It equipped only two RAF squadrons, being employed on low-level tactical work over Germany. Like its predecessors, it suffered from a high accident rate, but remained in service until March 1961. This photograph is of serial XD904. (*Aeroplane Monthly*)

The Hawker Hunter FR 10, based on the Hunter F6 interceptor, entered RAF service in March 1961 as a replacement for the Meteor FR 9 and the Swift FR 5. In addition to its armament of four 30 mm Aden guns, it carried three cameras in the nose. This Hunter FR 10 serial XF460 of 8 Squadron was photographed in 1969. These machines continued in active service until March 1971. (Flight Lieutenant A.S. Thomas RAF)

The Lockheed U-2A reconnaissance aircraft, painted all-black, first began operations over the Soviet Union on 4 July 1956, under the control of the US Central Intelligence Agency. The U-2R serial 68–10337 shown here was a later version which formed part of the 9th Strategic Reconnaissance Wing of the USAF. (Ex-Warrant Officer 1 (MAD) P.G. Crozier RCT)

The Vickers Valiant was the first of the RAF's 'V' bombers, entering squadron service in February 1955. In July of that year 543 Squadron was equipped with Valiant PR 1s for strategic reconnaissance, machines which continued in service until February 1965. This Valiant PR 1 of 543 Squadron was photographed in 1960, accompanied by a Canberra. (Flight Lieutenant A.S. Thomas RAF)

The Handley Page Victor B/SR2 was a version of the Victor B2 nuclear bomber, adapted for strategic reconnaissance. It entered service with 543 Squadron at Wyton in December 1964 as a replacement for the Vickers Valiant B(PR)1 and continued in this role until May 1974, when the squadron was disbanded. This photograph of serial XH672 of 543 Squadron was taken in 1970. The aircraft was eventually converted into a K2 tanker and transferred to 55 Squadron at Marham. (Flight Lieutenant A.S. Thomas RAF)

Lancaster GR 3s (later designated MR 3s) were employed by Coastal Command after the Second World War on maritime reconnaissance, replacing the lease-lend Liberators which were returned to the USA. They remained in service until Neptunes and Shackletons began to arrive. This photograph of Lancaster GR 3 serial RF307 of 203 Squadron was taken at Gibraltar on 10 March 1947. The RAF's last Lancaster in active service was an MR 3, serial RF325, which was retired on 15 October 1956. (Flight Lieutenant A.S. Thomas RAF)

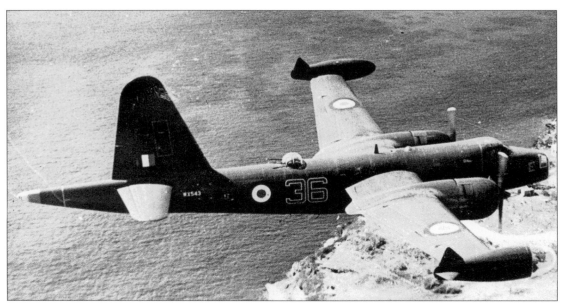

The Lockheed Neptune MR 1 entered RAF service with 217 Squadron in January 1952 as Coastal Command's long-range reconnaissance aircraft and anti-shipping bomber, eventually equipping four squadrons and one special flight. The aircraft was fitted with Magnetic Anomaly Detector (MAD) equipment in the tail, as well as radar and searchlights. All Neptunes were returned to the US Navy by 1957, when they were replaced by the latest versions of Shackletons. This Neptune serial WX543 of 36 Squadron was photographed over Bermuda in 1956. (Flight Lieutenant A.S. Thomas RAF)

The Avro Shackleton began to replace the RAF's long-range maritime reconnaissance aircraft, such as the Liberator and the Fortress, from April 1951 onwards. The MR 1 carried a chin radome but the MR 2, introduced in late 1952, was fitted with a semi-retractable radome behind the wings. The Shackleton, such as the MR 2 of 42 Squadron shown here, gave excellent service although it was known affectionately as '10,000 rivets flying in close formation'. The MR 2 continued in active service until April 1972, by which time some had been converted into Shackleton Advanced Early Warning aircraft. (Squadron Leader I.M. Coleman RAF)

near Sverdlovsk in the Ural Mountains, causing it to spin down out of control. The civilian pilot, Francis Gary Powers, had taken off from Peshawar in Pakistan and was heading for Bödö in Norway. He baled out and was imprisoned, in the glare of much dramatic publicity, although he was later exchanged for a Russian spy. The affair was a serious embarrassment to the Americans but soon afterwards, in August 1960, the first successful recovery of a capsule from the country's satellite 'Discoverer' took place, adding a new dimension to the watch over the Soviet Union.

During the period of the U-2 overflights, the RAF's photo-reconnaissance squadrons in England were whittled down once again. At Wyton, 542 Squadron had already been disbanded in October 1955, although it was re-formed a month later and a detachment of its Canberra PR 7s sent to Australia during Britain's nuclear tests. Also at Wyton, 540 Squadron with Canberra PR 7s was disbanded in September 1956. No 541 Squadron, which had been sent to Germany with Meteor PR 10s in June 1951, was disbanded in September 1957. However, 543 Squadron was re-formed in July 1955 at Gaydon in Warwickshire with Vickers Valiant B (PR) 1s, the reconnaissance version of Britain's first nuclear bomber, and then moved to Wyton the following November. No 192 Squadron, the electronic intelligence squadron, was renumbered 51 Squadron in August 1958 and equipped with both Canberra B2s and Comet C2s. It continued its highly secret work from Watton and then Wyton, where in July 1971 it received Nimrod R1s with additional electronic equipment.

At the same time, the RAF's photo-reconnaissance facilities in Germany were strengthened, four squadrons being equipped with Canberra PR 7s. No 69 Squadron was the first, in May 1954. It was followed by 31 Squadron in March 1955, 80 Squadron in

August 1955, and 17 Squadron in June 1956. Second Tactical Air Force was thus well served with photo-reconnaissance squadrons during this period of the Cold War. In January 1959 this Command was renamed RAF Germany.

Other units also underwent changes. In December 1953, JAPIC (UK) was given the revised title of the Joint Air Reconnaissance Intelligence Centre (UK) and three years later began to move from Nuneham Park to RAF Brampton, close to the reconnaissance squadrons at Wyton. Part of its organisation was the Joint School of Photographic Interpretation. In July 1957 the Central Reconnaissance Establishment was established and occupied the same building. In December 1965 the School of Photography, which in 1963 had moved from its quarters at Wellesbourne Mountford to temporary quarters at RAF Cosford in Shropshire, took over a new building on this station.

Meanwhile, RAF maritime reconnaissance assumed increasing importance with the growth of the Soviet Navy. In common with the remainder of the RAF, Coastal Command had been reduced drastically after the Second World War, but its squadrons were built up again in the early 1950s when it was believed that the Russians were constructing as many as 1,000 submarines, some of which could carry missiles with nuclear warheads. By mid-1953 Coastal Command had increased to eight Shackleton squadrons, four Sunderland flying boat squadrons, four Neptune squadrons, one Hastings squadron for meteorological reconnaissance, and one Sycamore helicopter squadron for search and rescue. Four years later the Sunderlands were withdrawn and the Neptunes returned to America, being replaced by Shackletons as the main aircraft engaged on surveillance of the Warsaw Pact naval and merchant shipping, as well as on fishery protection patrols and on the monitoring of sea pollution. To these were

The F117 cameras were developed as replacements for the hand-held versions of the F24 used by the RAF and the K20 used by both the USAAF and the RAF during the Second World War. The F117A was manually wound, capable of taking 120 exposures of 4½-inch by 4½-inch, with a 6-inch lens and shutter speeds of 1/60th, 1/125th and 1/400th of a second. The F117B was very similar, but it was rewound with an integral electric motor and the handle grips were slightly different. (J.K. Nesbit, courtesy RAF Cosford Museum)

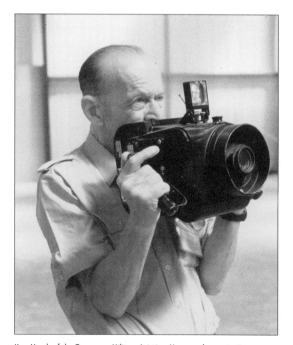

Ken Murch of the Tangmere Military Aviation Museum demonstrating an F117 from the museum exhibits. (B.M. Harris, courtesy Tangmere Military Aviation Museum)

Many women served as photographers and photo-interpreters during the Second World War. Leading Aircraftwoman Kay Davison, a photographer with Bomber Command at Driffield in Yorkshire, was allowed a flight on 17 July 1945 in Halifax letter Y over the devastated areas of the Ruhr. (Mrs K. Stevens née Davison)

eventually added the surveillance of the UK's offshore energy installations.

In spite of its somewhat ungainly appearance, the Avro Shackleton was one of the most successful and enduring aircraft used for long-range maritime reconnaissance, both at home and overseas. It was armed with cannons and machine guns, and could carry depth charges, homing torpedoes or bombs. As with its predecessors in the Second World War, it carried Air to Surface-Vessel (ASV) radar, the maritime equivalent of H_2S. The later versions were fitted with Magnetic Anomaly Detectors (MAD), used for spotting submarines underwater. In addition, these aircraft monitored innumerable naval and merchant vessels on the surface. Although there were a couple of retractable camera mountings in the rear fuselage, photography at low level was usually carried out by the hand-held F117 camera.

In April 1964 the functions of the Air Ministry, Admiralty and the War Office were absorbed into a reconstituted Ministry of Defence. Four years later (fifty years after its formation) the RAF in the UK began a radical alteration to its command structure when Fighter Command merged with Bomber Command to form Strike Command. No 90 (Signals) Group was incorporated into this new Command on 1 January 1969. Coastal Command followed on 28 November 1969, becoming No 18 Group. The Central Reconnaissance Establishment was disbanded on 1 October 1970 and control of JARIC (UK) was passed to No 1 (Bomber) Group within Strike Command. Finally, the former No 90 (Signals) Group was passed to Maintenance Command on 1 May 1972 and in turn this Command was merged with Training Command on 1 September 1973 to form the new Support Command.

Flying Officer Stan G.E. Payne, the Station Armament and Photographic Officer at RAF Aqir in Palestine, photographed in 1947. He was holding an F24 camera, which was still in service after its introduction in 1930. (Flight Lieutenant S.G.E. Payne C.Eng, MRAeS, RAF (Ret'd))

The Avro Lincoln, designed to replace the Lancaster as the RAF's main heavy bomber, arrived too late to take part in the Second World War but equipped many squadrons of Bomber Command until the last were withdrawn in May 1963. Lincolns served in operations against terrorists in Malaya and Kenya. A detachment of 214 Squadron, of which serial RE295 is shown here, was sent to Eastleigh near Nairobi from June to December 1954, during the Mau Mau uprisings; photographic reconnaissance formed part of their duties. (Squadron Leader P.J. Thompson RAF (Ret'd))

CHAPTER FOURTEEN

NEAR AND MIDDLE EAST COMMANDS

In common with squadrons at home, the photo-reconnaissance squadrons overseas suffered from the drastic cut-backs of the RAF in the immediate post-war years. Indeed, the problems resulting from the reductions overseas became even more acute, since some of the countries in which the squadrons were based entered a period of political turbulence and even armed conflict when released from the constraints imposed by the war. Meanwhile Britain felt compelled to fulfil her obligations to maintain law and order in the countries of the Commonwealth and Empire, while recognising the natural desire of indigenous peoples to govern themselves. At the same time, it became necessary to protect some of these peoples from the threat of international communism and dictatorship emanating from the Soviet Bloc under the guise of freedom from colonialism. The remaining photo-reconnaissance squadrons overseas played a full part in these extremely difficult years.

At the end of the war, the RAF squadrons in the Mediterranean were controlled by the Mediterranean Allied Air Forces, based at Caserta in Italy. This headquarters was disbanded in August 1945 and replaced by RAF Mediterranean and Middle East in Cairo, which covered the enormous area of North Africa, Malta, Greece, the Levant, Iraq, Egypt, the Sudan, Aden and East Africa. Serious trouble was brewing in all these areas, perhaps insufficiently appreciated by a British Government which was wrestling with the immense problems of turning its war economy back to civilian requirements.

Two long-range photo-reconnaissance squadrons in the area were disbanded. In September 1945 at Peretola in Italy, 682 Squadron lost its Spitfire PR XIXs and was disbanded. This fate befell 683 Squadron in the same month at San Severo in Italy, also equipped with these aircraft. However, 680 Squadron, equipped with Mosquito PR XVIs and based at Deversoir in Egypt and then Ein Shemer in Palestine, carried out aerial surveys of Iraq and Persia until September 1946 when it was renumbered 13 Squadron and received Mosquito PR 34s. In addition, 208 Squadron moved to Ein Shemer in June 1946 and was equipped with Spitfire XVIIIE fighter-reconnaissance aircraft two months later, flying on policing sorties.

Two squadrons operated in the maritime photo-reconnaissance role. These were 38 Squadron, which received Lancaster GR IIIs in November 1946 and moved from Luqa in Malta to Ein Shemer the following month, and 37 Squadron which was re-formed at Luqa in September 1947, also equipped with Lancaster GR IIIs, and then moved to Ein Shemer.

The gathering of these four reconnaissance squadrons at Ein Shemer, which lay mid-way between Haifa and Tel Aviv, was no coincidence. Palestine had been mandated by the League of Nations to Britain at the end of the First World War and the British Government was expected to create within it a national home for Jewish people without denying the aspirations of the Arabs who formed the majority of the population. But the Second World War had witnessed the appalling massacre of millions of Jews in occupied Europe and world sympathy had moved strongly in favour of the survivors, many of whom wished to create a new home in Palestine. The unenviable task of the British, including the RAF squadrons, was to prevent the illegal entry of these would-be immigrants and to try to arrange an equitable agreement with the Arabs.

A ship carrying immigrants was located on 17 January 1946 by a Warwick GR V of 621 Squadron, based at Ein Shemer, some months before the squadron was disbanded. The ship was then intercepted by a British destroyer and turned back. Seventeen such ships were located before the end of the year, with the Lancasters of 37 and 38 Squadrons playing a prominent part in the final months. An outcome of these operations was a series of attacks on RAF bases in Palestine by Jewish terrorists, resulting in much destruction and some loss of life.

The two maritime squadrons moved back to Luqa, 38 Squadron in November 1947 and 37 Squadron in April 1948. Malta had been given a certain amount of self-government in 1947 but Britain retained the right to base armed forces on the island. The Lancasters continued reconnaissance from this distant base until the United Nations decreed that Palestine should be partitioned between the Jews and the Arabs, resulting in the creation of the republic of Israel on 30 June 1948. The British forces gradually withdrew before this date, the RAF having located no less than forty-seven immigrant ships in all, to be dealt with by the Royal Navy. Most of the servicemen were glad to leave the country, knowing that the political situation was intractable and that they were leaving behind a divided country which could explode into conflict at any time.

The situation in Egypt was also fraught with problems but the British wished to remain in this country in order to protect the interests of the Western Allies in the Suez Canal. During 1947 British forces in the country were withdrawn to the Canal Zone in the hope of affording a compromise with Egyptian national aspirations. Within the RAF units, 13 Squadron with its Mosquito PR 34s moved to Fayid in February 1947, followed by 208 Squadron with its Spitfire XVIIIEs in November 1948. One of their main functions was to reconnoitre and photograph the border between Israel and Egypt, for there was bitter hostility between the two countries. By this time, the RAF Mediterranean and Middle East had been renamed the Middle East Air Force.

On 7 January 1949, four Spitfires of 208 Squadron were ordered to reconnoitre the incursion of Israeli troops over the Egyptian border. At the end of the operation, one was shot down by anti-aircraft fire and the pilot baled out over Egyptian territory. While the other three pilots were watching his descent they were attacked by Israeli Spitfires with the same camouflage and red spinners as their own aircraft, and all three were shot down. It is probable that the Israeli pilots of these intruding Spitfires had received their training in the RAF. One RAF pilot was killed, one managed to get back to Fayid, and two were captured by the Israelis within Egypt and imprisoned for a while before being released. On the same day as this episode, six more Spitfires of 208 Squadron escorted by seven Tempest VIs of 213 Squadron, searching for

Handley Page Halifax VII serial PP375 of 620 Squadron, at Aquir in Palestine in 1946. This version of the bomber was fitted with carburettor air filters for operations in tropical climates, as well as extra fuel capacity. Among the squadron's duties was maritime reconnaissance, searching for shipping carrying illegal immigrants headed for Palestine. (Flight Lieutenant S.G.E. Payne C.Eng, MRAeS, RAF (Ret'd))

A Canberra PR 9 (left) and a Canberra T4 two-seat trainer (right) of 39 Squadron at Luqa in Malta. The squadron was first equipped with Canberra PR 9s in October 1962, when based at Luqa and engaged on photo-reconnaissance during attachment to Nato. (Squadron Leader P.J. Thompson RAF (Ret'd))

their lost comrades, were similarly attacked. The pilots were also confused by the camouflage of the Israeli Spitfires and one Tempest was shot down.

The Israeli troops inflicted a number of reverses on the Egyptian forces before withdrawing, and serious tension continued. The need for survey and mapping was recognised by the re-establishment during November 1950 of 683 Squadron at Fayid, equipped with Lancaster PR 1s. The squadron carried out these duties before moving to Aden in January 1952 to continue the same tasks. Meanwhile, 208 Squadron was equipped with Meteor FR 9s for fighter reconnaissance in January 1951. Meteor PR 10s were supplied to 13 Squadron in November of that year, tactical photo-reconnaissance being of paramount importance in the Canal Zone.

The unpleasant political situation in the Middle East was further exacerbated in June 1951 by the action of the Persian Government in nationalising the Anglo-Iranian oil refinery at Abadan, with a threat to the safety of British nationals, many of whom were evacuated by air. At the same time, the British forces in Egypt faced increased hostility from nationalist bodies. Some of their number were murdered, local labour was withdrawn and the families of servicemen were evacuated. The RAF in the Canal Zone was reinforced with bomber and fighter aircraft. The situation worsened in July 1952 when King Farouk was deposed and Egypt came under the control of its military, eventually led by Colonel Gamal Abdel Nasser. By then Britain had begun to reassess its obligations and a decision was made to pull out of the country. A treaty was signed in July 1954, agreeing to withdraw British forces provided facilities were kept in the Canal Zone for their return in the event of an attack by the Soviet Union. The RAF decided to base its units in Cyprus, together

with the headquarters of Middle East Air Force, and this was achieved by May 1956.

Before this move to Cyprus was carried out, RAF photo-reconnaissance aircraft were involved in a dispute which, although very minor in military terms, was extremely important for their country's relations with Saudi Arabia. For many years, Britain had maintained a presence in the Trucial States on the Arabian side of the Persian Gulf, a territory which had been known previously as the Pirate Coast. With the development of huge deposits of oil, these Gulf States began to equal Saudi Arabia in significance.

The Buraimi Oasis, on the boundary between the state of Abu Dhabi and that of Muscat and Oman, had always been coveted by Saudi Arabia. In August 1952 a small force of Saudi militia crossed over Abu Dhabi territory and occupied part of the oasis. To avoid armed conflict with Saudi Arabia, it was decided to blockade this force, with Trucial Oman Levies intercepting camel trains carrying supplies. The reconnaissance of the surrounding desert was first carried out by Vampire fighters operating from RAF Sharjah but in April 1953 the work was taken over by four Meteor FR 9s of 208 Squadron detached from Abu Sueir in Egypt. Their range proved insufficient, however, and within a few weeks they were replaced by four Lancaster GR IIIs of 37 and 38 Squadrons from Malta, operating outside their normal maritime reconnaissance role. These returned to normal duties in July and were replaced by Lancaster PR 1s of 683 Squadron, which by then were engaged on a survey of Iraq from their base at Habbaniya. They flew down to Sharjah and carried on the work. However, this squadron was due for disbandment by November, and in September 1417 Flight, equipped with Ansons, was formed to take over the reconnaissance. The blockade was called off for a few weeks while negotiations took place but when these failed the British, tired of the matter and its cost, decided to remove the Saudi party by force. An operation was mounted in October and achieved success with little bloodshed. Relations with Saudi Arabia became even more soured and diplomatic relations were broken off.

In this period a rebellion of the most vicious and brutal kind broke out in Kenya. From 1952 the so-called Mau Mau sect of the Kikuyu people began committing atrocities against other Africans and white settlers, with the intention of occupying land which they believed had been taken from them unfairly. A State of Emergency was declared in October 1952 but the King's African Rifles, reinforced with a British battalion, were unable to contain all terrorist activities over the vast area of central Kenya. They were supported by light aircraft of the Police Air Wing and, from the spring of the following year, a flight of armed North American Harvards of the Rhodesian Air Training Group. These carried out some useful work but this was not sufficient to deal with all the Mau Mau gangs, who moved into the dense forests and rocky defiles of the Aberdare Mountains and Mount Kenya, at altitudes where light aircraft were less effective. In March 1954 two Meteor PR 10s of 13 Squadron were sent from Fayid for a short while to carry out photo-reconnaissance. On their return, vertical photography was undertaken by Lincolns of Bomber Command squadrons which were detached from Britain to RAF Eastleigh, near Nairobi. These photographs were duly interpreted and followed by bombing attacks which were so accurate that they destroyed the morale of the terrorists, who scuttled out of the area in droves to surrender. By early 1955 the Mau Mau activities were greatly reduced, although the work of mopping up the remainder continued for several months.

The renewed interest of the RAF in Cyprus coincided with the signing of the Baghdad Pact on 4 April 1955 by Britain, Turkey, Iraq and Pakistan. The United States became closely associated with this new group of states united in military defence, which provided a welcome extension of Nato's eastern boundary confronting the Soviet Union. The concentration of RAF units in Cyprus included 13 Squadron, which moved to the new airfield of Akrotiri in February 1956 and began to receive Canberra PR 7s three months later to replace its ageing Meteor PR 10s. However, 208 Squadron moved to Malta during January 1956 until sufficient accommodation for its Meteor FR 9s was available at Akrotiri two months later. Canberra bomber squadrons also arrived, providing an offensive capacity.

Living conditions in Cyprus proved far more agreeable than in the Canal Zone, but some Greek inhabitants began to stir up political trouble in the name of 'Enosis' (union with Greece) – a proposal which was bitterly opposed by the Turkish community. The leader of the Greek Cypriots was Archbishop Makarios, but his request for union with Greece was refused by the United Nations in early 1955. The initiative passed to Colonel Grivas who began a 'revolution' on 1 April 1955, leading a band under the acronym of Eoka (Ethniks Organosis Kypriou Agonistou). Bomb explosions and the murder of British servicemen followed, and counter-measures were taken. Nos 37 and 38 Squadrons, still based at Luqa but re-equipped with Avro Shackleton MR 2s, hunted for small vessels carrying arms to the terrorists, with considerable success. A collection of privately owned light aircraft was pressed into service to hunt for terrorists and these were joined by a flight of Bristol Sycamore HR14 helicopters. Two flights of Austers arrived, these 'Air Observation Post' aircraft being flown by Army pilots. When it became clear that Makarios was involved with the terrorists he was arrested and exiled to the Seychelles, but violence and rioting continued in Cyprus.

The RAF withdrew from Iraq in January 1956, following a long association with the country and without ill-feeling on either side. However, relations with Egypt reached crisis point when on 26 July 1956 Colonel Nasser announced that the Universal Suez Canal Company was to be seized, as retaliation for the withdrawal of the United States from a project to build the Aswan High Dam on the River Nile. Western interests, primarily those of Britain and France, were thus destroyed at a stroke, and the two countries decided that military action might have to be taken to counter this illegal seizure.

The first requirement was photo-reconnaissance and in early August 1956 a detachment of Canberra PR 7s of 58 Squadron was sent out from Wyton to Akrotiri, augmenting those with which 13 Squadron was re-equipping. They were followed by Republic F-84F fighter-reconnaissance aircraft of the French Air Force. Hunter Vs and Meteor NF 13s also flew out, reinforcing Venoms already based at Nicosia, the only other usable airfield. There were also transport aircraft such as Hastings and Valettas on the island. The congestion was such that many of the Meteors of 208 Squadron, which did not have the range to operate over Egypt, were sent back to Malta. Meanwhile, an aircraft carrier task group and other warships of the Royal Navy headed towards the eastern Mediterranean.

When diplomatic efforts failed and conflict seemed inevitable, detachments from eight squadrons of Canberra B2s and B6s of Bomber Command were sent to Cyprus, adding to the congestion. No more could be accommodated in the island and four other detachments of Canberra B2s together with four detachments of Vickers Valiant V-

bombers were sent to Malta, arriving in the latter part of October. The first reconnaissance was carried out by a Canberra PR 7 of 58 Squadron on 20 October, surveying the Egyptian coastline. Others began eight days later, carried out by both 13 and 58 Squadrons. One Canberra was damaged by a MiG fighter but returned safely.

The British and French plan of attack was given the code name of Operation 'Musketeer'. It began in the afternoon of 31 October 1956, the day after Israel invaded the Sinai Peninsula in north-east Egypt. During the early part of the day, eleven photo-reconnaissance sorties were flown by Canberras and F-84Fs, covering the Egyptian airfields. These airfields were attacked by Valiants and Canberras on the same day and the following night. Ground attacks by land-based and carrier-borne aircraft began the next morning. After a couple of days photo-reconnaissance revealed that 158 aircraft of the Egyptian Air Force, consisting originally of 216 modern aircraft, had been destroyed without loss to the attackers. Moreover, twenty-one of the surviving aircraft had disappeared from the country, possibly fleeing to Russia. Anglo-French attacks then began on other ground targets and one RAF Venom was lost in an accident at low level.

Airborne landings took place near Port Said on 5 November and seaborne forces followed the next day, accompanied by bombardments from the air and sea. However, the action of the Anglo-French intervention was severely criticised by the United Nations, led by the United States. An Emergency Force was raised by the Security Council, while a cease-fire was ordered to take effect from midnight on 6 November. The British and French, who had made rapid progress along the Suez Canal, were forced to cease operations and pull out of Egypt. It was a humiliating and frustrating end to a venture which was within sight of military success, even though politically ill-conceived in the first place. Somewhat incongruously, technical development soon demonstrated that the Suez Canal was of less strategic value than had been believed, for it could not be used by the new breed of supertankers which were coming into service and instead sailed round the Cape of Good Hope.

The work of photo-reconnaissance was not finished, however. Syria had forbidden over-flying on 1 October, in sympathy with Egypt, but the RAF continued clandestine flights over this country and others in the Middle East. On 8 November Canberra PR 7 serial WH799 of 13 Squadron, flown by a crew from 58 Squadron, was attacked while on a reconnaissance over Syria and came down over the Lebanese border. It was believed that the attacking aircraft was a Meteor or a MiG-15 of the Syrian Air Force, probably flown by a Czechoslovakian or a Russian pilot. The navigator of the Canberra was killed, but the pilot and second navigator were taken to the military hospital at Beirut and eventually repatriated.

Further conflicts occurred in the Trucial States in this period. The Sultan of Muscat nominally exercised authority over the vast territory of Oman but for many years had been thwarted in a remote part of the country by the leader of a sect which was supported by Saudi Arabia. In 1955 the Sultan decided to remove this rebel force with the aid of the British. Military operations began, while reconnaissance was carried out from an airstrip by 1417 Flight, which by then was equipped with Hunting Percival Pembrokes as well as the faithful Ansons. Four Lincolns of Bomber Command, formed into 1426 Flight at Bahrein, reinforced this reconnaissance. Some military progress was achieved but in 1956 an 'Oman Liberation Army' was formed and in June of the following year an armed force landed on the

coast and made its way into villages in the mountainous interior. Increased air photography was required, and several Shackleton MR 2s of 37 Squadron, which moved in July 1957 from Luqa to Khormaksar, were brought in from Aden to operate from the RAF station on the island of Masirah. A detachment of Meteor FR 9s of 208 Squadron also flew in from Malta, to carry out shorter range photo-reconnaissance at low level. Air attacks by Venoms were combined with attacks by the Sultan's forces and elements of the British Army but the rebels retreated to higher ground from where they proved more difficult to dislodge. In January 1958, 208 Squadron was transferred to the fighter role back in the UK and then returned to Aden. The campaign in Oman was not wound up until February 1959.

Meanwhile, the measures against terrorists in Cyprus were strengthened by increasing the number of Sycamore helicopters and forming these into 284 Squadron during October 1956. Activities against these terrorists, who moved mainly in remote areas of the Troodos Mountains, became more effective and in March 1957 Eoka offered a truce provided Makarios was released. This was accepted by the British and the archbishop was released a few weeks later, although he was not allowed to return to the island. The violence continued.

The reconnoitring of terrorist activities was best carried out by light aircraft and helicopters, with the crews working visually in the manner of First World War pilots and observers but with the advantage of reporting immediately by R/T. The helicopters could also land small bodies of troops in areas highly inconvenient to the terrorists, who were then harried and often destroyed. Westland Whirlwind helicopters, with their larger carrying capacity, arrived in 284 Squadron the following month. With regard to the fixed-wing light aircraft, numerous Air

The Bristol Sycamore was the first helicopter designed and built in Britain to enter RAF service, in February 1952. The first was the Mark HR12, but the improved versions HR13 and HR14 followed. Sycamores were employed for reconnaissance and casualty evacuation, and saw service at home and overseas. They were withdrawn from front-line duties in October 1964 but continued on communications until August 1972. This Sycamore HC14 serial XG502 saw service with the Joint Experimental Helicopter Unit from March 1955 and was then employed on Operation 'Musketeer' in Suez during 1956. It was then reissued to 225 Squadron, which continued with Sycamore HC14s until March 1962. (Museum of Army Flying)

Observation Post squadrons had been formed in the RAF from 1941 onwards. These squadrons were usually equipped with Austers flown by Army pilots, using small hand-held cameras, and their work of close co-operation with ground troops had proved highly successful in Italy and Normandy. On 1 September 1957 the Army Air Corps was formed, the squadrons at last achieving independence from the RAF, and this new organisation operated with modern Austers in Cyprus. From November 1958 the Austers of the Army Air Corps were backed by RAF light aircraft, Scottish Aviation Pioneers of 230 Squadron and de Havilland Chipmunks of 114 Squadron.

These combined operations contained most of the activities of the Eoka terrorists but some violence continued. On 17 February 1959 an agreement was reached in London by Britain, Greece and Turkey, whereby Cyprus attained sovereign status but Britain retained control of Akrotiri and the Army base of Dhekelia. This agreement became effective the following September and terrorist activities against the British died away. Cyprus soon rejoined the British Commonwealth, but the peace between the Greeks and the Turks remained uneasy.

While these activities were in progress, the Canberras of 13 Squadron at Akrotiri continued their work, some of which was clandestine. Their crews were often joined by others from 58 Squadron from Wyton and their tasks included photo-reconnaissance of airfields in Middle Eastern countries which were being supplied with aircraft from the Soviet Union. Details of these operations have never been disclosed, but there is little doubt that they also included electronic intelligence of radar stations and other activities in the south of the Soviet Union itself.

The situation in Malta in this period was not altogether happy, in spite of the excellent relations which had existed between its people and the British forces during the Second World War. The dependence on Britain as an employer on the island had diminished with the run-down of the armed forces and in 1957 the Maltese Labour Party demanded total separation. The maritime Shackletons of 38 Squadron continued to fulfil their usual role from Luqa but in July 1958 Canberra PR 7s of 69 Squadron flew out to Malta from Laarbruch in Germany. They were renumbered 39 Squadron and also employed primarily on maritime photo-reconnaissance as part of Nato's southern flank, for a Russian fleet was active in the Mediterranean. The Canberras also flew on survey work in Libya and some were sent to Khormaksar in Aden, where they carried out a survey of the country and photographed ports in the Yemen, since arms were believed to be arriving from Egypt to encourage incursions into the Protectorate.

Meanwhile, a coup took place in Iraq during July 1958 and the King and Prime Minister were deposed. The country decided to withdraw from the Baghdad Pact during the following spring and on 20 August 1959 this was replaced with the Central Treaty Organisation (Cento), which worked effectively from headquarters in Turkey. On 1 March 1961 the Near East Command was formed in Cyprus and the Middle East Command in Aden. One of the first problems the latter faced concerned Iraq, for this country claimed that Kuwait, with an oil production which had expanded enormously since the Second World War, was part of its territory. In fact, Kuwait was a small and independent state which for many years had enjoyed friendly relations with Britain, to whom it looked for protection.

Throughout the turbulent post-war years, Aden and its Protectorates had remained fairly quiescent, apart from border incursions from the Yemen and inter-tribal conflicts which had been quelled by air and ground

The Westland Whirlwind entered RAF service in September 1954 as a helicopter with a larger capacity than the Dragonfly, serving with squadrons at home, in Germany, the Near East and the Far East. It was used for tactical transport, ground assault or search and rescue, the last continuing in squadron service until March 1982. This Whirlwind HAR 10 serial XP347 was photographed with a Wessex of the Royal Navy. (P. Batten)

The Hawker Siddeley Nimrod MR 1, evolved from the Comet airliner, entered service with the RAF in October 1969 for marine reconnaissance. Thereafter, the electronic equipment was updated to include 'Searchwater' radar and the aircraft became the MR 2, as with this photograph of XV238 of 42 (Torpedo Bomber) Squadron. In addition to its reconnaissance role, the machine could carry up to nine homing torpedos in its bomb bay and, during the Falklands campaign, was fitted with Sidewinder missiles. (Squadron Leader I.M. Coleman RAF)

operations. Indeed, between 1956 and 1959 the RAF squadrons in Aden had been strengthened considerably, Khormaksar being considered a suitable alternative for the loss of bases in other areas. Among the new arrivals was 37 Squadron, which moved its base from Luqa in July 1957 during the confrontation with the dissidents in Oman.

Kuwait was about 1,500 miles from the headquarters in Aden and it was obvious that operations could not be conducted from that distance. Bahrein, another friendly state in the Persian Gulf, was a suitable choice and RAF squadrons flew to RAF Muharraq in that country, from the UK and East Africa as well as from Khormaksar and a detachment from 13 Squadron at Akrotiri, which by then was equipped with Canberra PR 9s. These kept watch on the border between Kuwait and Iraq as well as the sea approaches. Other squadrons airlifted troops and sent fighter aircraft to Kuwait while Royal Navy vessels headed for the threatened state. A considerable build-up was achieved with such commendable rapidity that the Iraqis decided that discretion was the better part of valour and no attack materialised. The British forces were gradually withdrawn.

The Federation of South Arabia was formed on 11 February 1959 from Aden and its Protectorates, in the hope that a peaceful state would be the outcome. The rush for independence from Britain accelerated during the early 1960s. British and Italian Somaliland combined as an independent state in July 1960. Independence was achieved by Tanganyika in December 1961, by Uganda in October 1962 and by Kenya in December 1963. These moves were peaceful on the whole, but disturbances broke out in the Federation of South Arabia after a republican coup in the neighbouring state of the Yemen during September 1962. This was encouraged and supported by Egypt, which continued to foment incursions across the border.

Canberras of 13 Squadron were brought into Khormaksar from Akrotiri to keep watch on vessels carrying arms from Egypt, and these aircraft were joined by a detachment from 58 Squadron at Wyton. The Shackletons of 37 Squadron also operated in this role. Yemeni aircraft intruded across the border and an insurrection in this area had to be put down by combined operations in the spring of 1964, resulting in the defeat of the rebels. However, this success did nothing to limit terrorism within Aden, which increased alarmingly over the next two years. Heavy casualties were caused, primarily from mortars and the throwing of grenades. Britain determined to pull out of the territory by 1968 at the latest.

While arrangements for this withdrawal were under way, a further commitment fell on 37 Squadron at Khormaksar. The Federation of Rhodesia broke up in 1964, with Nyasaland becoming the independent state of Malawi and Northern Rhodesia becoming the independent state of Zambia. However, the British Government refused to grant sovereignty to the remaining country, Southern Rhodesia. This country, by then named simply Rhodesia, announced a Unilateral Declaration of Independence (UDI) on 11 November 1965. Britain duly declared that the regime was illegal and invoked economic sanctions by members of the United Nations. For the RAF, this move was followed by some bizarre episodes with their former friends and brothers-in-arms in the Rhodesian Air Force. The crew of an RAF Vulcan V-bomber which was unaware of UDI and landed at New Sarum, near the capital of Salisbury, found that the fuselage had been painted with the assegai and roundel motif of the RhAF before they took off the next morning, after enjoying the hospitality of the country. Javelin FAW9s of 29 Squadron, which flew into Ndola in Zambia from Akrotiri, to 'protect' the country from

Rhodesia, used the Flying Information Centre at Salisbury when flying from their base.

The most notable effect of sanctions against Rhodesia was the lack of oil. In March 1966 Shackletons of 37 Squadron were sent from Khormaksar to Majunga in Madagascar to work with the Royal Navy on the Beira Patrol, since it was known that supplies were arriving via Portuguese Mozambique, which was sympathetic to the Rhodesia cause. Thereafter Rhodesia obtained its oil via South Africa. The costly patrols continued, and other Shackletons were sent out from the UK after 37 Squadron was withdrawn.*

The departure of the British from Aden was complicated by the Arab/Israeli War of 3–9 June 1967, which ended in an Israeli victory but closed the Suez Canal. This move was accomplished before the end of the year, with some of the squadrons taking up new bases in the Persian Gulf, although 37 Squadron was disbanded at Khormaksar in September 1967, when its Shackletons were flown back to England. The increased presence of the RAF in the Gulf States remained amicable but the need diminished as the newly rich countries built up their own forces. Reconnaissance continued, with a detachment of Canberras of 13 Squadron from Muharraq keeping watch on the Iraqi/Kuwait border and the formation in November 1970 of 210 Squadron, equipped with Shackleton MR 2s, serving from Sharjah until disbanding a year later. The RAF pulled out of the Persian Gulf at the same time as this disbandment, leaving a high reputation with the rulers of these states and their peoples.

Meanwhile, Malta decided to achieve independence from Britain in September

---

* In 1973 the author saw a Royal Navy plaque, on the wall of the Leopard Rock Hotel in the east of Rhodesia, which read: 'With grateful thanks for your hospitality: HMS *Charybdis*, Beira Patrol'.

1964, although an agreement was reached whereby Britain was allowed to retain defence facilities for the next ten years. Thus the Shackletons of 38 Squadron and the Canberras of 39 Squadron were permitted to remain on the island. In addition, the Canberra PR 9s of 13 Squadron moved from Akrotiri to Luqa in September 1965, concentrating the whole Near East photo-reconnaissance force in Malta. But 38 Squadron was disbanded in March 1967 and its place in Malta was not taken until February 1968 when the Shackleton MR 3s of 203 Squadron flew out from Ballykelly in Northern Ireland, continuing the watch on Russian warships in the Mediterranean. This squadron began to receive new Hawker Siddeley Nimrod MR 1s in July 1971, replacing the ageing Shackletons. However, 39 Squadron was sent back to Wyton in September 1970.

All did not go well with the agreement between Britain and Malta, and the Maltese Government insisted on the complete withdrawal of British forces by March 1972. No 203 Squadron transferred to Sigonella in Sicily in January of that year, as part of Nato, but operated partly from Akrotiri. At the same time 13 Squadron, which was partly engaged on a survey of Kenya, moved its headquarters back to Akrotiri. However, the loss of the British forces created such massive problems for the Maltese economy that a reversal of the decision took place and the squadrons returned to Luqa, 203 Squadron in April 1972 and 13 Squadron in the following October.

When Turkey invaded the northern part of Cyprus in July 1974, the Vulcans based there carried out some of their duties from Malta, often in the maritime reconnaissance role. By this time it was clear that the Central Treaty Organisation was of little value, with two members of Nato fighting each other, and the nuclear bombers were withdrawn to the UK in early 1975. Only 84 Squadron, equipped with Whirlwind helicopters, remained in Cyprus.

The fairly gentle state of affairs in Rhodesia did not persist, for a bloody and vicious war broke out after the coup in Portugal in 1975. Major incursions were made into Rhodesia from Zambia and Mozambique and the matter was not settled until December 1979, when the white government of Rhodesia relinquished control.

In spite of the renewed presence of the RAF in Malta, relations were far from cordial, with the Maltese Government in sympathy with Libya and its new ruler Colonel Gaddafi, who had staged a military coup in the country during 1969, ousting the British forces from their bases and creating a strongly anti-Western society. It was decided to disband 203 Squadron at Luqa and its Nimrods flew back to Britain at the end of 1977 to be allocated to other squadrons. The Canberras of 13 Squadron flew home to Wyton in October 1979, severing the last formal links of RAF squadrons with the famous George Cross Island. Within the Mediterranean, only the bases of Gibraltar and Akrotiri remained to serve the RAF.

CHAPTER FIFTEEN
THE FAR EAST

The dropping of the atom bombs and the capitulation of Japan came as a complete surprise to almost all servicemen. The Japanese had been defeated in Burma apart from a few starving and harried remnants of their forces, but it was generally believed that those occupying other countries in the Far East and Japan itself would fight to the death. Plans for a huge invasion of the west coast of Malaya had been prepared, under the code name of Operation 'Zipper'. Some British troops had already entered the vessels when VJ-Day and the end of the Second World War was declared on 14 August 1945. Landing beaches had been identified by photo-reconnaissance carried out by Mosquito PR 34s of 684 Squadron and all was ready for the great enterprise, but the troops were able to arrive unopposed in Malaya after surrender documents had been signed by Japanese commanders. The first British to arrive in Singapore were the crew of a Mosquito PR 34 of 684 Squadron, which took off from the Cocos Islands on 31 August 1945 to photograph southern Malaya and developed an engine fault. They were received correctly by Japanese officers, before their commander signed the surrender document.

The area of South-East Asia Command, which already covered India, Ceylon, Burma, Siam, Malaya and Sumatra, was extended on 13 August 1945 to include Borneo, Java, the Celebes, and French Indo-China below the 16th parallel. Parts of the south-west Pacific, including New Guinea and the Solomons, were handed over to Australian control. The total area was thus immense and the problems faced by the British were almost insuperable, for some of the indigenous peoples had lost faith in the Western countries which had failed to protect them from years of brutal Japanese domination. Some nationalist bodies were intent on getting rid of European control and establishing communist states, even if this meant armed insurrection. At the same time the men of the British forces, particularly those conscripted into the services, were anxious to return home and resume civilian life, and insufficient transport was available for this purpose. These returnees included many ex-PoWs, almost all of whom were in an extremely debilitated condition after their inhuman treatment at the hands of the Japanese.

Although many RAF squadrons were disbanded after VJ-Day, there was still plenty of photo-reconnaissance work ahead. Thus 681 Squadron, equipped with Spitfire PR XIXs, and 684 Squadron, equipped with Mosquito PR 34s, remained operational for the time being. The former was based at Mingaladon in Burma at the time of the surrender and continued photographing roads, railways, airfields and PoW camps. It moved to Kai Tak at the end of the following month, to help with the re-establishment of civil administration in Hong Kong, a matter which was achieved speedily. The squadron then flew down to Kuala Lumpur for a few

Sunderland V serial RN290 of 230 Squadron, in maritime white livery, in the seaplane base at RAF Seletar in Singapore after the Japanese capitulation.
(The late Corporal C.E. Lloyd)

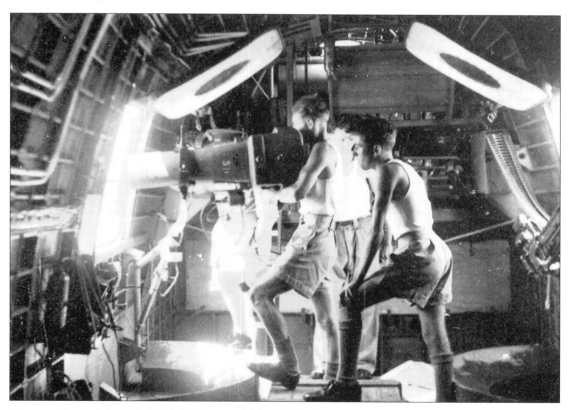

F52 camera oblique installation in a Sunderland. (Flight Lieutenant G.H. Parry RAF (Ret'd))

The RAF airfield at Seletar in Singapore after the Japanese capitulation. (Leading Aircraftman R.F. White RAFVR)

The Westland Dragonfly HC2 was based on the US Sikorski S-51 but manufactured in Britain. It first entered RAF service in 1950 with the Casualty Evacuation Flight (later 194 Squadron) in Malaya. This Dragonfly serial XD649, photographed in the mid-1950s, was fitted up with casevac panniers for jungle rescue work. Versions of this helicopter continued in service with the RAF until June 1956. (The Westland Group)

weeks before taking up its new base at Seletar in Singapore Island, where it arrived on 9 January 1946. Meanwhile the Mosquito squadron, based at Alipore in India at the time of the surrender but with detachments at Mingaladon and the Cocos Islands, moved to Tan Son Nhut near Saigon on 11 October 1945 to begin a photographic survey of French Indo-China. On 27 January 1946 the squadron crossed over to Don Muang near Bangkok to carry out similar work over Thailand (as Siam was more generally known by this time), including the Kra isthmus adjoining Malaya. These surveys were to prove highly beneficial in later years.

At this time, Britain faced the task of assuming control over many island communities of the south-west Pacific, including the Netherlands East Indies. The re-occupation of Sumatra, Borneo, New Guinea, Timor and Bali was carried out reasonably smoothly by the British or the Australians. However, an Indonesian Independence Movement in the Netherlands colony of Java managed to acquire weapons from the Japanese and was prepared to use them against all Europeans, seeing little distinction between the British and the Dutch. The RAF formed 904 Wing in Java, at Kemarojam airfield near Batavia, and a detachment of Spitfires PR XIXs flew down from Kai Tak in late October 1945 to join the fighter and transport squadrons allocated to the Wing. The main duties of the RAF were to help round up the Japanese forces and to locate camps containing internees before flying them to safety, or guarding road convoys. Photo-reconnaissance was an essential part of these tasks.

The situation in Java became unpleasant rapidly, with much of the country out of control. Before the end of the year the Army suffered over 1,000 casualties, and all the occupants of a Dakota which made a forced landing 5 miles from the airfield were captured and murdered. A detachment of

Mosquito PR 34s from 684 Squadron arrived, but the high humidity caused problems with the wooden construction of the aircraft. Auster Vs of 656 Squadron made a notable contribution to tactical reconnaissance. The difficulties continued for much of the following spring and the RAF and Army personnel were not sorry when their duties began to wind down in the summer of 1946 and there was a gradual handover to Dutch authorities. The last of the RAF units were withdrawn from the Netherlands East Indies at the end of November 1946. By this time, Java and Sumatra had been surveyed by the detachment of Mosquito PR 34s from 684 Squadron, in spite of the aircraft's structural problems.

In the following three years the area of South-East Asia Command was reduced drastically. India became an independent republic on 14 August 1947, but great tracts of its vast territory were partitioned to become the new Republic of Pakistan. Both countries remained in the Commonwealth. Burma became an independent country outside the Commonwealth on 4 January 1948. Ceylon assumed the status of a self-governing Dominion within the Commonwealth exactly a month later. During this period, 681 Squadron returned from Seletar to India in May 1946 but the squadron was renumbered 34 Squadron three months later. The Spitfire PR XIXs continued with aerial surveys for the next year but then the squadron was disbanded. Meanwhile the Mosquito PR 34s of 684 Squadron at Don Muang continued survey work but the squadron was disbanded on 1 September 1946, being immediately re-formed as 81 Squadron at Seletar, where it also received a flight of Spitfire PR XIXs and later a few Spitfire FR 18s. The squadron continued survey work, moving within Singapore to Changi on 1 October 1947 and Tengah on 1 February 1948. With a detachment at

Mingaladon, it completed surveying the remainder of Burma by August 1947. This was followed by a survey of British North Borneo by the end of the year, carried out by another detachment operating from the island of Labuan off the coast of Brunei.

South-East Asia Air Command left India, Pakistan and Burma. By 1 June 1949 it was whittled down to the Far East Air Force, with main headquarters at Changi in Singapore but with other headquarters in Ceylon and Hong Kong. By this time its manpower had shrunk from about 125,000 at the end of the war to under 9,000. Singapore proved an admirable centre for maintaining British interests in the Far East, in spite of its history of failure in the war against the Japanese. The island possessed four excellent airfields: Seletar, Tengah, Changi and Sembawang. The industrious Chinese and Malays harboured little resentment at the presence of the British while the climate, although hot and subject to heavy reain, was not oppressive. In addition to the photo-reconnaissance surveys completed by 81 Squadron, maritime reconnaissance was carried out by Sunderland squadrons operating from Seletar, which was an excellent flying boat base, as well as an airfield, close to the naval base.

The new Far East Air Force faced a serious problem in the mainland peninsula, however. This arose from the Malayan Communist Party, which had collaborated with the British during the Japanese occupation by providing a resistance movement which by the end of the war consisted of about 4,000 guerillas. These attempted to turn Malaya into a communist republic by a series of strikes and other disruptions but when these failed began a policy of murder, intimidation and sabotage in 1948, with the objective of gradually taking over the country area by area. They were opposed by the great majority of the Malayan and Chinese people of the country, who looked to Britain for

protection. The RAF played a full part in what became known as the 'Malayan Emergency' by providing reconnaissance, by moving troops and police, and by carrying out bombing or rocket attacks against terrorist bases. These were named Operation 'Firedog' and Kuala Lumpur was re-activated as an RAF station to co-ordinate the activities. At the same time, the Sunderlands at Seletar patrolled the Gulf of Siam and the South China Sea, photographing small craft which might be smuggling arms between China and the east coast of Malaya. This work was carried out in collaboration with sloops and destroyers of the Royal Navy.

Fortunately, the surveys previously completed by 81 Squadron gave the security forces accurate knowledge of the interior of Malaya, although much of this was covered by thick jungle which favoured the terrorists. The state of Perak in the north-west was one of the seriously affected areas, and a single photo-reconnaissance Spitfire accompanied by a mobile photographic and interpretation unit was sent to the civil airfield of Taiping in the centre of the state. For about a month, terrorist encampments were identified and photographed. When attacked, however, the survivors simply fled into the jungle. Collections of huts in the interior of several other states were photographed by 81 Squadron's Mosquitos and Spitfires and then attacked by Beaufighters and Spitfires with rockets, cannon fire and bombs, while security forces, transported to landing grounds or parachuted from Dakotas, laid ambushes for the fleeing terrorists. The troops and police were supplied from the air by Dakotas, using the techniques perfected in Burma against the Japanese. These operations achieved some successes but the remaining terrorists split up into smaller groups and hid in deeper jungle where identification was more difficult. Murders and attacks on road and rail convoys continued and even intensified, especially in

The Scottish Aviation Pioneer entered service with the RAF in the Far East during February 1954 as an Army co-operation and communications aircraft, capable of operating from short runways. Squadrons at home and in the Mediterranean were also equipped with this tough and reliable aircraft, which continued in service until January 1970. (*Aeroplane Monthly*)

The Scottish Aviation Twin Pioneer followed the single-engined version, entering RAF service during 1958. It possessed the same attributes as its predecessor, but with a larger carrying capacity and a longer range. Twin Pioneers remained in front-line duties until late 1968. (*Aeroplane Monthly*)

the monsoon period when air activity was curtailed. By early 1949 it became evident that a long struggle lay ahead.

No maps had been constructed from 81 Squadron's surveys and it was thought necessary to update its work before these were drawn up. Large-scale maps of 1 inch to 1 mile and 2½ inches to 1 mile were required for use by the Army on jungle patrols and by the RAF in picking out suitable dropping zones. This work was begun in 1949 by 81 Squadron, flying at a lower level in order to produce suitable photographs for these large-scale maps. Some Anson C19s were also employed on this task in the summer of 1949. The squadron moved back to Seletar on 16 March 1950 but detachments were frequently sent to Butterworth in north-west Malaya. The new survey was not completed until 1952.

Terrorist camps were also identified by 81 Squadron, although aircraft flying below about 15,000 feet could often be spotted from the ground and dispersal might take place before air and ground strikes could be carried out. The counter-measures certainly harried and dispersed the terrorists and kept them on the move but their activities did not diminish.

In 1950 the security forces began the far-sighted plan of moving Chinese and Malay settlements in the interior into safe havens where they could be protected and where social amenities were provided. This plan was carried out gradually by British and Gurkha troops and the police, with a kindliness and humanity which contrasted sharply with the brutality of the communists, thus benefiting the government cause. The scheme also had the effect of isolating the terrorists from their supplies of food, for they were unable to grow their own or keep livestock when kept constantly on the move. It also denied to them valuable sources of information, for they were no longer able to intimidate the villagers. Of course it was essentially a long-term plan and for the time being the results

were not conclusive. Nevertheless it was notable that, in a vain attempt to win over the villagers to their cause, the Malayan Communist Party changed its name during 1950 to the Malayan Races Liberation Army.

While the RAF was embroiled in operations in Malaya and the Middle East, war broke out in Korea. The communist state of the People's Democratic Republic north of the 38th parallel, which was fixed at the end of the Second World War as a demarcation line between the areas controlled by the Russians and the Americans, invaded South Korea on 25 June 1950. Although Britain was able to help the South Koreans and the United Nation's Forces, mostly Americans, with Army and Navy support against North Koreans backed by Chinese forces, other commitments prevented the RAF from making a major contribution. By this time, the personnel of the Far East Air Force had been whittled down to no more than 4,000. However, excellent photo-reconnaissance was provided by detachments of Sunderland Vs from 88 and 209 Squadrons which moved from Seletar to Iwakuni on the Japanese island of Honshu, using Hong Kong as an intermediate base. The aircraft were engaged on anti-submarine patrols as well as the photography and identification of surface vessels. Many of the carrier-borne attacks made by the American Navy and the Royal Navy stemmed from these long and tedious reconnaissance sorties. In addition, the RAF provided pilots who flew in US aircraft, as well as two flights of Austers which carried out some of the dangerous work of tactical reconnaissance. The war continued with heavy losses on both sides until a truce was signed on 27 July 1953.

In the course of the Korean War, there were signs that the security forces in Malaya were beginning to gain the upper hand over the communists. The terrorists intensified their attacks against soft targets but

RAF Whirlwind HAR 10 serial XP398, based at Kuching, landing at an Army outpost in May 1964 during the Indonesian confrontation. (P. Batten)

A logging site in Borneo, photographed from 1,500 feet by a Canberra PR 9 of 13 Squadron on 3 February 1966, during the confrontation with Indonesia. (Squadron Leader P.J. Thompson RAF (Ret'd))

The Westland Belvedere HC 1, with twin engines and twin rotors, entered RAF service in September 1961 as a transport and troop carrier, equipping three squadrons. This Belvedere serial XG456 of 66 Squadron was photographed in June 1964 at Nanga Gaat in North Borneo while transporting a downed Wessex 1 of the Royal Navy's 845 Squadron. Belvederes were retired in March 1969. (P. Batten)

identification of their positions improved and air attacks became more effective while the large-scale maps provided from 81 Squadron's surveys enabled the ground forces to dispose their units more accurately. The policy of gathering villagers into protected encampments began to pay dividends. Increased numbers of terrorists surrendered, and known communist sympathisers in the country were deported. The first Westland Dragonfly HC2 helicopters arrived in April 1950 and assisted in reconnaissance as well as casualty evacuation. By the middle of 1954 it was estimated that 7,500 terrorists had been killed or captured, leaving about 3,500 in the jungles. Some areas of Malaya had been completely cleared of terrorists.

The Far East Air Force was always the last to receive the RAF's new equipment, but at last modern aircraft began to arrive. The fighter-bomber squadrons were equipping with Vampires and then Venoms. Meteor PR 9s arrived to re-equip 81 Squadron in December 1953, and on 1 April 1954 the squadron enjoyed the distinction of flying the last operational sortie of any Spitfire. This was followed by the last operational sortie of any Mosquito on 15 December 1955. The venerable Sunderlands at Seletar were also beginning to wear out. On 1 October 1954, 88 Squadron was disbanded and its remaining flying boats were distributed among the other two squadrons. Then 209 Squadron was disbanded on 1 January 1955 and all the Sunderlands were concentrated in 205 Squadron. Bristol Sycamore helicopters arrived to form 194 Squadron at Kuala Lumpur in October 1954, improving both casualty evacuation and reconnaissance. Scottish Aviation Pioneers of 267 Squadron also supported these operations.

Both reconnaissance and air strikes were intensified in 1954 and co-ordinated even more precisely with ground operations. Large-scale maps were constantly updated by photo-reconnaissance carried out by 81 Squadron. Austers marked targets with smoke or flares and air strikes followed almost immediately, before the terrorists had time to disperse. The terrorists could no longer find hiding places, and by the end of the year it seemed that the security forces were within sight of winning the conflict.

The end came after the new Federal Government of Malaya offered an amnesty to the remaining terrorists in November 1955, in advance of the independence which had been arranged for the country. Sporadic violence continued but, when this independence within the Commonwealth was attained on 31 August 1957, any residual sympathy among the population for the communists evaporated. By 1 April 1959 it became possible for most RAF units to leave Malaya and hand over their duties to the emergent Royal Malayan Air Force and three RAAF squadrons. The Emergency regulations were finally lifted on 31 July 1960, by which time a hard core of only about five hundred communists remained in the interior, waiting impotently for a time when they might become a resurgent force. This brought to an end twelve years of campaigning in which photo-reconnaissance had played a major and vital part.

While Malaya was achieving its independence, a new organisation was formed. This was the South-East Asia Treaty Organisation (SEATO), which was born at a conference held in Manila in September 1954 attended by Australia, Britain, France, New Zealand, Pakistan, the Philippine Republic, the United States and Thailand. It came into force on 19 February 1955 and provided a defensive alliance against communist aggression, with headquarters in Bangkok. There were no standing military forces but joint exercises were held from time to time.

In August 1957 the RAF opened an important staging post on the island of Gan in the Maldives, thus providing a strategic link between the Middle East and the Far East which was independent of India, Pakistan and Ceylon. This was placed three months later under the control of the Far East Air Force. It was not used as a permanent base for any RAF squadrons but detachments could be sent there for exercises, including photo-reconnaissance Canberras.

After leaving the Malayan mainland, the Far East Air Force concentrated its squadrons at Singapore. Among these was 205 Squadron, which was equipped with Avro Shackleton MR 1As in May 1958 and moved from Seletar to Changi, and 81 Squadron, which received Canberra PR 7s in January 1960 when based at Tengah. After a few quiet years, the RAF in the region found itself involved in yet another confrontation, this time in Indonesia. This arose in 1962 from the proposal to incorporate Malaya, Singapore Island and British North Borneo into a new Federation of Malaysia, within the Commonwealth. British North Borneo consisted of the Crown Colonies of Sarawak, Sabah and Brunei, but to the south was the much larger Indonesian state of Kalimantan, and the Indonesian Republic laid claim to the whole island and indeed even to Singapore and Malaya.

Rebellion and terrorism fomented by the Indonesian Government, which included a strong communist influence, began in Brunei and Sarawak during December 1962. British and Gurkha troops were flown from Singapore to support the local police and other forces, landing at the RAF base in the island of Labuan, which was easy to protect. Most of the pockets of revolutionary forces were then suppressed but incursions by bands of armed irregulars from Kalimantan occurred. These intensified when the Federation of Malaya was proclaimed on 16 September 1963, until an undeclared state of war existed between Malaysia and Indonesia. Fortunately the new Federation was supported by the majority of its Malayan and

Chinese population in North Borneo, although the oil-rich state of Brunei chose to remain a separate Sultanate within the Commonwealth. Nevertheless the incursions became so threatening that it was decided to evacuate many British residents to Singapore.

The terrain in North Borneo is similar to that of Malaya but the jungle is even thicker and the mountains are higher, while the climate is wetter. The country had been surveyed by the Mosquito PR 34s of 81 Squadron in 1947 and the defending troops had the additional advantage of experience in Malaya and the use of advanced helicopters. The frontier was enormous, about 800 miles, but the aerial survey disclosed that there were only a few feasible points of entry and these were guarded by troops who were often landed by Westland Whirlwind HAR 10 helicopters of 225 Squadron, which had been sent out from Odiham in 1960 and were based at Kuching in Sarawak but operated from various airstrips. These were reinfoced by a detachment of Westland Belvedere HC 1 heavy-lift helicopters from 66 Squadron sent out from Khormaksar. Supplies were either parachuted to the troops or landed by these helicopters. Naval helicopters also joined in this work, and at a later stage Whirlwinds of 103 and 110 Squadrons also arrived.

Tactical photo-reconnaissance was of course essential, and this was supplied mainly by the Canberra PR 7s of the ubiquitous 81 Squadron, which were detached to Labuan from Singapore, occasionally supported by Canberra PR 7s of 13 Squadron detached from Malta. The earlier photographic survey had been on too small a scale for tactical use on the ground but the great endurance and better performance of the Canberra and its camera equipment provided large-scale photography of jungle tracks and crossing points, as well as longhouses which might harbour the terrorists. Moreover, the processing of the films and photo-interpretation was carried

A Wessex HU 5 of the Royal Navy's 848 Squadron, based at Bario in North Borneo, delivering supplies to troops of the Gurkha Regiment in September 1965.
(P. Batten)

out with remarkable speed. The intelligence gained was superior even to that acquired in Malaya, giving the troops an advantage which the Indonesian Air Force did not provide for the invaders.

At the same time, a detachment of Shackletons from 205 Squadron at Labuan provided maritime photo-reconnaissance in liaison with the Royal Navy, although it seems that the Indonesians made few attempts to land insurgents or supplies from the sea in North Borneo. The presence of these aircraft and the Royal Navy persuaded Indonesian naval vessels to retire to safety. However, in August 1964 a party of about a hundred regular Indonesian troops was landed by small craft on the west coast of Johore in Malaya, and about the same number were dropped inland from a Hercules several days later. Some sabotage followed and more Indonesian troops were landed. Their locations were identified by air reconnaissance and air strikes and ground attacks followed. In all, 451 Indonesian soldiers arrived and every one was either killed or captured before the attempts at invasion ceased during the following March. They caused irritation but very little damage.

Meanwhile regular Indonesian troops joined in the infiltration of North Borneo and the defending forces were permitted to cross the border for a distance of up to 10,000 yards as a counter-measure. The Indonesian Air Force took little part in these operations, knowing that RAF fighter squadrons provided an effective defence and would be eager to shoot down their aircraft. Nevertheless the ground incursions continued into 1965, although the troops showed no desire for conflict with the British or the Gurkhas.

In August 1965 Singapore decided to leave the Federation of Malaysia and to pursue its own policy of expansion, but it remained within the Commonwealth and continued to support the counter-insurgency operations.

The conflict dragged on in Borneo, but an important event followed in the next month when the Indonesian Communist Party failed in an attempt to stage a coup in the country. Popular feeling moved against the communists and, although the armed incursions continued into 1966, a peace treaty was signed between Indonesia and Malaysia in August of that year. The campaign ended and the RAF and the other security forces began to withdraw from Borneo.

In spite of the successful conclusion of the Indonesian confrontation, the expense involved caused concern at home, coming as it did at the same time as other conflicts in the Middle East. By 1966 Britain decided that it could no longer afford expensive commitments abroad and must provide for emergencies by retaining at home a 'rapid reaction' force which could be transported quickly by air to any trouble spots. A programme of training the Royal Malayan Air Force and the emergent Singapore Air Force began to achieve success. The area remained quiet, while Britain did not participate in the Vietnam War which began with the direct involvement of American forces in 1965 and ended with the surrender of Saigon in 1975.

RAF squadrons were disbanded or withdrawn to the UK. The remaining forces were withdrawn from Borneo. In January 1970, 81 Squadron, which had performed for so long and so magnificently in the Far East, was disbanded at Tengah. This was followed by 205 Squadron at Changi in October 1971, when the RAF finally left the island. The Far East Asia Command and the Far East Air Force closed down. RAF Gan continued as a staging post until March 1976 and the South East Asia Treaty Organisation was finally wound up in June 1977. Soon afterwards, only 28 Squadron in Hong Kong represented the RAF in the Far East, equipped with Westland Wessex HC2 helicopters.

CHAPTER SIXTEEN

STRIKE COMMAND

When it was formed in April 1968, Strike Command possessed only two long-range strategic reconnaissance squadrons. Both had formed part of Bomber Command, which was incorporated into the new organization as No 1 Group. Of these, 543 Squadron at Wyton had acquired Handley Page Victor SR 2s in January 1966 after its ageing Vickers Valiant B (PR) 1s were grounded in the previous year. These aircraft were normally employed on high-altitude work in daylight, when the bomb bays were fitted with up to eight F96 cameras, each with a focal length of 48 inches, arranged in a fan so as to cover a wide area from horizon to horizon. Improvements in film emulsions, automatic exposure in varying conditions of light, and the introduction of computerised techniques in the design of lenses added to the effectiveness. Radar photography had also improved with later and better versions of the H_2S, and more advanced methods were being developed. Although American satellites were steadily replacing such manned aircraft in the strategic reconnaissance role, 543 Squadron continued as a photograpic unit until it was disbanded in May 1974.

Meanwhile, 27 Squadron at Scampton in Lincolnshire was equipped in November 1973 with Avro Vulcan SR 2s and continued in a similar capacity as the RAF's strategic reconnaissance squadron, with the additional duties of mapping and ocean surveillance. However, the squadron was disbanded in March 1982, although re-formed a few

months later with the new Panavia Tornado GR 1 in the tactical role. Another unit was 51 Squadron, also based at Wyton, equipped with de Havilland Comet R1s in the electronic intelligence and radar reconnaissance roles. As related in Chapter Thirteen, these were supplemented by Hawker Siddeley Nimrod R1s in July 1971 but the Comets continued alongside the new aircraft for three more years. The work of this squadron is considered so vital that it continues in 1996, still equipped with three Nimrod R1s.

The only home-based photo-reconnaissance unit in 1968 equipped with Canberra PR 7s and PR 9s was 58 Squadron at Wyton. Detachments were in course of completing a number of surveys overseas before the squadron was disbanded in September 1970.

Coastal Command became part of Strike Command in November 1969, forming No 18 Group in the new organisation. It brought with it six squadrons equipped with the redoubtable Avro Shackleton. These included the earliest MR 1, which had first entered service in April 1951, the 'extended' version known as the MR 2 which was introduced almost two years later, and the MR 3, with a tricycle undercarriage and various other improvements, which was supplied to squadrons from August 1957 onwards. The search for a jet replacement for this venerable aircraft had been continuing for some time, however, and it was found in another

The Hawker Siddeley Buccaneer first entered service with the RAF in October 1970, primarily as a maritime strike aircraft, and eventually equipped five squadrons. Buccaneers also served in Germany and later in the Gulf War, where one of their tasks was to act as target designators for Tornados carrying Paveway laser-guided bombs. This photograph shows Buccaneer serial XN981 of 12 Squadron from Lossiemouth in Morayshire. It is armed with Martel anti-shipping missiles, AJ168 TV guided with the blunt nose and AS37 anti-radar with the pointed nose. Behind it is Buccaneer serial XZ432 of 237 Operational Conversion Unit from the same station. (Flight Lieutenant I. Gilchrist RAF)

Above, left: The F126 reconnaissance camera, size 25-inch by 16-inch, takes about 300 exposures of 9-inch by 9-inch. It is primarily designed for medium or high altitude in daylight, without flash facility, but is fitted with an automatic exposure control which enables photography at dusk. The movement of the camera over the ground is balanced by an 'image movement compensation' system, controlled remotely by input data of velocity and height, so that the aircraft can be flown at a wide range of altitudes and speeds. *Above, right*: The F135 camera was designed for low-altitude reconnaissance, both day and night. In size, it is about 12-inch by 8½-inch by 9-inch. It has a twin lens arrangement which allows photographs to be taken in alternate sequence, giving a good overlap of 50 per cent. The picture size is 2¼-inch by 2¼-inch, and 1,000 exposures can be taken (500 on each track). An automatic exposure control sets both the aperture and shutter to suit light conditions, both at day and night. The mechanism also incorporates 'image movement compensation', to correct the effect of speed of the aircraft. (Both photos: Flight Lieutenant G.H. Parry RAF (Ret'd))

Nine Avro Vulcan B2s were modified as Vulcan MM2s to carry out the role of long-range marine reconnaissance. They entered service with 27 Squadron at Waddington in Lincolnshire in November 1973 and continued in service until March 1982. This Vulcan B2 serial XM598 continued as a bomber and is now on display at the Aerospace Museum at Cosford in Shropshire. (Squadron Leader P.J. Thompson RAF (Ret'd))

Lockheed Hercules C3 serial XV301 of 47 Squadron, fitted with a refuelling probe, at Lyneham in Wiltshire in 1991. These aircraft first entered RAF service in 1966 and, in their modified form, were the standard military transport in 1995. (R.C. Nesbit)

adaptation of the civilian Comet airliner. This entered RAF service in October 1970 as the Hawker Siddeley Nimrod MR I and, with its fin-mounted radome, integrated navigational system and digital computer, quickly replaced all the RAF's Shackletons apart from those supplied to 8 Squadron soon after it was re-formed at Kinloss in Morayshire on 1 January 1972. This new version was the Shackleton AEW which was converted from the MR 2 and carried a huge radome under the nose. Eleven of these Shackleton aircraft were converted and they remained the only Airborne Early Warning aircraft supplied to the RAF until Boeing E–3D Sentries were purchased from America and entered service with 8 Squadron in 1991. By this time, Shackletons had served for forty years.

Coastal Command also contributed five squadrons of helicopters, equipped with either the Westland Wessex HC 2 or the Westland Whirlwind HAR 10. Helicopters had proved their worth overseas in casualty evacuation and Army support and their development in this capacity continued apace in Britain. However, the Wessexes and Whirlwinds of No 18 Group were employed primarily in the search and rescue role around the coasts of Britain, although they could also be used for photo-reconnaissance. The transport of troops by helicopter was carried out by Air Support Command, as Transport Command had been renamed in 1967.

Conventional cameras continued in widespread use in the tactical role. This function was carried out by aircraft of the former Fighter Command, which had become No 11 Group of Strike Command. The cameras were fitted in fast and manoeuvrable interceptors adapted for the purpose, and many of these served in RAF Germany as a separate Command under Nato. The Canberra PR 7s in Germany were being phased out at this stage, in favour of these

newer jets. No 80 Squadron was disbanded at Brüggen in September 1969, followed by 17 Squadron at Wildenrath three months later. No 31 Squadron at Laarbruch soldiered on until March 1971 but was then disbanded.

By 1972 seven squadrons equipped with new tactical reconnaissance jet aircraft were based at Brüggen, Laarbruch and Wildenrath, from where they confronted the potential enemy, the Soviet Union. Four of the squadrons were equipped with the McDonnell Douglas Phantom FGR 2, which had first entered RAF service three years previously. This aircraft carried up to five day or night cameras in a reconnaissance pod made by the electronics group EMI. During the day, these usually consisted of four F95 cameras and one F135 camera. At night, four F135 cameras were carried, together with electronic sensors such as the new Sideways-Looking Reconnaissance Radar (SLRR), which could pick up fairly large objects at night, and a heat-seeking Infra-Red Linescan (IRLS), which recorded the relative temperatures of objects on the surface. In addition, the pod carried a Modulator Data Converter which recorded the position, speed and direction of the aircraft on the film strip.

The remaining three tactical squadrons in Germany employed the British Aerospace Harrier GR 1, which came into service in July 1969. Apart from its remarkable Short Take-Off and Vertical Landing (STO/VL) capabilities with a full load, this aircraft carried a single F95 camera facing obliquely to port. It could also carry a reconnaissance pod, often fitted with four F95 cameras facing alternately to port and starboard, a single F135 camera and a data unit. Of course, these cameras could be replaced with others or the combination altered as each sortie demanded.

Since these two types of tactical photo-reconnaissance aircraft flew at very low level and at high speed over their targets, blurring

An Air Transportable Reconnaissance Exploitation Laboratory (ATREL) at RAF Cosford in 1991. These laboratories can be flown to the area of operations, where several can be joined by vestibules to form a complete imagery exploitation laboratory. (J.K. Nesbit)

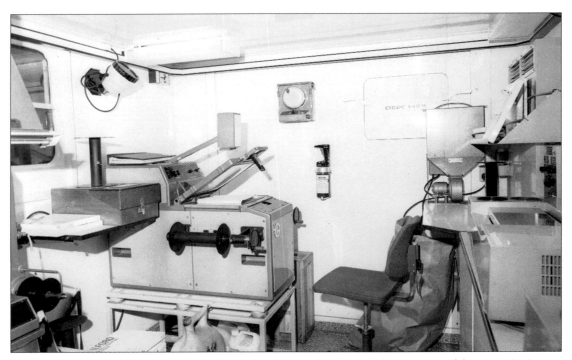

Interior view of an Air Transportable Reconnaissance Exploitation Laboratory showing an electronic printer and a print processor. (Flight Lieutenant G.H. Parry RAF (Ret'd))

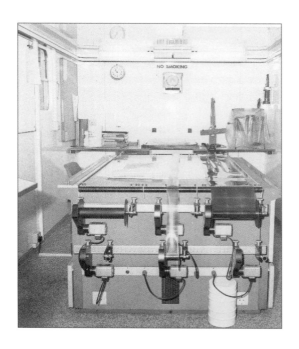

Interior view of an Air Transportable Reconnaissance Exploitation Laboratory showing a 'seven-strand viewing table'. (Flight Lieutenant G.H. Parry RAF (Ret'd))

Moveable Air Reconnaissance Exploitation Laboratories (MARELS), which can be transported to an area of operations on low-loader trucks. (Flight Lieutenant G.H. Parry RAF (Ret'd))

of the exposure would have ruined the result without the Image Movement Compensation (IMC) which had been introduced in the Second World War and thereafter steadily improved. This ensured that the film in the camera was set to move in such a way as to match the relative speed of the aircraft over the ground, by means of direct inputs giving speed and altitude.

The RAF's School of Photography at Cosford continued its work, but in 1972 became the Joint School of Photography (JSOP) when the Royal Navy's school at Lossiemouth, which had trained both Navy and Army students, closed down. From this time, JSOP at Cosford came under the joint control of the three services, and officers have been appointed from each to command the school.

Other improvements at this stage concentrated on reducing the time taken from the moment the reconnaissance aircraft landed to the provision of intelligence information about the enemy. Mobile Reconnaissance Intelligence Centres (RICs) were provided, on the lines of the mobile units which were employed with great success in the Second World War but with the addition of Air Transportable Reconnaissance Exploitation Laboratories (ATRELs) which could be flown at short notice to the area of operations, usually in the Lockheed Hercules of Air Support Command, formerly named Transport Command. This joined Strike Command in September 1972 to become No 46 Group. The structure of Strike Command thus became far simpler than the numerous Commands which had preceded it.

RAF photographic activities continued to concentrate on tactical work and in March 1974 the Sepecat Jaguar GR 1 was introduced, replacing the Phantom in Germany and at home. This could also carry a reconnaissance pod, containing an Infra-Red Linescan and four F95 cameras, two of which were sometimes replaced with F126 vertical cameras. Eight RAF squadrons were equipped with this machine, three in Strike Command and five in RAF Germany. In 1995, the Jaguar GR 1A was still in service with the RAF.

On 10 April 1975 the whole of the RAF's Strike Command was added to Nato, becoming known within this organisation as United Kingdom Air Forces. The area of Nato extended from the North Pole to the Tropic of Cancer and included much of Europe and the Atlantic within its sphere of operations. The role of this powerful organisation remained that of vigilance, providing a potent deterrent against any threat from the Soviet Bloc, fortunately without having to resort to hostilities.

When the home-based RAF squadrons were eventually drawn into conflict, it was in an unexpected part of the world, the South Atlantic, after the Falklands Islands were invaded by Argentine forces on 2 April 1982. The dependency of South Georgia was invaded the following day. British rule in the Falklands had prevailed for over two hundred years and its inhabitants looked to their home country for protection, even though they were about 8,000 miles distant from London. At this time, Britain's overseas commitments were largely concentrated in Germany but her response was remarkably swift. The first vessels of the South Atlantic Task Force left Portsmouth on 5 April, while intense but fruitless diplomatic efforts were made to persuade Argentina to withdraw.

The war was fought by British combined forces, with the majority of the soldiers and marines landed from ships, but of course aircraft of the Royal Navy, Army and the RAF also played a crucial role in the ultimate victory. Numerically, the Sea Harriers and helicopters of the Fleet Air Arm formed the greater part of the strike force, although some of its Sea Harriers were flown by RAF pilots.

The fighter and reconnaissance version of the McDonnell Douglas Phantom, the FRG, first entered service with the RAF in Germany in June 1970. This aircraft, serial XV406 of 43 Squadron at Leuchars in Fife, was photographed in November 1970 while carrying four Raytheon Sparrow air-to-air missiles and a reconnaissance pod. (Hawker Siddeley Aviation)

A camera pod being fitted on a Phantom FGR 2 of 2 Squadron in 1973, when the squadron was based at Laarbruch in Germany. (*Aeroplane Monthly*)

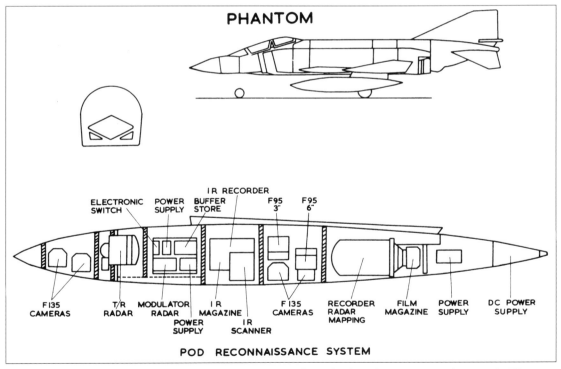

PHANTOM

POD RECONNAISSANCE SYSTEM

An example of the contents of the sensors on the pod carried by the Phantom FGR 2 when employed on night reconnaissance. In this instance the F95 cameras would be fitted but not used. (Flight Lieutenant G.H. Parry RAF (Ret'd))

They were backed by light helicopters of the Royal Marines and the Army Air Corps. The contribution of the RAF consisted of Vulcans, Hercules, Victors, Harriers, Nimrods and VC10s, with Sea King and Chinook helicopters. They were opposed by the Argentine Air Force, one of the strongest in Latin America, with some aircraft already installed on the short runway of 4,200 feet at Port Stanley airfield in the Falklands but with the majority of their modern fighters 400 miles distant in their home country.

The British could not have attempted to regain the Falklands without the facility provided by the Americans of their Wideawake staging airfield at Ascension, a British island in the Atlantic roughly equidistant between England and the war zone. Nevertheless the logistical problems were formidable, with supplies carried by RAF Hercules refuelled in flight by Victors. The first elements of the Task Force sailed from Ascension Island on 16 April for the Falklands, led by the carriers HMS *Hermes* and *Invincible*. At this stage its air component consisted of twenty Sea Harriers of the Fleet Air Arm, together with Westland Sea King, Wessex, Lynx and Wasp helicopters from the same service. The Army Air Corps and the Royal Marine Commandos of the Task Force were supported by their own Westland Scout and Aerospace/Westland Gazelle helicopters, employed mainly on reconnaissance.

The first maritime photo-reconnaissance sorties were carried out from Wideawake by Nimrod MR 1s of the RAF's 42 Squadron, which flew from their base at St Mawgan in Cornwall. The aircraft carried Harpoon anti-ship missiles and were additionally fitted with pylons which enabled them to carry four Sidewinder missiles, although these weapons were never used. This detachment from 42 Squadron was replaced on 12 April by Nimrod MR 2s of 120, 201 and 206

Squadrons from Kinloss in Morayshire, fitted with more effective Searchwater radar equipment.

Some of the Victors also carried out photo-reconnaissance sorties, after being converted from their tanker role with equipment taken from retired Vulcan SR 2s. The first sortie took place on 20 April from Wideawake over South Georgia, in a flight of over fourteen hours, and this was followed by two more flights. The dependency was retaken on 25 April by a small task force under the command of the Royal Navy which left Gibraltar in early April, headed by two destroyers and carrying Lynx and Wessex helicopters. The tasks of the Victors were to supply intelligence about the Argentine forces and the presence of any pack ice or icebergs in the vicinity of South Georgia. Each sortie required four refuelling tankers on both the outward and return flights. Meanwhile the Nimrod MR 2s from Kinloss were modified by installing in-flight refuelling probes which, from 9 May, enabled them to fly on maritime photo-reconnaissance sorties of up to nineteen hours.

There is little doubt, however, that the RAF felt the loss of Airborne Early Warning aircraft with sufficient range and modern equipment for the task in hand. A long-standing programme to convert Nimrods to this role was in progress but never came to fruition. It was eventually cancelled in December 1986, when the Boeing E–3D Sentry was ordered. Meanwhile, it was believed by some aviation observers that Sentries of the USAF may have supported the RAF in the Falklands campaign.

While these maritime reconnaissance flights were taking place, the Argentine forces on Aeroporto Malvinas, as they had confidently renamed Stanley airport, received a foretaste of their unpleasant future. At a very early hour on 1 May a stick of twenty-one 1,000–lb bombs was dropped across the

The Sepecat Jaguar was first introduced into the RAF in 1974 as a supersonic fighter which could also be employed on ground attack and tactical reconnaissance. This Jaguar GR 1A was painted in desert pink for the Gulf War and fitted with a reconnaissance pod, a Sidewinder missile and an electronic counter-measures fit. (Senior Aircraftman N. Green RAF)

The British Aerospace Harrier GR 3 was updated from the GR 1 which, in July 1969, was the first 'vertical take-off and landing' aircraft to enter any air force in the world. Although designed as a single-seat aircraft in the ground attack role, these early marks also had a photo-reconnaissance capability, with one F135 vertical and four F95 oblique cameras in a pod. This Harrier GR 3 of 1 (Fighter) Squadron at Wittering in Cambridgeshire participated in the Falklands campaign. (Flight Lieutenant R.D. Chalmers RAF (Ret'd))

The last version of the long-lived Avro Shackleton was the Advanced Early Warning adaptation, twelve of which were converted from MR 2s from 1971 onwards. The bulky radome under the nose carried the special equipment. All were supplied to 8 Squadron, at first based at Kinloss in Morayshire but moving to Lossiemouth in August 1973. Shackleton AEW 2s remained in service until 1991. They were named after characters in the children's BBC TV programme *Magic Roundabout*, serial WR963 in this programme being *Ermintrude*. (Flight Lieutenant R.D. Chalmers RAF (Ret'd))

runway by a Vulcan B2 of 44 Squadron from Wideawake, with a crew from 101 Squadron. This bomber arrived over the airfield after being refuelled on numerous occasions by Victors. The main purpose of this attack was to deny the airfield to the Mirages and Super Etendards of the Argentine Air Force on the mainland, which might have been able to use the short runway with the aid of arrester gear. It was followed at dawn by a low-level strike by Sea Harriers of the Task Force, against both the airport and a grass airfield at Goose Green. The counter-invasion had begun, and the Falkland Islanders knew that liberation would follow.

The first RAF tactical strike aircraft employed on the enterprise were nine Harrier GR 3s of 1 Squadron at Wittering, which had made record flights of over nine hours to Wideawake between 3 and 5 May, refuelled en route by Victors. Six of these embarked on 8 May for the Falklands in the container ship *Atlantic Conveyor*. The other three followed later, together with five more, after their defensive role at Wideawake had been taken over on 24 May by Phantom FGR 2s of 29 Squadron from Coningsby in Lincolnshire. The first six RAF Harriers together with Sea Harriers, were transferred between 18 and 19 May to the aircraft carrier HMS *Hermes*, joining other Sea Harriers and the Sea Kings of the Fleet Air Arm. Four Boeing Vertol Chinook HC 1 helicopters from the RAF's 18 Squadron based at Odiham in Hampshire were also carried by *Atlantic Conveyor*, but the Sea King HAR 3 helicopters provided by the RAF's 202 Squadron at Brawdy in Pembrokeshire remained at Ascension Island, where they were employed on search-and-rescue duties and on transporting stores.

The battle for the Falklands was bitter and bloody, fought by all arms of the British forces, although thick fog reduced flying activities for the first three weeks of May.

Operating from the mainland, the Argentine Air Force attacked the Task Force with great determination and courage. In spite of heavy losses, its pilots sank the destroyer HMS *Sheffield* on 4 May, the frigate HMS *Ardent* on 21 May, the frigate HMS *Antelope* on 23 May and the destroyer HMS *Coventry* on 25 May. They damaged the container ship *Atlantic Conveyor* so badly on 25 May that she sank three days later. Three of the RAF's four Chinook helicopters were destroyed when the latter vessel was hit by an Exocet missile, but the remaining aircraft carried out magnificent service until the end of the campaign. The Royal Fleet Auxiliary *Sir Galahad* was sunk by air attack on 8 June, while *Sir Tristram* was badly damaged.

Once the RAF Harriers arrived, the FAA Harriers were able to concentrate on defensive operations and air combat, in which they proved superior to the attacking aircraft. The RAF Harriers acquitted themselves extremely well in attacks against heavily defended ground targets, the first of which took place against fuel dumps on 20 May, the day before the main landings of troops began. By 9 June, they also operated from a short aluminium strip at St Carlos Bay. No records have yet been released of any photo-reconnaissance work, but of course the aircraft were capable of carrying out such duties.

Ten FAA or RAF Harriers were lost, of which five were in accidents. Much tactical reconnaissance was carried out by Scout and Gazelle helicopters. Of the 23 helicopters, were lost, 19 of them accidentally or sunk in vessels. It was estimated that 117 Argentine aircraft were destroyed or probably destroyed, over half of which were helicopters, and about 30 more were captured. The campaign ended with a complete victory for the British forces on 14 June when the demoralised Argentine troops surrendered.

The Westland/Aérospatiale Puma was one of the products of a joint Anglo-French manufacturing arrangement, which first entered RAF squadron service in June 1971. It is used for casualty evacuation, troop carrying and as a gunship. (The Westland Group)

The Westland Wessex first entered RAF service in 1964, for tactical reconnaissance and ground assault. Some are still in use for search and rescue duties. This Wessex HC2 serial XT601 of A Flight 22 Squadron at Chivenor in Devon was photographed on 15 December 1986 when the photographer Jane Cowderoy, dressed in orange survival suit, was about to be winched up with the assistance of the navigator Flight Lieutenant Bob Lander. (R.C. Nesbit)

The winchman of Wessex HC2 serial XT601, Flight Sergeant Ken Tucker, being lowered on to a tiny rock off the steep cliffs of Lundy Island, 300 feet below, during a practice exercise. He reached it while the sea was foaming and spray blowing over him. (Jane Cowderoy)

Westland Sea King HAR 3 helicopters were delivered to the RAF from December 1977 onwards for long-range search and rescue work. They replaced the Whirlwinds and are also replacing the Wessexes. This Sea King serial ZE368 is on the strength of 202 Squadron, based at Finningley in Yorkshire with detached flights at various stations. (The Westland Group)

The EH101 is a multi-role helicopter produced by EH Industries, a company formed by Westland Helicopters and Augusta. The Royal Navy variant, named 'Merlin' is fitted with the latest detection equipment and can carry four homing torpedos. The Military-Utility variant was under order for the RAF in 1995. The Westland Group)

The Panavia Tornado GR 1 arrived in RAF service slightly too late to participate in the Falklands War. The first operational unit to receive this formidable two-seater was 9 Squadron at Honington in Suffolk during January 1982, but eventually ten squadrons were equipped with the aircraft. The GR 1 was (and remains) a low-level, tactical aircraft fitted with radar which enabled it to find its target in all weathers and at night. It was followed in 1984 by the Tornado F2 interceptor version. In 1990 the Tornado GR 1A arrived, a low-level reconnaissance version which acts as a pathfinder for the GR 1 and other aircraft, or records the results of their attacks. It is fitted with the TIRRS (Tornado Infra-Red Reconnaissance System). Part of this equipment consists of an Infra-Red Line Scanner which sweeps from side to side along the track of the aircraft. However, since the aircraft flies at low level, the picture definition near either horizon is less well defined. To compensate for this defect, two Sideways Looking Infra-Red sensors are also fitted, providing high resolution near the horizons. Computers 'stretch' these distant recordings so that the results, combined with those of the Infra-Red Line Scanner, are similar to vertical photography at a high level. This system is positioned below the fuselage in place of two 27–mm cannons of the GR 1, with the recordings displayed on a TV-type screen in the navigator's position. The GR 1A was not designed to carry conventional cameras but the imagery of the system is of high quality and the results are video-taped for later analysis. Moreover, it is effective both by day and at night without the use of photo-flashes. In addition to its remarkable reconnaissance work, the machine has a secondary attack role.

The next major conflict in which the RAF participated was the Gulf War of 1991/2. This arose from Iraq's claim to Kuwait, a sheikdom which had been granted independence by the British in 1961. The Iraqis had never recognised this new state and, when their long war with Iran ended in the late 1980s, felt strong enough to invade the Sheikdom and acquire its oil resources. On 2 August 1990 troops of the Iraqi Republican Guard crossed the frontier, brushed aside isolated pockets of Kuwaiti resistance and soon occupied the whole country.

The government of Saudi Arabia invited foreign countries to send troops to protect its country from potential aggression, while the Security Council of the United Nations imposed strict sanctions on trade with Iraq. From 7 August strong contingents of the USAF flew to Saudi Arabia and two days later the British Government announced that its forces would also move to that country and the Gulf States, forming part of what became known as the Coalition Force. Strategic and radar reconnaissance of Iraq was provided by aircraft of the USAF, including the U–2R, while satellites were also employed.

By 16 January 1991, the day before Operation 'Desert Storm' began to retake Kuwait, about 600,000 troops, 4,000 tanks and 150 warships were available within Saudi Arabia, the Gulf States and Turkey, apart from the air forces. It was estimated by the Iraqis that the equivalent of the force designed to combat the entire Warsaw Pact countries was ranged against them.

By this time the RAF had contributed 18 Tornado F3 interceptors, 40 Tornado GR 1s for tactical bombing operations, 6 of the new Tornado GR 1As for reconnaissance, 12 Jaguar GR 1As for tactical attacks and photo-reconnaissance, 17 Victor K2 or VC10 K2 tankers, 3 Nimrod MR 2s, 12 Chinook HC 1 helicopters, 19 Puma helicopters, 7 Hercules transports and 1 BAe 125 communications aircraft. These aircraft were detached from various squadrons, none of

The Hawker Siddeley Nimrod was developed from the Comet airliner as a maritime reconnaissance aircraft, first entering RAF service in October 1969. This Nimrod MR 2 of 42 Squadron was photographed at RAF St Mawgan in Cornwall in November 1985, showing bomb doors open to receive McDonnell Douglas *Harpoon* anti-shipping missiles and Electronic Support Measures (ECM) on top of the fin. Magnetic Anomaly Detector (MAD) equipment, developed to pick up alterations in the Earth's magnetic field from a submarine or surface vessesl, was in the tail. (R.C. Nesbit)

The five screens of a Marconi AQS-901 digital processing and display system in a Nimrod MR 2. These are known as the 'wet' equipment, which deals with signals received from sonobuoys dropped from the aircraft. These detect the position of a submarine prior to launching torpedos from the bomb bay. (R.C. Nesbit)

The Electronics Support Measures (ESM), or Searchwater radar, are known as the 'dry' equipment. Signals returned from a surface vessel are processed by computer and displayed on the screen. (R.C. Nesbit)

The tactical position in the navigators' compartment of a Nimrod, with the input data from the 'wet' and 'dry' operators displayed on a 24-inch screen (switched off in this photograph). The weapons system for anti-submarine torpedos is on the right, with the author sitting in front of the equipment. (R.C. Nesbit)

which flew out in their entirety, and formed composite squadrons in the Gulf. However, the total strength of about 7,000 personnel included squadrons of the RAF Regiment. The aircraft were followed by other detachments, including twelve Hawker Siddeley Buccaneer S2Bs. This ageing aircraft had been introduced into the RAF in 1969. It had been employed initially in the maritime strike role but was also capable of operating over land and in the event was to give a good account of itself. The Royal Navy and the Army also contributed helicopters, both for strike and reconnaissance.

The air attack, once launched, was awe-inspiring in its ferocity and effectiveness. Among the first to participate were the Tornado GR 1s, whose crews were given the highly dangerous task of putting Iraqi runways out of action with JP233 cluster bombs, in night attacks. Four Tornados were lost in four days, but eight Iraqi airfields were closed. Then they operated against Iraqi supply lines, storage dumps and hardened shelters, often working in combination with Buccaneer S2Bs. The Tornados used thermal imaging and laser guided bombs while the Buccaneers were fitted with laser designator pods which further directed these bombs to their targets. Three more Tornados were lost, one in an accident, but all the Buccaneers returned.

The Tornado GR 1As carried out reconnaissance at night from 18/19 January, each bringing back up to one hour's material for analysis. The first task given to them was the hunt for Iraqi Scud missiles, which were mobile and elusive. They were causing damage and casualties with random attacks against population centres in Israel. Several of these missiles and launchers were located and destroyed, after photo-interpreters of the Reconnaissance Intelligence Centre at Dhahran had examined the expanded imagery on large TV screens. The GR 1As

also carried out other pre- and post-attack reconnaissance, including searches for suitable infiltration routes to be used by Special Forces. Although they formed only part of the reconnaissance units within the Coalition Air Forces, these six aircraft flew on 125 sorties, most of which were classed as successful.

The three Nimrods employed their Searchwater radar to good effect, not only supplementing the information provided by E–3 Sentries of the USAF but largely replacing it. They provided picture images for the US aircraft carrier *Midway* and tactical directions for Lynx helicopters armed with Sea Skua missiles.

The Jaguars flew by day, concentrating at first on naval targets by using high velocity rockets. After sinking or damaging fifteen such vessels, they turned to Iraqi missile sites and artillery batteries along the Kuwaiti coast. These were mobile but moved only at night. Thus pods were fitted to the Jaguars for oblique photography during daylight. The aircraft operated in pairs, one carrying cameras of long focal length and the other with cameras of short focal length. After photo-interpretation, the targets were attacked on the same day, when American clusters bombs were dropped with devastating results. No Jaguars were lost throughout the entire war.

By the time the Coalition ground forces attacked, on 24 February, most of the aircraft of the Iraqi Air Force had been destroyed while some of the remainder had fled the country. The Iraqi Army then suffered enormous casualties as they retreated from Kuwait and fled towards Baghdad. After Iraq surrendered on 28 February, it was estimated that some 3,400 of her tanks had been destroyed, as well as 2,400 armoured personnel carriers, 2,000 artillery pieces, 25 warships or auxiliary vessels, with probably over 100,000 lives lost. The RAF contributed

Stanley Airport in the Falklands, which the Argentines had optimistically renamed Aeroporto Malvinas, photographed on 16 June 1982, two days after the Argentines capitulated. Fake bomb craters made from dirt had been placed on the runway, close to the genuine bomb craters, to deceive British photo-interpreters into believing that attacks made by Vulcan bombers from Ascension Island had scored direct hits on the airport's only runway. (*Aeroplane Monthly*)

The Panavia Tornado GR 1A is a version of the supersonic tactical strike aircraft which first entered operational service in January 1981. It carries infra-red scanners and can operate at a very low level, sweeping large areas and recording the results on a TV-type screen in the navigator's compartment. (British Aerospace)

The Boeing E-3D Sentry began service during 1991 with 8 Squadron at Waddington in Lincolnshire, replacing the venerable Shackleton Airborne Early Warning aircraft. The enormous rotadome antenna mounted on the Boeing 707 airframe is the most distinctive feature of this remarkable aircraft, which is capable of maritime reconnaissance as well as acting as a command post and detecting aircraft at all altitudes. This photograph shows serial ZH101, one of seven Sentries with which 8 Squadron was equipped in 1995 (British Aerospace)

A Hawker Siddeley Buccaneer, painted in 'desert sand', at RAF Lyneham in Wiltshire shortly after the end of the Gulf War. The 'Hello Sailor' motif was particularly suitable for maritime strike and reconnaissance, but the main role of the robust Buccaneer in the Gulf War was laser designation for bombs dropped by Tornados. (R.C. Nesbit)

The Canberra PR 9, fitted with two Rolls-Royce engines of 11,250-lb thrust, first entered service with 58 Squadron in January 1958 as the RAF's high-altitude photo-reconnaissance aircraft, capable of flying above the enemy fighters of that time. Some were still in service in 1995 with 39 (No 1 PRU) Squadron at Marham in Norfolk, such as serial XH168 shown here. (39 (No 1 PRU) Squadron)

The Hycon Type B camera, originally designed for the U-2 project, was fitted with a smaller magazine for use in Canberra photo-reconnaissance aircraft. The camera was built by the Hycon Corporation of California to a specification written by Dr Edwin Land, the inventor of the Polaroid camera. The lens, which has a focal length of only 36 inches, was designed by Dr James Baker and manufactured by new computer-driven techniques of grinding and polishing. A thin plastic film was devised by Eastman Kodak, allowing the U-2 to carry two rolls, each over 5,000 feet in length. About 4,000 paired negatives could be obtained from a single mission, each covering an area 6 miles square from an altitude of about 52,000 feet, in which objects as small as 30 inches across could be distinguished. The camera weighed about 500 lb and only some twenty-five were built. Known as the System 111B, it is at present in use by 39 (No 1 PRU) Squadron at Marham in Norfolk, which is engaged on survey work with Canberra PR 9s and PR 7s. This example is on display with the Imperial War Museum at Duxford in Cambridgeshire. (Chris Pocock)

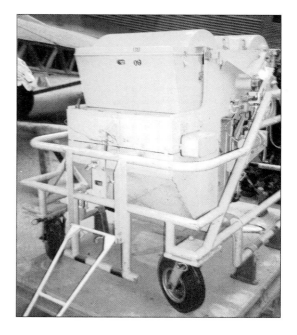

When the Eurofighter EF2000 enters RAF squadron service, it will be fitted with wingtip pods containing electronic surveillance measures and electronic counter-measures. This Eurofighter serial ZH588 is one of three prototypes in existence in 1995. (British Aerospace)

A corner of the museum in the Joint School of Photography at RAF Cosford. The long black exhibit behind the glass case is a German FK3M, an infra-red camera with a 3-metre focal length used for recording British shipping in the English Channel during the Second World War. The white exhibit on the right is a Cintel Electronic Printer, which was used by the RAF for printing negatives of 9-inch by 9-inch, with controllable density correction. Models for planning the D-Day invasion of June 1944 can be seen top left. (Sergeant D. Jenkins RAF (Ret'd), courtesy RAF Cosford Museum)

to this decisive and awesome victory by flying the second largest number of missions of all the air forces in the Coalition Forces.

Soon after the Gulf War ended, 8 Squadron at Waddington in Lincolnshire became operational with the Boeing E–3D Sentry, the crews having trained initially at the Nato air base of Geilenkirchen in Germany. At present, this complex Airborne Early Warning aircraft is the most modern version of a machine which entered service with the USAF in the late 1970s. Capable of undertaking flights of up to twelve hours without refuelling, it is fitted with an enormous rotodome which tracks both airborne and maritime targets from a distance of hundreds of miles. It acts as a flying headquarters for Command, Control, Communications and Intelligence, and the RAF squadron forms part of any Nato rapid reaction force.

Since the Gulf War, the Russian communist system has collapsed and the Cold War is at an end. The RAF is pulling out of Germany and in course of contracting yet again. Reconnaissance and policing duties are still required over Iraq and the fragmented countries of the former Yugoslavia, although fortunately actual conflict is a rarity. Another area which has been reconnoitred extensively by the RAF is Northern Ireland, although no information on this subject has yet been released.

In early 1995, the tactical reconnaissance strength of the RAF consisted of 6, 41 and 54 Squadrons, equipped with Jaguar GR 1As and based at Coltishall in Norfolk, and 2 and 13 Squadrons, equipped with Tornado GR 1As and based at Marham in Norfolk. For maritime patrol, there are 120, 201 and 206 Squadrons, equipped with Nimrod MR 1s and based at Kinloss in Morayshire. Electronic intelligence is provided by the Nimrod R1s of 51 Squadron at Waddington in Lincolnshire, while 8 Squadron at the same

station is equipped with E–3D Sentries for airborne early warning. The names of two famous photo-reconnaissance units of the past have now been combined, forming 39 (No 1 PRU) Squadron at Marham. This squadron is equipped with Canberra PR 9s and PR 7s, and is engaged primarily on reconnaissance duties with the System 111B camera and survey work with Zeiss RMK 15/23 and RMK 30/23 cameras.

In 1995, the Joint Air Reconnaissance Intelligence Centre (UK) – JARIC (UK) – still continued its work at RAF Brampton. The Joint School of Photographic Interpretation (JSPI) is now based at RAF Wyton where it is sponsored by the Ministry of Defence but under the operational control of the Commandant of the Intelligence Centre at Ashford in Kent. Also in 1995, the Joint School of Photography (JSOP) at RAF Cosford celebrated the 80th year since it began its existence as an RFC unit at Farnborough.

The Association of RAF Photography Officers (ARAFPO), which was formed in December 1965, is run from RAF Brampton. Another association is the Medmenham Club, which was formed in July 1946 from wartime photo-interpreters and later became available to officers who passed the Long Photographic Interpretation course at the JSPI. A more recent association is the Boy Entrant Photographers' Association (BEPA), which was formed in 1987 for boys who trained pre-war at the RAF School of Photography when it was located at Farnborough. This also has a 'brother' association, the 'One Niners', which was formed in 1991 for post-war Boy Entrant and Craft Apprentices who trained in photography at the school at RAF Cosford.

The pace of technological advance in reconnaissance increases steadily. The introduction of the video tape in the system fitted to the Tornado GR 1A has removed the

The Zeiss KS-153 camera is used by the RAF for low- to medium-altitude photo-reconnaissance at high speed. The Trilens version shown here has an assembly of three 80-mm lenses with an aperture range of f/2.56 to f/16 and a focal plane shutter giving speeds of up to 1/2,000th of a second. It utilises a single film of 240 mm width and up to 152 metres in length, giving a coverage of 143.5 degrees laterally and 48.5 degrees along the track, with three across-track images per frame. The camera has forward movement compensation and automatic exposure control, achieving results of remarkable clarity. (Carl Zeiss Ltd)

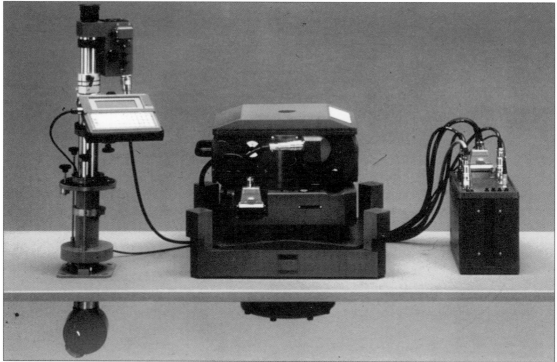

The Zeiss RMK A camera system and the newer RMK TOP camera system are similar in their application, being employed mainly for aerial survey. Both use interchangeable camera body/lens units which have lenses of different focal lengths and angular coverage. The cameras have rotating disc shutters giving a wide range of speeds and incorporate forward movement compensation and automatic exposure control. The film used is 240 mm wide and 150 metres long. This picture shows a typical camera with its magazine, peripheral control units and a navigation telescope. (Carl Zeiss Ltd)

processing which was required with 'wet' film. If circumstances permit, the navigator can pass back information on his screen by radio, as it appears. As a further refinement, the combination of a data-link with the system is now enabling interpreters on the ground to examine a copy of the tape as it appears, so that commanders can assess enemy territory and formations while the aircraft is in flight.

Another item of equipment which can be used for reconnaissance is TIALD (Thermal Imaging Airborne Laser Designator), although this pod was first fitted to Tornado GR1s in the Gulf War for the purpose of guiding bombs dropped at medium level by other aircraft. The pod contains an infra-red sensor, either for use at night or over targets with a strong thermal contrast against their backgrounds. It also includes a laser designator, a target tracker and a transceiver unit. When the target is acquired on the video display in the navigator's cockpit, the tracker is locked on to it and guides the bomb. However, it has been found that the system is also admirable for the purpose of medium-level reconnaissance, giving the RAF a useful tool for surveillance over Iraq and other countries under the authority of Nato.

Yet another introduction takes the form of electro-optical sensors which replace film in conventional cameras, recording imagery on tape with a very high degree of resolution. Once again, these can be transmitted to the ground by data-link.

Technology is advancing to the point where enemy formations will be visible to RAF commanders in all weathers, by day and night, at all times. It is a far cry from the airsick observer in his spinning and buffeting balloon at the turn of the century, peering at the enemy through binoculars and dropping messages or reporting when back on the ground, but the essential principles and value of aerial reconnaissance remain the same.

BIBLIOGRAPHY

Place of publication given only if outside London.

Aart, Dick van der. *Aerial Espionage*. Shrewsbury, Airlife, 1984.

Ashworth, Chris. *RAF Coastal Command 1936–1969*. Sparkford, Patrick Stephens, 1992.

Association of Royal Air Force Photography Officers. *The History of Air Photography in the Royal Air Force* (5 Parts). Private printing, 1977–1982.

Barker, Ralph. *Aviator Extraordinary*. Chatto & Windus, 1969.

Brabazon of Tara, Lord. *The Brabazon Story*. Heinemann, 1956.

Braybrook, Roy. *Battle for the Falklands (3) Air Forces*. Osprey, 1982.

Brooks, Andrew J. *Photo Reconnaissance*. Ian Allan, 1975.

Burrows, William E. *Deep Black*. Bantam Press, 1988.

Campbell, Duncan. *The Unsinkable Aircraft Carrier*. Michael Joseph, 1984.

Cooke, Ronald C. and Nesbit, Roy Conyers. *Target: Hitler's Oil*. William Kimber, 1985.

Crickmore, Paul F. *Lockheed SR–71 Blackbird*. Osprey, 1986.

Deuel, Leo. *Flights into Yesterday*. MacDonald, 1969.

Falls, Cyril. *The First World War*. Longmans, 1960.

Foster, Peter R. *RAF Buccaneer*. Ian Allan, 1987.

Fox, Alan. *A Very Late Development*. University of Warwick, Industrial Relations Research Unit, 1990.

Halley, James J. *The Squadrons of the Royal Air Force & Commonwealth 1918–1988*. Tonbridge, Air Britain, 1988.

Hinsley, F.H. et al. *British Intelligence in the Second World War*. 6 volumes, HMSO, 1979–1990.

Jackson, Paul. *RAF Strike Command*. Ian Allan, 1984.

James, John. *The Paladins*. MacDonald, 1990.

Joint Air Reconnaissance Centre (UK). *A Short History*. RAF Brampton, private printing, 1971.

Jones, H.A. and Raleigh, Sir Walter. *The War in the Air*. 7 volumes, Oxford University Press, 1928.

Jones, R.V. *Most Secret War*. Hodder & Stoughton, 1978.

Kennedy, Colonel William V. *The Intelligence War*. Salamander, 1983.

Lee, Air Chief Marshal Sir David. *Eastward*. HMSO, 1984.

——. *Flight from the Middle East*. HMSO, 1980.

——. *Wings in the Sun*. HMSO, 1989.

Lewis, Peter. *British Aircraft 1809–1914*. Putnam, 1962.

Mead, Peter. *The Eye in the Air*. HMSO, 1983.

Middlebrook, Martin and Everitt, Chris. *The Bomber Command War Diaries*. Penguin, 1990.

Morse, Stan. *Gulf War Debrief*. Aerospace, 1991.

Pocock, Chris. *Dragon Lady*. Airlife, 1989.

Powys-Lybbe, Ursula. *The Eye of Intelligence*. William Kimber, 1983.

Price, Dr Alfred. *The Spitfire Story*. Jane's, 1982.

——. *Panavia Tornado*. Ian Allan, 1988.

Public Record Office (select references only):
AIR 14/4078 RAF Benson, Photo-Reconnaissance Convention 1950/1.
AIR 41/6 1945 Photo-Reconnaissance 1914–Apr 1941.
AIR 41/7 1948 Photo-Reconnaissance May 1941–May 1945.

Pyner, Alf. *Air Cameras RAF & USAAF, 1915–1945*. Burnham-on-Crouch, private printing, 1988.

Rawlings, John D.R. *Coastal Command and Special Squadrons of the RAF and their Aircraft*. Jane's, 1982.

——. *The History of the Royal Air Force*. Temple Press, 1984.

Richards, Denis and Saunders, Hilary St G. *Royal Air Force 1939–45*. 3 volumes, HMSO, 1954.

Ross, Tony, *75 Eventful Years*. Canterbury, Wingham Aviation Books, 1993.

Smith, Constance Babington. *Evidence in Camera*. Chatto & Windus, 1958.

Spooner, Tony. *Warburton's War*. William Kimber, 1987.

Stanley, Colonel Roy M. *World War II Photo Intelligence*. Sidgwick & Jackson, 1982.

Sturtivant, Ray. *The Squadrons of the Fleet Air Arm*. Tonbridge, Air-Britain, 1984.

Taylor, John W.R. *Combat Aircraft of the World*. Ebury Press and Michael Joseph, 1969.

Thetford, Owen. *Aircraft of the 1914–1918 War*. Harborough, 1954.

——. *Aircraft of the Royal Air Force since 1918*. Putnam, 1988.

Willis, Steve and Holliss, Barry. *Military Airfields in the British Isles 1939–1945*. Enthusiasts Publications, 1989.

SECOND WORLD WAR PHOTO-RECONNAISSANCE STRATEGIC UNITS AND SQUADRONS

NORTH-WEST EUROPE

HESTON FLIGHT
Heston	Sep 1939–Nov 1939

Lockheed 12A	Sep 1939–Nov 1939
Beechcraft	Sep 1939–Nov 1939
Blenheim IV	Sep 1939–Nov 1939
Spitfire PR I	Oct 1939–Nov 1939

Wg Cdr F.S. Cotton	Sep 1939–Nov 1939

On 1 November 1939 Heston Flight was renamed No 2 Camouflage Unit.

NO 2 CAMOUFLAGE UNIT
Heston	Nov 1939–Jan 1940

Lockheed 12A	Nov 1939–Jan 1940
Spitfire PR I	Nov 1939–Jan 1940
Blenheim IV	Nov 1939–Jan 1940

Wg Cdr F.S. Cotton	Nov 1939–Jan 1940

On 17 January 1940 No 2 Camouflage Unit was renamed the Photographic Development Unit.

SPECIAL SURVEY FLIGHT
(DETACHED FROM NO 2 CAMOUFLAGE UNIT)
Lille/Seclin	Nov 1939–Nov 1939
Coulommiers	Nov 1939–Feb 1940

Spitfire PR I (various)	Nov 1939–Feb 1940

Wg Cdr F.S. Cotton	Nov 1939–Feb 1940

On 10 February 1940 the Special Survey Flight was renamed 212 Squadron.

212 SQUADRON
Coulommiers	Feb 1940–Jun 1940

Spitfire PRI (various)	Feb 1940–Jun 1940

Wg Cdr F.S. Cotton	Feb 1940–Jun 1940

On 18 June 1940, 212 Squadron was absorbed by the Photographic Development Unit.

PHOTOGRAPHIC DEVELOPMENT UNIT
Heston	Jan 1940–Jly 1940

Lockheed 12A	Jan 1940–Jun 1940
Spitfire PR I (various)	Jan 1940–Jly 1940
Hudson I	Feb 1940–Jly 1940
Blenheim IV	Jan 1940–Jly 1940

Wg Cdr F.S. Cotton	Jan 1940–Jun 1940
Wg Cdr G.W. Tuttle	Jun 1940–Jly 1940

On 8 July 1940 the Photographic Development Unit was renamed the Photographic Reconnaissance Unit.

PHOTOGRAPHIC RECONNAISSANCE UNIT
Heston	Jly 1940–Nov 1940

Spitfire PR I (various)	Jly 1940–Nov 1940
Blenheim IV	Jly 1940–Nov 1940
Hudson I	Jly 1940–Nov 1940

Wg Cdr G.W. Tuttle	Jly 1940–Nov 1940

On 16 November 1940 the Photographic Reconnaissance Unit was renamed No 1 Photographic Reconnaissance Unit.

NO 1 PHOTOGRAPHIC RECONNAISSANCE UNIT

Heston	Nov 1940–Dec 1941
Benson	Dec 1941–Oct 1942

Spitfire PR I (various)	Nov 1940–Oct 1942
Spitfire PR IV	Mar 1941–Oct 1942
Blenheim IV	Nov 1940–May 1941
Hudson I	Nov 1940–Dec 1940
Maryland I	Jun 1941–Oct 1942
Mosquito PR 1	Aug 1941–Oct 1942
Mosquito PR IV	Aug 1942–Oct 1942

Wg Cdr G.W. Tuttle	Jly 1940–Nov 1941
Wg Cdr J.A.C. Stratton	Nov 1941–Apl 1942
Wg Cdr S.L. Ring	Apl 1942–Oct 1942

On 19 October 1942 No 1 Photographic Reconnaissance Unit was disbanded and its parts formed into 540, 541, 542, 543 and 544 Squadrons.

540 SQUADRON

Leuchars	Oct 1942–Feb 1944
Benson	Feb 1944–Mar 1945
Coulommiers	Mar 1945–May 1945

Mosquito PR IV	Oct 1942–Sep 1943
Mosquito PR IX	Jun 1943–Dec 1944
Mosquito PR VI	Nov 1944–May 1945
Mosquito PR XVI	Jun 1944–May 1946

Wg Cdr M.J.B. Young	Oct 1942–May 1943
Wg Cdr Lord Douglas-Hamilton	May 1943–Mar 1944
Wg Cdr J.H.R. Merrifield	Mar 1944–Sep 1944
Wg Cdr A.H.W. Ball	Sep 1944–May 1945

541 SQUADRON

Benson	Oct 1942–May 1945

Spitfire PR IV/PR VII	Oct 1942–Nov 1943
Spitfire PR IX	Nov 1942–Dec 1943
Spitfire PR XI	Jan 1943–May 1945
Spitfire PR X	May 1944–Jan 1945
Mustang III	Jun 1944–May 1945
Spitfire PR XIX	Sep 1944–May 1945

Sqn Ldr D.W. Steventon	Oct 1942–Jly 1943
Sqn Ldr E.A. Fairhurst	Jly 1943–Nov 1943
Sqn Ldr J.H. Saffey	Nov 1943–Sep 1944
Sqn Ldr E.A. Fairhurst	Sep 1944–May 1945

542 SQUADRON

Benson	Oct 1942–May 1945

Spitfire PR IV/PR VI/PR VII	Oct 1942–Mar 1943
Spitfire PR IX	Feb 1943–Jly 1943
Spitfire PR XI	Feb 1943–May 1945
Spitfire PR X	Jun 1944–May 1945
Spitfire PR XIX	May 1944–May 1945

Sqn Ldr D. Salway	Oct 1942–Jun 1943
Sqn Ldr D.L. Lee	Jun 1943–Jly 1943
Sqn Ldr D.M. Furniss	Jly 1943–Dec 1943
Sqn Ldr D.B. Pearson	Dec 1943–Mar 1944
Sqn Ldr A.H.W. Ball	Mar 1944–Sep 1944
Sqn Ldr G.B. Singleton	Sep 1944–May 1945

543 SQUADRON

Benson	Oct 1942–Oct 1943

Spitfire PR IV/PR VII	Oct 1942–Oct 1943
Spitfire PR IX	Nov 1942–Oct 1943

Sqn Ldr A.E. Hill	Oct 1942–Oct 1942
Sqn Ldr G.E. Hughes	Oct 1942–Oct 1943

On 18 October 1943, 543 Squadron was disbanded.

544 SQUADRON

Benson	Oct 1942–May 1945

Wellington IV	Oct 1942–Apl 1943
Anson I	Oct 1942–Mar 1943
Spitfire PR IV	Oct 1942–Oct 1943
Maryland I	Dec 1942–Feb 1943
Mosquito PR IV	Mar 1943–Sep 1943
Spitfire PR XI	May 1943–Oct 1943
Mosquito PR IX	Sep 1943–Mar 1945
Mosquito PR XVI	Mar 1944–May 1945

Sqn Ldr W.R. Acott	Oct 1942–Jly 1943
Sqn Ldr J.P.H. Merrifield	Jly 1943–Oct 1943
Wg Cdr D.C.B. Walker	Oct 1943–Nov 1943
Wg Cdr D.W. Steventon	Nov 1943–May 1945

NO 3 PHOTOGRAPHIC RECONNAISSANCE UNIT

Oakington	Nov 1940–Aug 1941

Spitfire PR I	Nov 1940–Aug 1941
Wellington IC	Nov 1940–Aug 1941
Sqn Ldr P.B.B. Ogilvie	Nov 1940–May 1941
Sqn Ldr N.H.E. Messervy	May 1941–Aug 1941

On 21 August 1941 No 3 Photographic Reconnaissance Unit was disbanded.

MALTA, AFRICA AND ITALY

431 (GENERAL RECONNAISSANCE) FLIGHT

Luqa	Sep 1940–Jan 1941
Maryland I	Sep 1940–Jan 1941
Skua	Sep 1940–Dec 1940
Blenheim IV	Oct 1940–Nov 1940
Sqn Ldr E.A. Whiteley	Sep 1940–Jan 1941

On 10 January 1941, 431 (General Reconnaissance) Flight became 69 Squadron.

69 SQUADRON

Luqa	Jan 1941–Oct 1941
Takali	Oct 1941–Nov 1941
Luqa	Nov 1941–Feb 1944
Montecorvino	Feb 1944–Apl 1944
Maryland I/II	Jan 1941–Sep 1942
Hurricane I/II	Jan 1941–Feb 1942
Beaufort I	Aug 1941–Sep 1941
Blenheim IV	Sep 1941–Oct 1941
Mosquito PR I	Jan 1942–Mar 1943
Beaufighter IC	Jan 1941–Feb 1942
Spitfire PR IV	Mar 1942–Feb 1943
Baltimore I/II	Jun 1942–Apl 1943
Wellington VIII	Aug 1942–Feb 1943
Baltimore III/IV	Apl 1943–Apl 1944
Baltimore V	Jan 1944–Apl 1944
Sqn Ldr E.A. Whiteley	Jan 1941–Jun 1941
Sqn Ldr R.D. Welland	Jun 1941–Jly 1941
Sqn Ldr E. Tennant	Jly 1941–Sep 1941
Wg Cdr J.N. Dowland	Sep 1941–Jan 1942
Wg Cdr E. Tennant	Jan 1942–Jun 1942
Plt Off J. Foster	Jun 1942–Jly 1942
Plt Off R. Munro	Jly 1942–Aug 1942
Sqn Ldr/Wg Cdr A. Warburton	Aug 1942–Mar 1943
Wg Cdr R.C. Mackay	Mar 1943–May 1943
Wg Cdr T.M. Channon	May 1943–Apl 1944

On 8 February, B Flight 69 Squadron became 683 Squadron. On 2 April 1944 the remainder of 69 Squadron began moving to the UK.

683 SQUADRON

Luqa	Feb 1943–Nov 1943
El Aouina	Nov 1943–Dec 1943
San Severo	Dec 1943–Aug 1945
Spitfire PR IV	Feb 1943–Jly 1943
Spitfire PR XI	Apl 1943–Sep 1943
Mosquito PR IV/PR VI	May 1943–Jun 1943
Spitfire PR XIX	Sep 1944–Aug 1945
Wg Cdr A. Warburton	Feb 1943–Oct 1943
Sqn Ldr H.S. Smith	Oct 1943–Aug 1944
Sqn Ldr R.T. Turton	Aug 1944–Apl 1945
Sqn Ldr E.R. Pearson	Apl 1945–Aug 1945

INTELLIGENCE PHOTOGRAPHIC FLIGHT

Heliopolis	Jun 1940–Mar 1941
Hudson I	Jun 1940–Mar 1941
Hurricane I	Jan 1941–Mar 1941
Sqn Ldr H.C. Macphail	Jun 1940–Mar 1941

On 17 March 1941 the Intelligence Photographic Flight was renamed No 2 Photographic Reconnaissance Unit.

NO 2 PHOTOGRAPHIC RECONNAISSANCE UNIT

Heliopolis	Mar 1941–Nov 1942
LG 219	Nov 1942–Feb 1943
Hudson I	Mar 1941–Apl 1941
Hurricane I/II	Mar 1941–Feb 1943
Electra 10A	Apl 1941–Feb 1943
Beaufighter IC	Sep 1941–Feb 1943
Spitfire PR IV	Apl 1942–Feb 1943
Sqn Ldr H.C. Macphail	Mar 1941–Jun 1942
Sqn Ldr J.R. Whelan	Jun 1942–Feb 1943

On 1 February 1943 No 2 Photographic Reconnaissance Unit became 680 Squadron.

680 SQUADRON

LG 219	Feb 1943–Dec 1943
Matariva	Dec 1943–Aug 1944
San Severo	Aug 1944–Feb 1945
Deversoir	Feb 1945–May 1945
Beaufighter IC	Feb 1943–Feb 1943
Spitfire PR IV	Feb 1943–May 1944
Hurricane I/II	Feb 1943–May 1945
Spitfire PR IX	Feb 1943–May 1945
Spitfire PR XI	Aug 1943–May 1945
Baltimore IIIA/V	Feb 1944–May 1944
Blenheim IV	Feb 1944–Jly 1944
Mosquito IX/XVI	Feb 1944–May 1945
Wg Cdr J.R. Whelan	Feb 1943–Oct 1944
Wg Cdr J.C. Paish	Oct 1944–Mar 1945
Sqn Ldr P.A. Friend	Mar 1945–May 1945

NO 4 PHOTOGRAPHIC RECONNAISSANCE UNIT

Benson	Sep (1942–Sep 1942
(then en route to North Africa)	
Maison Blanche	Nov 1942–Feb 1943
Spitfire PR IV	Oct 1942–Feb 1943
Sqn Ldr A.H.W. Ball	Oct 1942–Feb 1943

On 1 February 1943 No 4 Photographic Reconnaissance Unit became 682 Squadron.

682 SQUADRON

Maison Blanche	Feb 1943–Jun 1943
La Marsa	Jun 1943–Dec 1943
San Severo	Dec 1943–Sep 1944
Peretola	Sep 1944–May 1945
Spitfire PR IV	Feb 1943–May 1944
Spitfire PR XI	Apl 1943–May 1945
Mosquito PR IV/PR VI	Apl 1943–Jly 1943
Spitfire PR XIX	Sep 1944–May 1945
Sqn Ldr A.H.W. Ball	Feb 1943–Jly 1943
Sqn Ldr J.T. Morgan	Jly 1943–Jly 1944
Sqn Ldr R.C. Buchanan	Jly 1944–Mar 1945
Sqn Ldr H.B. Oldfield	Mar 1945–May 1945

1437 (STRATEGIC RECONNAISSANCE) FLIGHT

Fuka	Nov 1941–Dec 1941
Tmimi	Dec 1941–Jan 1942
Wadi Natrun	Jan 1942–Apl 1942
Burg el Arab	Apl 1942–Nov 1942
Tmimi	Nov 1942–Dec 1942
Benina	Dec 1942–Dec 1942
Magrun	Dec 1942–Jan 1943
Marble Arch	Jan 1943–Jan 1943
Tamet	Jan 1943–Jan 1943
Darragh	Jan 1943–Feb 1943

1437 (STRATEGIC RECONNAISSANCE) FLIGHT (cont.)

Castel Verde	Feb 1943–Apl 1943
Senem	Apl 1943–May 1943
Monastir	May 1943–Jly 1943
Sorman West	Jly 1943–Jly 1943
Luqa	Jly 1943–Aug 1943
Francesco	Aug 1943–Oct 1943
Foggia	Oct 1943–Oct 1943
Maryland I	Nov 1941–Apl 1942
Baltimore I/II	Apl 1942–Jly 1943
Mustang A–36	Jly 1943–Oct 1943
Sqn Ldr S. Ault	Nov 1941–Jun 1943
Sqn Ldr S.G. Welshman	Jun 1943–Oct 1943

On 13 October 1943, 1437 (Strategic Reconnaissance) Flight was disbanded.

60 (SAAF) SQUADRON

Heliopolis	Jly 1941–Nov 1941
Fuka	Nov 1941–Dec 1941
Tmini	Dec 1941–Jan 1942
Heliopolis	Jan 1942–Jly 1942
Beirut	Jly 1942–Aug 1942
Abbassia	Aug 1942–Aug 1942
LG 100	Aug 1942–Sep 1942
LG 201	Sep 1942–Nov 1942
Tmini	Nov 1942–Dec 1942
Benina	Dec 1942–Jan 1943
Marble Arch	Jan 1943–Jan 1943
Darragh	Jan 1943–Feb 1943
Castel Benito	Feb 1943–Mar 1943
Senem	Mar 1943–Apl 1943
El Djem North	Apl 1943–Apl 1943
Monastir	Apl 1943–May 1943
Sorman	May 1943–Jly 1943
Sabratha	Jly 1943–Sep 1943
Ariana	Sep 1943–Nov 1943
El Aouina	Nov 1943–Dec 1943
San Severo	Dec 1943–May 1945
Maryland I/II	Aug 1941–Jun 1943
Baltimore II	Oct 1942–Jun 1943
Baltimore III	Oct 1942–Aug 1943
Mosquito PR IV	Feb 1943–Oct 1943
Mosquito PR VI	Jly 1943–Dec 1943
Mosquito PR IX	Jly 1943–Sep 1944
Mosquito PR XVI	Feb 1944–May 1945
Maj S.B.F. Scott	Jly 1941–Oct 1941
Maj E.U. Brierley	Oct 1941–Jun 1942
Maj O.G. Davis	Jun 1942–Jly 1943
Maj E.U. Brierley	Jly 1943–Apl 1944
Maj O.G. Davies	Apl 1944–Aug 1944
Maj D.W. Allan	Aug 1944–Jan 1945
Maj P.P. Daphne	Jan 1945–May 1945

200 SQUADRON (PR FLIGHT)

Jeswang (Gambia)	Dec 1941–Mar 1943
Hudson III	Dec 1941–Mar 1943
Maryland I	Jan 1942–Mar 1942
Wg Cdr B.O. Dias	Mar 1942–Sep 1942
Wg Cdr W.H. Ingle	Sep 1942–Mar 1943

128 SQUADRON (PR DETACHMENTS AT JESWANG)

Hastings (Sierra Leone)	Oct 1941–Mar 1943
Hurricane IIB	Oct 1941–Mar 1943
Spitfire PR IV	Oct 1942–Dec 1942
Sqn Ldr B. Drake	Oct 1941–Mar 1942
Sqn Ldr J.I. Kilmartin	Mar 1942–Aug 1942
Sqn Ldr H.A.B. Russell	Aug 1942–Mar 1943

On 8 March 1943, 128 Squadron was disbanded.

INDIA AND SOUTH EAST ASIA

NO 4 PHOTOGRAPHIC RECONNAISSANCE UNIT

Seletar	Nov 1941–Feb 1942
Beaufort	Nov 1941–Nov 1941
Buffalo	Nov 1941–Feb 1942
Sqn Ldr C.G.R. Lewis	Nov 1941–Feb 1942

On 15 February 1942 No 4 Photographic Reconnaissance Unit was disbanded.

NO 3 PHOTOGRAPHIC RECONNAISSANCE UNIT (AT FIRST NAMED NO 5 PRU)

Dum-Dum	Apl 1942–May 1942
Pandaveswar	May 1942–Jun 1942
Dum-Dum	Jun 1942–Jan 1943
B–25C Mitchell	Apl 1942–Jan 1943
Hurricane IIA/IIB/IIC	May 1942–Jan 1943
Spitfire PR IV	Oct 1942–Jan 1943
Sqn Ldr A.C. Pearson	Apl 1942–May 1942
Wg Cdr S.G. Wise	May 1942–Jan 1943

On 25 January 1943 No 3 Photographic Reconnaissance Unit was renamed 681 Squadron.

681 SQUADRON

Dum-Dum	Jan 1943–Dec 1943
Chandina	Dec 1943–Jan 1944
Dum-Dum	Jan 1944–May 1944
Alipore	May 1944–May 1945
Mingaladon	May 1945–Aug 1945
B–25C Mitchell	Jan 1943–Sep 1943
Hurricane IIB	Jan 1943–Nov 1943
Spitfire PR IV	Jan 1943–Dec 1944
Spitfire PR XI	Oct 1943–Aug 1945
Mosquito PR VI/PR IX	Aug 1943–Sep 1943
Spitfire PR 19	Aug 1945–Aug 1945

681 SQUADRON (cont.)

Wg Cdr S.G. Wise	Jan 1943–Dec 1943
Wg Cdr F.D. Procter	Dec 1943–Apl 1945
Wg Cdr D.B. Pearson	Apl 1945–Aug 1945

On 29 September 1943 the twin-engined aircraft of 681 Squadron were transferred to the newly formed 684 Squadron, together with their crews.

684 SQUADRON

Dum-Dum	Sep 1943–Dec 1943
Comilla	Dec 1943–Jan 1944
Dum-Dum	Jan 1944–Apl 1944
Alipore	Apl 1944–Aug 1945
Mitchell B–25C	Sep 1943–Aug 1945
Mosquito PR II	Sep 1943–May 1945
Mosquito PR VI	Sep 1943–May 1945
Mosquito PR IX	Sep 1943–May 1945
Mosquito PR XVI	Feb 1944–Aug 1945
Beaufighter VI/X	Aug 1945–Aug 1945
Mosquito PR 34	Jly 1945–Aug 1945
Sqn Ldr B.S. Jones	Sep 1943–Dec 1943
Wg Cdr W.B. Murray	Dec 1943–Nov 1944
Wg Cdr W.E.M. Lowry	Nov 1943–Aug 1945

160 SQUADRON (CEYLON)

Ratmalana	Feb 1943–Aug 1943
Sigiriya	Aug 1943–Aug 1944
Kankesanturai	Aug 1944–Feb 1945
Minneriya	Feb 1945–Aug 1945
Liberator III/IIIA	Feb 1943–Jun 1945
Liberator V	Jun 1943–Aug 1945
Liberator VI	Jun 1944–Nov 1944
Wg Cdr C.A. Butler	Feb 1943–Jan 1944
Wg Cdr G.R. Brady	Jan 1944–Nov 1944
Wg Cdr J.N. Stacey	Nov 1944–May 1945
Wg Cdr G. McKenzie	May 1945–Aug 1945

INDEX